Development Centre Studies

Start-up Latin America 2016

BUILDING AN INNOVATIVE FUTURE

OECD DEVELOPMENT CENTRE

This work is published under the responsibility of the Secretary-General of the OECD. The opinions expressed and arguments employed herein do not necessarily reflect the official views of the member countries of the OECD or its Development Centre.

This document and any map included herein are without prejudice to the status of or sovereignty over any territory, to the delimitation of international frontiers and boundaries and to the name of any territory, city or area.

Please cite this publication as:
OECD (2016), *Start-up Latin America 2016: Building an Innovative Future*, Development Centre Studies, OECD Publishing, Paris.
http://dx.doi.org/10.1787/9789264265660-en

ISBN 978-92-64-26565-3 (print)
ISBN 978-92-64-26566-0 (PDF)

Series: Development Centre Studies
ISSN 1563-4302 (print)
ISSN 1990-0295 (online)

The statistical data for Israel are supplied by and under the responsibility of the relevant Israeli authorities. The use of such data by the OECD is without prejudice to the status of the Golan Heights, East Jerusalem and Israeli settlements in the West Bank under the terms of international law.

Photo credits: Cover © design by the OECD Development Centre.

Corrigenda to OECD publications may be found on line at: *www.oecd.org/about/publishing/corrigenda.htm*.

Foreword

Founding new enterprises and innovation are key elements of production transformation strategies. Innovative start-ups can contribute to closing productivity gaps and moving countries towards inclusive development. There is growing worldwide interest in actions to promote the creation and expansion of start-ups. Today's start-up world is diverse, and public policies for start-ups exist in OECD countries and developing countries. Although the innovation and production systems of emerging countries are still nowhere near as dense as those of OECD countries, the start-up landscape has become more dynamic, with innovative solutions emerging and mindsets changing in emerging and developing countries.

Based on the 2013 OECD study *Start-up Latin America: Promoting Innovation in the Region*, this report reviews mechanisms to promote start-ups in Chile, Colombia, Mexico and Peru and is part of the OECD Development Centre's work on production development and innovation. Drawing on the experiences of countries in the region, the document proposes guidelines to improve the design and implementation of such policies to make them more effective.

Acknowledgements

This report was produced by the OECD Development Centre. Annalisa Primi, Head of the Structural Policies and Innovation Unit at the Development Centre, directed the project, with guidance from Mario Pezzini, Director of the OECD Development Centre, and Federico Bonaglia, Acting Deputy Director of the OECD Development Centre. Lucía Pérez-Villar, Junior Policy Analyst at the Development Centre, and Annalisa Primi drafted the report. Manuel Toselli, Junior Economist at the OECD Development Centre, contributed to the drafting of Chapter 2. The authors would like to thank Jiyeon Chang for her valuable contribution to revising the report, and Kim Millin for her support as project manager. Meritxell Fernández-Barrera edited the Spanish edition and Timothy Barton translated the Spanish report into English. Delphine Grandrieux and Vanda Legrandgérard co-ordinated the publication process. We are grateful to the OECD colleagues who contributed to the report, especially Rolando Avedaño and Sebastián Nieto Parra. We are also grateful to Nadim Ahmad, Mariarosa Lunati, Kate Eklin and the Latin America Team at the OECD Development Centre for their comments, as well as to Anne-Lise Prigent for her editorial advice and Aída Buendía and Irit Perry for their contributions to producing the graphics. We would also like to thank the OECD Mexico Centre and its Director Roberto Martínez for their support.

This report is the result of a long, fruitful period of collaboration between the OECD Development Centre and the Government of Mexico. We are particularly grateful to the National Institute of Entrepreneurship (INADEM) for encouraging the review of good practices in Mexico and Latin America regarding policies to promote start-ups and entrepreneurial ecosystems in Latin America. We are also most grateful to Enrique Jacob Rocha, President of INADEM, for his leadership. We would also like to thank Alejandro González, General Co-ordinator of Strategic Planning, Evaluation and Monitoring and Chairman of the SME Working Group; Iván Ornelas, Director of International Relations; Adriana Tortajada, Director General of Entrepreneurship Programmes and Financing; and Liliana Reyes, Director of Venture Capital. The Mexican Delegation to the OECD encouraged the sharing of experiences and dialogue regarding innovation and production-transformation policies in global economies, while the Ambassador of Mexico to the OECD, Dionisio Pérez-Jácome, provided valuable support. The contribution made by Flavia Farinetti, Counsellor for Economic Affairs for the Permanent Delegation of Mexico to the OECD, was essential to ensure that the project ran smoothly.

This report benefited from a broad consultation process and interviews with many stakeholders in Latin America's entrepreneurship ecosystems. We would like to thank the Economic Commission for Latin America and the Caribbean (ECLAC), especially Sebastián Rovira for his feedback and for providing access to data. We are grateful for the co-operation of organisers and participants at three events: the Startup Nations Summit held in Monterrey from 22 to 24 November 2015, the Global Entrepreneurship Congress held in Medellín from 14 to 17 March 2016, and the 6th PRODEM Seminar-Workshop for entrepreneurial ecosystem professionals held in Lima from 9 to 12 May 2016. We are also grateful for the support we received from private-sector representatives, from experts and from policy makers for the Chilean, Colombian, Mexican and Peruvian governments, who took part in the consultation rounds between November 2015 and May 2016. Specifically, we would like to thank the following:

In Chile: Eduardo Bitran, President of the Production Development Corporation (CORFO); Inti Núñez and Felipe Jara, Manager and Deputy Manager of CORFO's Entrepreneurship Management Division (Gerencia de Emprendimiento); Rocío Fonseca, Manager of Start-Up Chile; Bernardo Troncoso, General Manager of the Technical Co-operation Service (SERCOTEC); Gonzalo Miranda, General Manager of Austral Capital; Fernando Prieto, President of Gal&Leo; and Germán Echecopar, professor at Adolfo Ibáñez University (at the date of consultation).

In Colombia: At iNNpulsa Colombia, Mary Luz Escobar Rivera, Director of Innovation and Entrepreneurship; Luisa Vergel, an advisor for the Innovation and Entrepreneurship Directorate; Sergio Ademar, an Executive at the Development and Innovation Unit; and Sergio Mendoza, Business Hyper-Growth Executive. At the Ministry of Commerce, Industry and Tourism, Adriana Vargas, Director of Foreign Investment and Services (at the date of consultation); Claudia Janneth Sepúlveda, Productivity and Competitiveness Advisor; Sandra Gisella Acero, Director of MSMEs; and Jorge Madrid, an Entrepreneurship and Innovation advisor. We are also thankful to Daniel Arango, Deputy Minister for Business Development at the Ministry of Commerce, Industry and Tourism; Juliana Ossa, Hyper-Growth Business Director at Bancóldex Daniel Quintero, General Manager of iNNpulsa Colombia; Andrés Mauricio León López, Science Technology and Innovation Consultant for the National Planning Department; Isabella Muñoz, Executive Director of ColCapital; Adriana Suárez, Executive Director of Endeavor Colombia; Antonio María Díaz Arz, Executive Director for Colombia at the Association of Entrepreneurs in Latin America (ASELA); and Tomás Mejía, Economic Development Secretary for the Municipality of Medellín.

In Mexico: The team of INADEM experts led by Alejandro González, General Co-ordinator of Strategic Planning, Evaluation and Monitoring and Chairman of the SME Working Group, and Iván Ornelas, Director of International Relations. We are particularly thankful to Adriana Tortajada, Director General of Entrepreneurship Programmes and Financing, Liliana Reyes, Director of Venture Capital, and María del Sol Rumayor, Director General of Business Development Programmes, for their contributions to the report. We are also grateful to Carlos Cobb, Director of Alternative Promotion Channels and Venture Capital Trust Officer at NAFINSA; Marcus Dantus, General Manager of Startup México; Hernán Fernández, General Manager of Angel Ventures Mexico; Roberto Charvel, Executive Director of Vander Capital; Rogelio de los Santos, Executive Director of Alta Ventures Mexico; Tim Kessler and Narciso Suárez of ABT Associates; Alberto Saracho of C230 Consultores; Celso Garrido, a senior lecturer at Metropolitan Autonomous University (UAM); and Mónica Caselet, a research professor at the Mexican branch of the Latin American Social Sciences Institute (FLACSO).

In Peru: Alejandro Bernaola Cabrera, Director General of Innovation, Technology Transfer and Business Services at the Ministry of Production; Sergio Rodríguez, Director of Innovation at the Ministry of Production; Renzo Reyes, Co-ordinator of the Start Up Perú programme; Liszett Butrón, of Start Up Perú's Innovation Directorate; Luis Terrones and Gina Medrano, Chief Development Officer and Deputy Manager, respectively, of the Development Finance Corporation (COFIDE); Karen Weinberger and Edilberto Salazar, Director and Head of Incubations at Emprende UP, the entrepreneurship and innovation centre of the University of the Pacific in Peru; Gisella Orjeda, President of the National Science and Technology Council (CONCYTEC); Hugo Wiener, Executive Director of CienciActiva (CONCYTEC); and Luis Mesías and María del Carmen Vergaray, Director General of Foreign Trade Development Policies and Economist at the Ministry of Foreign Trade and Tourism, respectively.

We also appreciate the contributions made by Gonzalo Brahms, Executive Director of ASELA; Ángeles Undurraga, Executive Director of Mujeres del Pacífico (Women of the Pacific); Hugo Kantis and Sabrina Ibarra, Director and Economist at PRODEM respectively; Cristina Fernández, Director for Policy and Research for the Global Entrepreneurship Network; Dane Stangler, Arnobio Morelix and Amisha Miller of the Ewing Marion Kauffman Foundation; Rhett Morris, Director of Endeavor Insight; Cate Ambrose and Eduardo Roman from the Latin American Private Equity & Venture Capital Association (LAVCA); and Marc Penzel and Jean-François Gauthier of the Compass team (formerly Startup Genome).

This document could not have been drafted and published without the financial support of INADEM.

Table of contents

Figures

Tables

Acronyms and abbreviations

ACAFI	Chilean Association of Investment Fund Administrators (Asociación Chilena de Administradoras de Fondos de Inversión)
AMEXCAP	Mexican Association of PE & VC Funds (Asociación Mexicana de Capital Privado)
ANDI	National Association of Entrepreneurs (Asociación Nacional de Empresarios de Colombia)
ASELA	Association of Latin American Entrepreneurs (Asociación de Emprendedores de América Latina)
CAF	CAF – Development Bank of Latin America (Banco de Desarrollo de América Latina)
CMIC	Mexican Capital Investment Corporation (Corporación Mexicana de Inversión de Capitales)
CNBV	National Banking and Securities Commission, Mexico (Comisión Nacional Bancaria y de Valores)
COMFEI	Mexico-France Council on Entrepreneurship and Innovation (Consejo México–Francia sobre Emprendimiento e Innovación)
CONACYT	National Council on Science and Technology, Mexico (Consejo Nacional de Ciencia y Tecnología)
CONCYTEC	National Science and Technology Council, Peru (Consejo Nacional de Ciencia, Tecnología e Innovación Tecnológica)
CORFO	Production Development Corporation, Chile (Corporación de Fomento de la Producción)
ECLAC	Economic Commission for Latin America and the Caribbean
EPM	Empresas Públicas de Medellín
FINCyT	Fund for Innovation, Science and Technology, Peru (Fondo para la Innovación, la Ciencia y la Tecnología)
FOMITEC	Fund for Innovation, Science and Technology, Peru (Fondo Marco para la Innovación, Ciencia y Tecnología)
FUMEC	United States-Mexico Foundation for Science (Fundación México–Estados Unidos para la Ciencia)
GDP	Gross Domestic Product
GEDI	Global Entrepreneurship and Development Institute
GEM	Global Entrepreneurship Monitor
GEN	Global Entrepreneurship Network
ICTs	Information and Communication Technologies
IDB	Inter-American Development Bank
INADEM	National Institute of Entrepreneurship, Mexico (Instituto Nacional del Emprendedor)
ITESM	Monterrey Institute of Technology and Higher Education, also know as Tecnológico de Monterrey (Instituto Tecnológico y de Estudios Superiores de Monterrey)
LAVCA	Latin American Private Equity & Venture Capital Association (Asociación Latinoamericana de Capital de Riesgo)
MIF	Multilateral Investment Fund
MinCIT	Ministry of Commerce, Industry and Tourism, Colombia (Ministerio de Comercio, Industria y Turismo)
MinTIC	Ministry of Information Technologies and Communications, Colombia (Ministerio de Tecnologías de la Información y las Comunicaciones)
MSMEs	Micro, small and medium-sized enterprises
MSTI	Main Science and Technology Indicators, OECD
MUSEIC	Mexico-United States Entrepreneurship and Innovation Council

NAFINSA	Nacional Financiera (Mexican development bank)
OECD	Organisation for Economic Co-operation and Development
PRODEM	Entrepreneur Development Programme (Programa de Desarrollo Emprendedor)
PRODUCE	Ministry of Production, Peru
PYMEs	Small and medium-sized enterprises
R&D	Research and development
RICYT	Network for Science and Technology Indicators *(Red de Indicadores de Ciencia y Tecnología)*
SENA	National Learning Service, Colombia (Servicio Nacional de Aprendizaje)
UNCTAD	United Nations Conference on Trade and Development
UNECE	United Nations Economic Commission for Europe
UNESCO	United Nations Educational, Scientific and Cultural Organization
USAID	United States Agency for International Development
USPTO	United States Patent and Trademark Office

Preface

In the global knowledge economy, the ability of countries to grow sustainably and redistribute income depends largely on whether they can translate productivity gains into better welfare for the population. Innovation and the creation of new firms are essential in this virtuous process of productivity growth. Start-ups of all kinds – those that use new technologies, those that offer new services and products, and those that provide solutions to emerging problems – play an important role in transforming a country's production and can boost and diversify the economy. Today, start-ups are no longer exclusive to Silicon Valley; many ecosystems have emerged in other regions too. However, start-ups must overcome major hurdles to get up and running and to expand, especially in developing countries. Despite the growing number of start-ups in emerging and developing countries, data on start-up ecosystems, pro-startup policies and the impact of support instruments are still in short supply. This report provides valuable new knowledge about the state of start-ups and policy actions implemented by emerging and developing countries.

How can public policies promote start-ups? How can they operate efficiently and have a local and global impact? This report presents a policy framework to promote start-ups that takes into account the different needs of companies at the seed, start-up, growth and expansion stages. The instruments identify financing, services, demand, regulations and the entrepreneurial culture as areas that public policies can target to help create a dense, dynamic, innovative start-up ecosystem.

In 2013, the OECD Development Centre published its first diagnosis of policies to promote start-ups in Latin America. The report (OECD, 2013, *Start-up Latin America: Promoting Innovation in the Region*) analysed policies and programmes at the design stage and during their initial implementation. The 2016 report provides an updated overview of the promotion of start-ups in Latin American countries. It begins with an update of the set of instruments used to promote start-ups, then it reviews and compares the mechanisms that currently exist in Chile, Colombia, Mexico and Peru.

The report shows that Latin American countries are structuring and strengthening their pro-startup policies. Countries are creating new institutions and support instruments and they are reforming existing programmes to make them more effective. Despite the rather unfavourable macroeconomic climate, the start-up scene is revealing a more dynamic side of Latin America that is seeking new solutions and reforming instruments, and where start-ups are a burgeoning reality.

The pro-startup policies of some countries are more developed than those of others, and each country has its own policy model. Chile has been consolidating and structuring its pro-startup policy as part of its production-development strategy. Colombia, meanwhile, has been looking to develop an inclusive financial market for start-ups. Mexico has been strengthening its institutional framework and closing the financing gap in early stages. Finally, Peru has made progress in consolidating the Start Up Perú programme and has begun to introduce seed capital. It is still too early to assess the impact of these policies, but the efforts currently underway suggest that countries have learned lessons in designing and managing support instruments and that the start-up culture has become more widespread, with ecosystems developing and expanding.

As countries in the region rethink their development strategies to bring about productive diversification and move towards sustained, inclusive growth patterns, this document is an important contribution, outlining the lessons that Latin America has learned in promoting start-ups and proposing ways forward for the future. Public policies can play an important role by generating incentives to create new firms, promoting a change in mindset regarding entrepreneurship and fostering productive diversification. Monitoring and assessing the results and impact of actions to promote start-ups is essential to ensure that public resources are spent wisely and that policies generate the expected results and are in line with the latest trends in the dynamic start-up environment. It is therefore important for countries in the region to share their experiences and to discuss policies so that they can mutually benefit from each other's experiences and reflect upon how to deal with emerging challenges. This report, compiled to strengthen dialogue on productive transformation, makes an important contribution to the present debate on how to mobilise private-sector initiative and the creation of businesses for development.

Mario Pezzini
Director, OECD Development Centre

Executive summary

Sustainable, inclusive growth depends largely on a country's ability to translate productivity gains into better welfare for the population. Innovation and the creation of new firms are essential to drive this virtuous process of productivity gains. Start-ups bring new products and services to the market based on scientific discoveries and new applications of existing knowledge. They create new markets and business models and offer novel solutions to emerging problems. Start-ups also bolster competition for innovation and encourage the development of a dynamic business environment, and they have the potential to boost and diversify the economy. However, these enterprises must overcome major hurdles to get up and running and to expand, especially in developing countries. Start-ups do not emerge in a vacuum. They need entrepreneurial talent, technical skills, business management capabilities, services and legal frameworks that foster their creation and expansion. They also need investment in infrastructure. Public policies can adopt various courses of action to reduce the barriers encountered by those looking to create or expand start-ups, and governments can work with the private sector on actions to support the development of an ecosystem in which there are dynamic start-ups.

This report analyses the experience of Latin American countries in promoting start-ups, focusing on Chile, Colombia, Mexico and Peru. It is an update of the first diagnosis conducted in the 2013 OECD study *Start-up Latin America: Promoting Innovation in the Region*. The report shows that Latin American countries are structuring and strengthening their pro-startup policies. Countries are creating new institutions and support instruments and they are reforming existing programmes to make them more effective. Even though the region's macroeconomic climate is rather unfavourable, the start-up scene is revealing a more dynamic side of Latin America, where start-ups are a burgeoning reality and governments are looking to design and reform instruments to capitalise on the opportunities of entrepreneurship.

Some countries have better developed pro-startup policies than others, and each country has its own policy model. Chile has been consolidating its pro-startup policy as a pillar in its national production-development strategy. Colombia, meanwhile, has been boosting its ecosystem and developing an inclusive financial market for start-ups. Mexico has been strengthening its institutional framework, promoting an entrepreneurial culture and closing the finance gap for early-stage enterprises. Finally, Peru has made progress in consolidating the Start Up Perú programme and is introducing seed capital. Overall, instruments to promote start-ups became more modern between 2010 and 2016. The countries of the region have introduced new, more flexible mechanisms that are in line with the ones operating in more advanced ecosystems, including mentoring networks and collaborative workspaces to streamline the functioning of traditional incubators. They are also finding new ways of channelling resources towards start-ups, such as crowdfunding. Although the region has improved at promoting start-ups, venture-capital and angel investors are still weak links in the financing chain.

Latin America is learning lessons on how to manage policies to support start-ups. Countries in the region have learned that it is important to create synergies between pro-startup policies and strategies for production transformation and innovation, that the quality and density of the production and innovation ecosystem affect the success rate of start-ups, that mechanisms to promote start-ups should strive to ensure that production benefits all sectors of society in all parts of the country, and that the programmes need to be flexible and reactive to respond to market needs.

Start-ups will not be the ultimate solution for development in the region, but creating a startup-friendly environment, facilitating investment in start-ups, creating flexible, modern services for new entrepreneurs, and investing in measures to promote an entrepreneurial culture can help to diversify and transform the region's economies. Policies to promote start-ups do not need big investments to have an impact, but they do need to be flexible and co-ordinated, with the aim of establishing partnerships with the private sector and with universities, technology centres and regions across the country. The policies also need flexible instruments, as well as experimentation and policy dialogue among different countries so that they can learn from each other and adopt best practices.

The countries of the region are structuring their policies to promote start-ups. They share four pressing challenges:

1. **Map start-ups and measure their impact.** Start-ups are a recent phenomenon in the region. As countries consolidate their pro-startup programmes, they are tweaking the criteria they use to determine which enterprises are eligible to benefit from public programmes and their role in the national innovation system. It is important for countries to improve official company registries and use the broad scope of such records to generate data on the performance of start-ups, that they could then use to analyse the features of businesses that fail or cease trading. Countries could obtain additional data on the nature and behaviour of start-ups that import and export goods by combining the information in official company registries with the statistical records of customs agencies. Meanwhile, information and communication technologies, the platform economy and new policy tools provide opportunities to generate new data and to map the development of the start-up scene in Latin American countries. It is important for countries to monitor the implementation of programmes and conduct impact assessments at a reasonably early stage to ensure that they use their resources efficiently. Data from new sources, such as the platform economy, could also be used to map the profile of start-uppers in the region and to design indicators suited to the unique nature of start-ups, especially their closer connection with the innovative entrepreneurs who founded them. These sources would reveal what impact the profile of entrepreneurs (gender, age and education) and the environment in which they operate have on the founding and expansion of start-ups, and indirect pro-startup policies would therefore be better informed. Countries could also explore to what extent start-up policies change the organisational structure of traditional policies to support innovation and production development. Programmes to support start-ups might also be modernising and invigorating traditional systems by introducing new ways of planning, managing and implementing public policies and by requiring changes to the profiles of the people in charge.
2. **Simplify and consolidate support programmes and bring them more in line with the needs of the target population.** Although initial experimentation with different programmes and mechanisms are helping to determine what works best in each context, if there are too many instruments, they are not effective for defining a policy that is easy for entrepreneurs to use. It is also important to work towards completing the financing chain and improving service provision and legislation for these businesses, given their potential needs at the scale-up and expansion stages.
3. **Facilitate productive investment.** Although the situation has improved in recent years, the region still adopts a conservative approach and is averse to the risks associated with productive investment. Financial institutions, private investors and investment funds could make a decisive contribution to boosting investment in the region. If the region's capital and funds were steered towards productive

investment, they could create a more dynamic business environment. For this to happen, countries need to reform legislation and create tax incentives to enable and facilitate productive investment. They also need to change mindsets and focus on investment.

4. **Increase regional co-operation.** The countries in the region can capitalise on and increase the impact of start-ups through greater regional co-operation. By co-operating with each other, countries can speed up the learning process and the transfer of best practices, as well as help regional initiatives achieve critical masses for market opportunities and financing. The community that supports start-ups in Latin America is young, and it already meets together and co-ordinates more than traditional areas of public policy. Countries could speed up learning processes and create good practices by improving the structure of these spaces for dialogue and by introducing peer review. Regional co-operation could also help close funding gaps and attract larger levels of investment, responding to the challenges that the countries face in terms of finance and target markets. Regional funds like the Pacific Alliance initiatives to promote start-ups and entrepreneurship are therefore important, and countries should do more to encourage such initiatives.

Assessment and recommendations

Start-up Latin America 2016 presents an overview of policies to support start-ups in Chile, Colombia, Mexico and Peru. This overview presents the main results and recommendations from the study. Even though there is an unfavourable macroeconomic climate and there are still innovation gaps between Latin America and more advanced countries, start-ups are revealing a different, more dynamic side to the region. Since 2010, the concept of start-ups has attracted growing attention from the media, investors and policy makers in Latin America, and countries have implemented various programmes to support start-ups. These policies to promote start-ups have evolved rapidly, and in the space of just six years, their design, focus and structure have changed significantly, showing initial results and revealing a change in people's perceptions of the region as a place for entrepreneurship and innovation.

Start-ups are now a reality in Latin America, though they are still in their infancy.

The global heartland of disruptive start-ups is still California, which was home to nine of the 20 highest market value start-ups in 2016, including Uber, Airbnb and Pinterest (Fortune, 2016), but today, many countries worldwide have a growing entrepreneurial culture. Latin America is also on board. Governments, the private sector and universities have begun to support the creation of start-ups, and they are increasingly aware of the potential of these enterprises to transform the economies of the region.

Although Latin America has made little progress in boosting its innovation systems, start-ups reveal a different, more dynamic side to the region. Latin American countries continue to invest little in science, technology and innovation. Investment in research and development (R&D) grew from 0.63% of GDP in 2009 to 0.74% in 2014, a small increase that leaves the region's countries trailing far behind the OECD countries, which invest around 2.3% of GDP in R&D (in 2014). Latin American countries have increased their use of information and communication technologies (ICTs) over the last decade, but there remains a large gap with the OECD countries (ECLAC, 2013). Connections are slow in most of Latin America. The average broadband download speed was 7.3 Mbps in 2014, compared with an average of 32.2 Mbps among OECD countries. Only Brazil, Chile, Mexico and Uruguay had speeds that were faster than the regional average (ECLAC, 2015).

At the time of the first review of Latin America's experience in promoting start-ups, their founding and growth appeared as something distant to the culture of the countries of the region (OECD, 2013). Today, the perception is different, with start-ups emerging and growing in Latin America. Venture capital is also growing, with investments having doubled between 2011 and 2015 (LAVCA, 2016). But what, exactly, is a start-up? And what is the profile of Latin American start-ups? Exhaustive, comparable data measuring the dynamic and impact of Latin American start-ups are still missing. There are no official databases on them, and the myriad of ways that countries use to define start-ups makes it difficult to measure them.

The implementation of programmes to promote start-ups is generating new information about them. For instance, thanks to data from the Production Development Corporation (CORFO), we know that Chile has 1 unicorn, 4 centaurs and 31 little ponies, and thanks to the Mexican Association of PE & VC Funds (AMEXCAP), we know that Mexico has 1 centaur and 26 little ponies. These figures are similar to those found in economies like Singapore, which has 2 unicorns, 12 centaurs and 27 little ponies among its 1 000 start-ups (CORFO, 2015). Countries are also generating information by monitoring programmes. For instance, the implementation of Start-Up Chile between 2010 and 2015 revealed that 80% of the beneficiaries were male, 75% were non-Chilean (mainly from the United States, Argentina, India and Brazil), and the survival rate of businesses was higher among Chileans (55%) than among foreigners (less than 50%).

Online platforms are also generating data about start-ups in the region. According to AngelList – a database that investors often use to find basic information about start-ups before making investment decisions – Brazil has the largest number of start-ups in Latin America, followed by Mexico. Mexico has the most even distribution of start-ups across the country, with 32% located in Mexico City, 10% in Guadalajara and 8% in Monterrey. Chile is at the other end of the spectrum, with 80% of start-ups registered in the capital, Santiago (Figure 0.1).

Figure 0.1. **Start-ups in Latin America and their distribution by city, 2016**
(number of start-ups and their distribution by city according to data from AngelList)

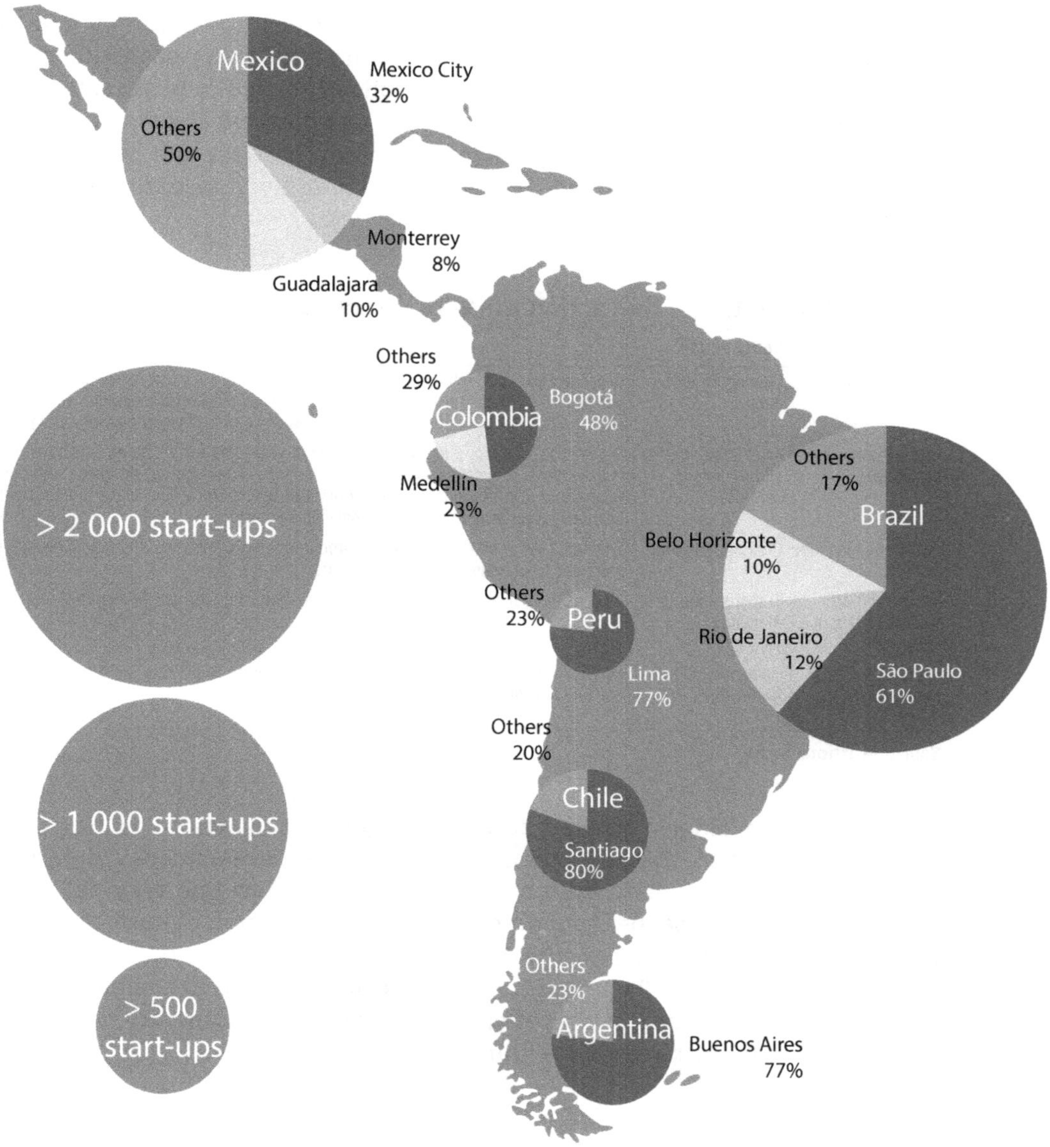

Source: Authors' work based on AngelList (2016).

Start-ups do not flourish in a vacuum; they need markets, institutions and networks in order to emerge and expand.

There is a broad consensus that new, innovative enterprises play a vital role in determining how dynamic a country's innovation will be. Start-ups reinvigorate the business community, increase competition for innovation, introduce new products, services and business models, create new markets and offer innovative solutions to emerging problems. Their creation and expansion depend on several factors: a solid scientific base, a business-friendly environment, and a financial sector willing to make medium-term investments in high-risk projects, among others.

Why should governments support the founding of start-ups, and how can they do so? Many countries have shown that national and local governments, in partnership with the private sector, can play a major role in setting the right environment for innovative entrepreneurship. Public policies can support start-ups both directly and indirectly. Indirect measures are essential because they shape the socio-economic environment in which start-uppers operate. They include policies related to science, technology and innovation, education, production development and physical and digital infrastructure. Direct policies to support start-ups reduce the main barriers that hinder the founding and growth of start-ups. Such policies also benefit intermediary institutions, universities and stakeholders in the financial system (Table 0.1).

Table 0.1. **The five action areas of direct policies to promote start-ups**

Gap	Policy action	Types of programmes/actions
Funding gap	Closing funding gaps	Seed-capital programmes and borrowing for start-ups, as well as incentives for the financial sector to work with start-ups, such as the promotion of venture capital, angel investors, etc. In recent years, countries have also introduced actions to support crowdfunding.
Information asymmetry	Facilitating linkages and providing services	Support services for start-uppers. In recent years, platforms, mentoring networks and collaborative workspaces have grown in number. They operate alongside traditional intermediary institutions like incubators and accelerators. New platforms to facilitate linkages between large firms and start-ups have also emerged.
Absence of demand	Creating markets	The inclusion of start-ups in public procurement programmes and initiatives that challenge start-ups to provide innovative solutions.
Little tradition for business and innovation	Transforming mindsets	Actions to raise awareness about start-ups (including prizes and events).
Legal and administrative barriers	Reforming legal frameworks	Legal and administrative reforms to suit the needs of start-ups, such as easier procedures for starting and winding up a business.

Source: Authors' work.

There is no single, optimal formula for promoting start-ups. Each ecosystem develops its own focus based on the country's features, development vision, and science, technology and production system. Instruments for start-ups vary according to the gap they serve to close, be it funding, information, demand, culture or the regulatory framework, and according to the development stage of businesses (seed, start-up, growth and expansion) (Figure 0.2). Recently, countries tend to combine financing and services in new programmes that offer integrated support to simplify the policy mix and respond better to the needs of start-ups.

Figure 0.2. **Policy mix to support start-ups**

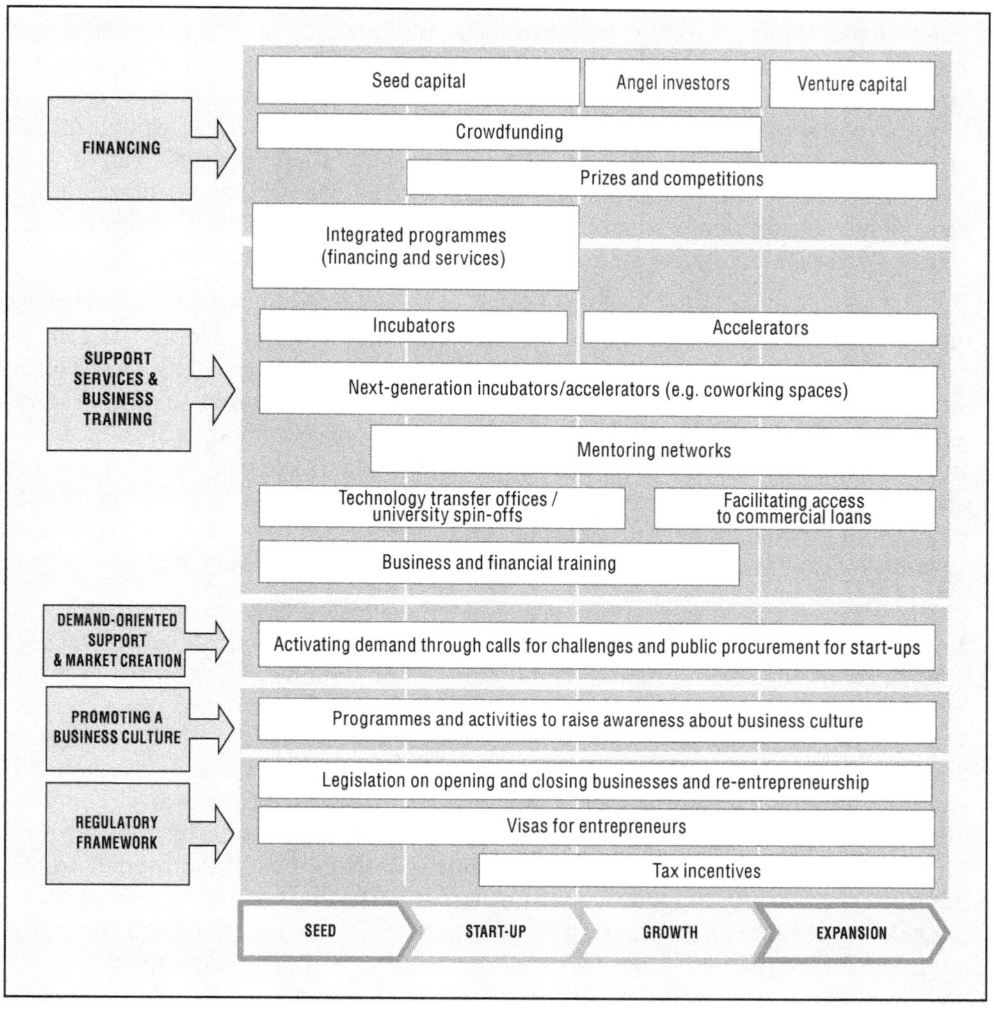

Source: OECD (2013), *Start-up Latin America: Promoting Innovation in the Region*, http://dx.doi.org/10.1787/9789264202306-en, updated and expanded.

Since 2010, start-up promotion has been an important part of Latin American countries' production-development and innovation strategies.

Since 2010, several countries in Latin America have introduced programmes to support start-ups, including Argentina, Brazil, Chile, Colombia, Mexico, Panama, Peru and Uruguay (OECD, 2013, 2015). Unlike more traditional policies to support innovation and competitiveness, these programmes have evolved rapidly. In the space of a few years, they have taken on a different design, focus and structure. Results are beginning to emerge, especially regarding people's perceptions of the region and its image as a place for innovative entrepreneurship.

Each country adopts a different approach (Figure 0.3):

Chile, since it launched Start-Up Chile in 2010, has moved from a pilot phase of pro-startup programmes to a more structured policy linked to its national production-transformation strategy. Chile has reformed the policy based on the results of the monitoring and evaluation it conducted, and the country now prioritises retaining more talent and businesses in the country. Chile also promotes the creation of start-ups in the regions outside Santiago and supports the founding of firms that offer innovative solutions to social problems in one of the country's strategic sectors (smart mining, the food industry and engineering, for instance). The country is aiming to close the early-stage funding gap; it has modernised services to entrepreneurs through more flexible mechanisms tailored to the needs of start-uppers, such as collaborative workspaces and mentoring networks and it has simplified the regulations for starting a business (a new law allows people to start a business in a single day). Private investment at the expansion stage and angel investors are still weak links in the financing chain in Chile.

Colombia has joined the wave of interest for start-ups in the region, and in 2012 it set up iNNpulsa Colombia to promote entrepreneurship. Today, Colombia is reforming the programme by introducing a voucher scheme to give new businesses access to financing and services managed by accredited intermediary organisations. Colombia is seeking to encourage financial institutions to invest in start-ups at all stages of their development and is promoting the strengthening of the business culture in the country. A distinctive feature in Colombia is the development of start-ups in cities; Bogotá and Medellín have seen rapid growth in start-up numbers and they are aiming to become start-up hubs by promoting the founding of start-ups through public-private partnerships.

Mexico is the country that has made the most progress in promoting start-ups between 2012 and 2016. The creation of the National Institute of Entrepreneurship (INADEM) in 2013 strengthened the institutional framework for start-ups. Meanwhile, the reintroduction of seed capital has closed the early-stage funding gap, thus achieving one of the challenges identified in the 2013 review (OECD, 2013). Mexico has also improved the financial inclusion of start-ups. Venture capital has taken off in the country, which now has the second most active industry in Latin America, behind Brazil (LAVCA, 2016). Mexico has reformed regulations to make it easier to start a business, the Express Companies Act being a notable example. It has also modernised services for entrepreneurs by launching mentoring networks and collective workspaces. Finally, Mexico has invested in promoting an entrepreneurial culture in the country and creating an image of Mexico as a place for entrepreneurship with a global impact.

Peru introduced the Start Up Perú programme in 2012. Since then, it has improved the programme design and it has increased the budget for start-ups, which now receive resources from the innovation fund. The Start Up Perú programme has been expanded, and today it includes seed capital and support for angel-investor networks. Peru also promotes the founding of start-ups based on scientific research through a competition organised by the National Science and Technology Council (CONCYTEC). Universities and the private sector are actively promoting the founding of start-ups in Peru, and the national development bank COFIDE has just made promoting start-ups one of its strategic lines of action. COFIDE is looking to promote venture capital and the financial inclusion of new enterprises.

Figure 0.3. **Policy mix for start-up promotion in Chile, Colombia, Mexico and Peru, 2016**

B. 2016

● Operational ◍ Developing ○ Non-operational ▨ Recently created

Category	Instrument	Chile	Colombia	Mexico	Peru
Financing	Seed capital	Operational	Developing	Operational	Developing
	Crowdfunding	Developing	Recently created	Recently created	Recently created
	Angel investors	Non-operational	Recently created	Operational	Recently created
	Venture capital	Operational	Developing	Operational	Recently created
	Prizes	Developing	Non-operational	Operational	Recently created
Integrated support	Integrated public/private programmes (financing and services)	Operational	Developing	Developing	Developing
Support services and business training	Incubators	Operational	Operational	Operational	Developing
	Accelerators	Operational	Operational	Operational	Developing
	Next-generation incubators and accelerators (coworking)	Recently created	Recently created	Recently created	Recently created
	Mentoring networks	Developing	Recently created	Developing	Recently created
	Support for developing commercial loans for startups	Non-operational	Developing	Non-operational	Non-operational
	Technology transfer and university spin-offs	Developing	Recently created	Operational	Recently created
	Business and financial training	Operational	Operational	Operational	Operational
Demand-oriented support & market creation	Public procurement and other	Recently created	Developing	Developing	Non-operational
Promoting a business culture	Raising awareness about the innovative business culture	Developing	Operational	Operational	Developing
Regulatory framework	Legal framework for starting, expanding and closing businesses	Operational	Developing	Developing	Developing
	Tax incentives and special taxes	Operational	Operational	Developing	Recently created
	Special visas for start-ups	Operational	Non-operational	Non-operational	Non-operational

Note: This table is not meant to present an international classification. It is based on qualitative information gathered in the country case studies in Chapters 3 to 6 of this report. The goal is to summarise visually the variety of tools to support start-ups and how developed they are in the countries in the region.

Source: Based on Chapters 3, 4, 5 and 6 of this document.

There are five areas in which all four countries have made progress:

1. **They have strengthened the institutional framework for supporting start-ups**, especially Mexico, which created INADEM in 2013, and Chile, which has made policies to support start-ups part of its national production-development strategy and has opened a division within CORFO devoted to start-ups. The region has also reformed its development banks, with start-ups becoming priorities for Bancóldex in Colombia, NAFINSA in Mexico and COFIDE in Peru. In Chile and Mexico, pro-startup policies have shifted from an experimental phase to a consolidation in their national strategies. To institutionalise these policies in such a way, they need to find ways to create synergies between these bottom-up pro-startup schemes and the more selective nature of production-development policies so that they can increase their impact in priority areas, like the automotive sector in Mexico and smart mining in Chile.

2. **The countries have prioritised social and regional inclusion in their pro-startup policies** and have introduced measures to enable start-ups to develop in regions beyond the capital city. These measures aim to place start-ups in a better position to transform regional economies, taking into account the specific features of production ecosystems and societies in the regions. Mexico has the largest variety of ecosystems outside the capital city, followed by Colombia; Chile is the country that most needs to increase opportunities for founding start-ups in the regions.
3. **The countries recognise that it is important to invest in transforming mindsets and promoting a culture of entrepreneurship.** Transforming ideas into a business is still not very common in the region. Risk aversion is high in Latin American societies, and relatively few people see entrepreneurs as key contributors to national development. Legal incentives, tax breaks and services for entrepreneurs are all important, but so too are measures to create an entrepreneurial culture, since they change people's mindsets. Start-Up Chile's media impact has helped to make Chile a talking point around the world and has inspired young people to become entrepreneurs. In Mexico, meanwhile, the launch of INADEM has raised awareness of the crucial role that entrepreneurship plays in the country's development, inspiring the Mexican youth and the diaspora to create new firms.
4. **The countries have modernised support instruments,** become more aware that instruments need to take all stages of start-up development into account (seed, start-up, growth and expansion), and introduced next-generation instruments that are more flexible and in keeping with global trends. All four countries have introduced new pro-startup schemes that are more modern, more comprehensive and better suited to the needs of start-uppers. Collaborative workspaces are one example. The countries have also reformed instruments to streamline new forms of financing, such as crowdfunding. In the area of pro-startup measures, because governments have worked together with entrepreneurs and the private sector, they have reformed instruments and improved practices more quickly than in other policy areas. The new policy mix consists mainly of integrated services that combine access to infrastructure, finance, services, and access to contacts and networks. In addition, policy makers have worked in partnership with the private sector and with research and technology institutes, which has improved policy effectiveness and ensured that these policies properly address the needs of start-ups.
5. **The countries have streamlined procedures and reformed legislation** to make it easier to create and expand businesses. Chile and Mexico have passed legislation enabling people to start a business in a single day, but in the four countries, procedures are still complex and tax incentives for new, highly innovative businesses are still insufficient.

To consolidate the progress made, increase the impact of pro-startup policies and strengthen start-up ecosystems in the region, it is important for countries to:

Map start-ups and improve the definition of start-ups as beneficiaries of public policy. Start-ups are a recent phenomenon in Latin America, and the countries in the region still lack comparable data. For instance, there is no single definition of what constitutes a start-up, even though each country has been adjusting the criteria it uses to determine which enterprises are eligible to benefit from start-up programmes. Chile and Mexico, for instance, use performance-based definitions (growth potential) and target different instruments to different stages of development ("emerging" for start-ups less than two years old and "expansion" for those that are older). They also take into account the firms' innovation intensity, target market (local vs. global) and capacity to meet the specific needs of the areas where they are located. It is important for countries to improve official company registries and use the broad scope of such records to generate data on the performance of start-ups. Countries could obtain additional data on the nature and behaviour of start-ups that import and export goods by combining the information in official company registries with the statistical records of customs agencies. Further information is also being generated as countries improve their public programmes to promote start-ups and as the platform economy grows. Countries could use these new data to map out the profile of start-uppers in the region, quantifying the impact of aspects such as gender, age, training and the environment on the emergence and expansion of start-ups. This information can improve indirect pro-startup policies such as those related to education, training, science and technology.

Monitor policy implementation, measure impact and use the results of assessments to improve policies. If countries monitor the implementation of programmes and conduct impact assessments at a reasonably early stage, they will be able to learn how to design and implement the best policies more quickly and ensure that they use resources efficiently. Monitoring and assessment are particularly important for start-up programmes, since countries often experiment new forms of support in response to the changing needs of the environment. Chile is the country in the region that has best monitored and assessed the impact of policies at an early stage. Since it introduced Start-Up Chile in 2010, it has reviewed the results of its implementation on two occasions. The analyses showed, for example, that the instruments need to include conditions to prevent too much support going to the capital city (Santiago), since this was hindering linkages between start-ups and the country's productive sectors, such as mining and agriculture. Assessments of policies to promote start-ups could also explore to what extent they change the organisational structures of the traditional institutions that promote production development and innovation. Programmes to support start-ups might also be modernising and invigorating traditional systems by introducing new ways of planning, managing and implementing public policies and by requiring changes to the profiles of the people in charge: pro-startup programmes need to be fast and flexible, and cannot be run using the same approach that is used for traditional entrepreneurship programmes.

Simplify and consolidate support programmes and bring them more in line with the needs of the target population. Although initial experimentation with different programmes and mechanisms are helping to determine what works best in each context, if there are too many instruments, they are not effective for defining a policy that is easy for entrepreneurs to use. Programmes can have a greater impact if they are integrated and incorporate both services and financing for entrepreneurs and they offer incentives to accompany start-uppers at the various stages of a company's development.

Find ways to create synergies between measures to promote start-ups and production-development strategies. While it is important to preserve the specific characteristics and the bottom-up approach of programmes to promote start-ups, it is also important to find mechanisms to ensure that support for start-ups contributes to driving innovation in key national industries, such as intelligent mining in Chile and the automotive sector in Mexico. Countries need to identify industries in which it would be beneficial to co-ordinate actions to promote start-ups with national production-development strategies. This was one of the reasons why Chile decided to include regional location among the conditionalities of its programmes to promote start-ups.

Include performance-based conditionalities and create exit mechanisms. Incentives work best when there are clear performance conditions. Start-Up Chile, for instance, made it compulsory for beneficiaries to set up business in Chile, having seen that, without this condition, few businesses had their base in the country. Almost all countries in the region now only support incubators that can prove that they are able to incubate businesses with the potential to grow and expand. Some countries, like Mexico and Peru, introduced conditions to ensure that companies generate new businesses and innovations in key national industries, while Chile made gender inclusion mandatory. Measures to support the venture-capital industry are much more effective when exit timeframes and conditions for the support are clearly established beforehand.

Act in the short term, but plan for the medium and long term. Seldom do start-ups become so successful that they scale up. When they do succeed, however, they do so very quickly, and the system needs to be ready to meet the needs of these emerging enterprises. Measures to promote the founding of start-ups should take into account what start-ups might need in the future if they become successful in order to get the necessary mechanisms up and running in terms of financing and regulation. For example, if a country wants to support biotech start-ups, it needs to analyse legislation on clinical trials and other factors that might not be ready for companies to operate using global standards. The European Union, for instance, has a strategy for creating a barrier-free, single digital market for purchases and sales throughout Europe, which enables companies to take full advantage of the opportunities furnished by the digital economy.

Facilitate productive investment. There is still a conservative approach to productive investment in the region, though the situation has improved in recent years, with venture capital growing. Commercial banks, development banks and investment funds could boost the region's entrepreneurial ecosystems. The region still needs to channel more private capital towards productive investment, but for this to happen, countries will need to reform legislation to foster private investment, while investors will need to change their mindsets.

Building partnerships with the private sector. Large companies are stepping up their investment in founding start-ups to increase opportunities to innovate by drawing on the talent of young people and learning more about consumer preferences. In 2010, only 1% of large companies had corporate venture capital shares, but by 2016 this figure had risen to 44% (Boston Consulting Group, 2016). Furthermore, large companies are expanding their action areas, and increasingly they are providing seed capital, incubation and mentoring as part of their open-innovation strategies. Meanwhile, the growing importance of start-ups has led to the creation of private associations that are giving voice to the needs and visions of entrepreneurs in the region. These associations reveal the needs of new entrepreneurs in real time. One such organisation is the Association of Latin American Entrepreneurs (ASELA), which was formed in 2013 as part of the Pacific Alliance. ASELA brings together the entrepreneur associations of Chile, Colombia, Mexico, Peru and Argentina and encourages those countries to share experiences and introduce reforms, such as the laws introduced in Chile and Mexico to enable people to start a business in a single day. By building partnerships with the private sector, countries can create opportunities to raise the impact of public policies.

Increase regional co-operation. Regional co-operation would enable Latin American countries to learn from each other and share good practices more quickly. It would also open up regional markets and facilitate the emergence of enterprises operating region-wide. The community that supports start-ups in Latin America is young, and it already meets together and co-ordinates more often than traditional areas of innovation or industrial policy. Countries could speed up learning processes and create good practices by improving the structure of these spaces for dialogue and by introducing peer review. Regional co-operation could also help to close funding gaps and attract larger levels of investment, which would respond to the challenges that the countries face in terms of finance. In this sense, regional funds like the Pacific Alliance initiatives to promote start-ups and entrepreneurship are important, and countries should do more to encourage such initiatives.

Recognise and assess the specificities of each context. Many lessons can be drawn from the experiences of others in promoting start-ups, and identifying best practices is crucial to improve policies. However, in addition to looking outside, countries also need to carefully analyse their own system and its specific features. Instruments that are successful in one country or region might not be suitable for another. Entrepreneurship is a process that involves experimenting, so standardising support instruments can be counterproductive.

Progress in education, innovation and production development and a more widespread entrepreneurial culture will also lead to better and more start-ups.

For start-ups to flourish in Latin America, the innovation and production systems need to become denser, private investors must begin to back start-ups, and countries need to strengthen their science and technology capabilities and close the gap in the digital economy. Start-ups do not operate in a vacuum and successful enterprises aspire to operate in the global market. Efforts are therefore needed to ensure that the production system and the science and technology system match the potential of innovative Latin American entrepreneurs.

Start-ups will not be the ultimate solution for development in the region, but creating a startup-friendly environment, channelling public investment (especially in the early stages) and private investment (especially at the expansion stage) towards start-ups, and creating flexible, modern services for entrepreneurs are essential parts of the transformation strategies of Latin American countries. Policies to promote start-ups do not so much need huge budgets as they need smart planning and a flexible design. They also require simple, rapid instruments, as well as partnerships with the private sector, universities and technology centres.

The current climate for the region is marked by sluggish growth and the depletion of traditional sources of growth, with low commodity prices and low external demand, which in recent years has been driven mainly by the People's Republic of China. Diversifying production and joining the new digital economy are therefore important objectives for the countries of the region. If Latin American countries can achieve these objectives, they will be able to make the necessary strides towards more inclusive, long-term growth to meet the growing demands of their societies, especially young people. It is therefore important and urgent to capitalise on these experiences in promoting start-ups, to strengthen the instruments and programmes that work, and to reform those that are not producing the desired results.

References

Boston Consulting Group (2016), *Corporate Venturing Shifts Gears*, The Boston Consulting Group. available at: www.bcgperspectives.com/Images/BCG-Corporate-Venturing-Shifts-Gears-Apr-2016_tcm80-208404.pdf.

CORFO (2015), *The Chilean Experience in Developing a Global Enrepreneurship Hub*, Bitrán E., October, mimeo.

ECLAC (2015), *La nueva revolución digital: de la Internet del consumo a la Internet de la producción*, Economic Commission for Latin America and the Caribbean, United Nations, Santiago, Chile.

ECLAC (2013), *Entre mitos y realidades. TIC, políticas públicas y desarrollo productivo en América Latina*, Economic Commission for Latin America and the Caribbean, United Nations, Santiago, Chile.

LAVCA (2016), *Latin America Venture Capital: Five Year Trends*, Latin American Private Equity & Venture Capital Association, available at: http://lavca.org/2016/07/15/new-vc-latin-america-venture-capital-five-year-trends/, accessed July 2016.

OECD (2015), *Entrepreneurship at a Glance 2015*, OECD Publishing, Paris, http://dx.doi.org/10.1787/entrepreneur_aag-2015-en.

OECD (2013), *Startup América Latina: Promoviendo la innovación en la región*, Estudios del Centro de Desarrollo, OECD Publishing, Paris, http://dx.doi.org/10.1787/9789264202320-es.

Online resource:

Fortune (2016), The Unicorn List, available at: http://fortune.com/unicorns/ , accessed July 2016.

Chapter 1

Why support start-ups, and how?

There is growing interest worldwide in actions to promote the creation and expansion of start-ups. Until a few years ago, start-ups were associated almost exclusively with Silicon Valley, but today they are much broader in scope and can be found outside the United States. Start-ups provide innovative solutions, create new markets and reinvigorate the business community. The emergence of start-ups depends not only on entrepreneurial spirit, but also on an environment (services, infrastructure, financing and regulatory framework) that is conducive to their emergence and expansion. National and local governments, in conjunction with the private sector, actively promote start-ups and seek to create incentives for their development. This chapter summarises definitions of start-ups and presents the rationale behind state intervention in this area and the matrix of instruments used to promote start-ups. The chapter concludes by identifying the lessons learned from other countries in designing and managing pro-startup policies.

The statistical data for Israel are supplied by and under the responsibility of the relevant Israeli authorities. The use of such data by the OECD is without prejudice to the status of the Golan Heights, East Jerusalem and Israeli settlements in the West Bank under the terms of international law.

Introduction

Start-ups are very popular right now, and not just in Silicon Valley. France, Chile, India, Italy, Mexico and Poland all have new programmes to foster start-ups in order to sustain competitiveness, promote innovation and tap into the opportunities offered by the new global digital economy.

There is a broad consensus that new, innovative enterprises play a vital role in determining how dynamic a country's innovation will be. Through start-ups, new products and services based on scientific discoveries and new applications of existing knowledge can be released, creating new markets and furnishing novel solutions to emerging problems. They also bolster competition for innovation and encourage the development of a dynamic business environment. The start-up and growth of these businesses depends on several factors: a solid scientific base, a business-friendly environment, and a financial sector willing to make medium-term investments in high-risk projects, among others.

Why, though, should governments support the founding of start-ups, and how can they do so? Many countries have shown that national and local governments, in partnership with the private sector, can play a major role in building the right environment for innovative entrepreneurship. This chapter reviews the definition of start-ups and discusses what elements are currently lacking for start-ups to emerge and grow and how these elements determine public policy action areas. It also presents a matrix of instruments based on the experience of OECD countries and emerging countries in promoting start-ups. The instruments in the matrix are classified by business development stage (seed, start-up, growth and expansion) and action area (financing, services, market activation, business culture and regulatory framework). The chapter concludes with a brief summary of the lessons learned from pro-startup programmes in various countries.

What are start-ups?

What is a start-up? This might seem an easy question to answer today, since start-ups have become a global phenomenon and everybody, whether an expert or not, has at least an idea of what they are. Generally speaking, start-ups are associated with new, disruptive, dynamic businesses, often arising from innovative ideas that require financial capital more than physical infrastructure for their development. The narrative of start-ups developed following the rise of Silicon Valley and new technology-based firms that make intensive use of information and communication technologies (ICTs). These enterprises emerged as spin-offs from ICT giants and technological universities. Silicon Valley remains the heartland of the world's disruptive start-ups. As of 2016, nine of the 20 highest market value start-ups are located in California, including Uber, Airbnb and Pinterest (Fortune, 2016).

Today, however, start-ups exist far beyond the confines of Silicon Valley. The phenomenon is expanding and adapting to the places where these new innovative businesses are being founded. Thanks to the spread of ICTs, globalisation and the growing aspirations of societies in emerging and developing countries, as well as public policies that now seek to create the right conditions for innovation, start-ups are emerging not only in Europe, but also in Africa, Asia and Latin America, where an emerging group of start-uppers are operating, creating innovative solutions and changing local mindsets (OECD, 2013a, 2013b; Bayrasli, 2015).

Over the last decade, start-ups have attracted growing attention from the media, market analysts, innovation experts and policy makers (IDB, 2009; Kantis and Federico, 2012; OECD, 2013a; UNECE, 2012; Kantis et al., 2015; Fortune, 2016). However, there is no single definition of what a start-up is. Public policy makers, researchers, market analysts and start-uppers all have different definitions. The most common criteria refer to ideas, networks, market opportunities, disruption to business models, and communities.

Despite the many definitions, two criteria stand out: one based on market performance, and one based on the nature of the business, including its innovativeness and disruptiveness. Public policy actions tend to be guided by hybrid definitions that refer both to the nature of the business and to its performance potential (Table 1.1).

According to the performance-based approach, start-ups are newly established firms with a high potential impact, strong growth, or a market value above a certain level. The OECD, for instance, defines high-growth enterprises as those that have an average annualised growth in employees or turnover greater than 20% over a three-year period and ten or more employees at the beginning of the observation period. It defines gazelles as the subset of the above that are less than five years old (OECD, 2015a; Figure 1.1). In Silicon Valley, start-ups are categorised according to their market value: "unicorns" are start-ups worth at least USD 1 billion, "centaurs" are those worth between USD 100 million and USD 1 billion, and "little ponies" are those worth between USD 10 million and USD 100 million.

The approach based on the nature of the business uses basic criteria related to the firm's age, nature and technology or innovation intensity. Under this approach, start-ups are new enterprises (usually less than five years old) that: i) were created based on business ideas related to the industrial application of scientific, technological and business innovations; ii) provide novel solutions to emerging problems; or iii) create new demand by developing new forms of business.

The definitions that best reveal the essence of start-ups are those created by the start-uppers themselves. Warby Parker co-CEO Neil Blumenthal defined a start-up as "a company working to solve a problem where the solution is not obvious and success is not guaranteed" (Business Insider, 2014). However, when start-ups could benefit from public- or private-sector support, the criteria used to define them, monitor their performance and assess their impact must be more tangible. Countries that have designed and implemented pro-startup policies have generally adopted hybrid definitions that use performance indicators as well as indicators regarding the business's nature and type. This document uses the term "start-up" to refer to innovation-intensive or high-impact new enterprises for which support mechanisms are being implemented in Latin American countries, based on each country's own definitions.

Table 1.1. **Some definitions of start-ups**

Performance-based definitions		Source
High-growth enterprises	Enterprises that have increased their number of employees (or turnover) by more than 20% a year over a three-year period and had ten or more employees at the beginning of the observation period.	OECD (2015a)
Gazelles	High-growth enterprises less than five years old.	OECD (2015a)
High-impact entrepreneurs	Individuals that launch and lead companies with above-average impact in terms of job creation, wealth creation and the development of entrepreneurial role models.	Endeavor-GEM (2011)
Definitions based on the nature of the business or innovation intensity		**Source**
Start-ups	Enterprises that are less than three years old that use technologies or innovation-intensive business practices or that have a significant growth potential in terms of turnover or jobs.	European Startup Monitor (2015)
	Enterprises that have been operating for less than two years.	Calvino et al., (2016)
	A company working to solve a problem where the solution is not obvious and success is not guaranteed.	Neil Blumenthal, co-executive director of Warby Parker; Business Insider (2014)
	A human institution designed to deliver a new product or service under conditions of extreme uncertainty.	Ries (2010)
Mixed definitions		
Start-ups	Innovative or technological firms targeting the global market with the potential to grow 20% during the first three years and achieve turnover in excess of USD 1 million.	Start-up Chile (2016)
	Companies not more than five years old, with turnover of less than INR 250 million (Indian rupees, about USD 3.7 million) in the last five years, that are working towards innovation, development and the commercialisation of new products, processes or services driven by technology or intellectual property.	Ministry of Commerce and Industry of India (2016)
	Entrepreneurial venture designed to search for a repeatable and scalable business model. Usually highly innovative and typically based on ideas, technologies or business models that did not exist before.	European Digital Forum (2016)

Source: Update and expansion of OECD (2013), *Start-up Latin America: Promoting Innovation in the Region*, http://dx.doi.org/10.1787/9789264202306-en.

Figure 1.1. **Gazelles by main sector, selected OECD countries, 2008-15**

(number of gazelles, measured by turnover growth [+20%], as a percentage of all enterprises with at least ten employees)

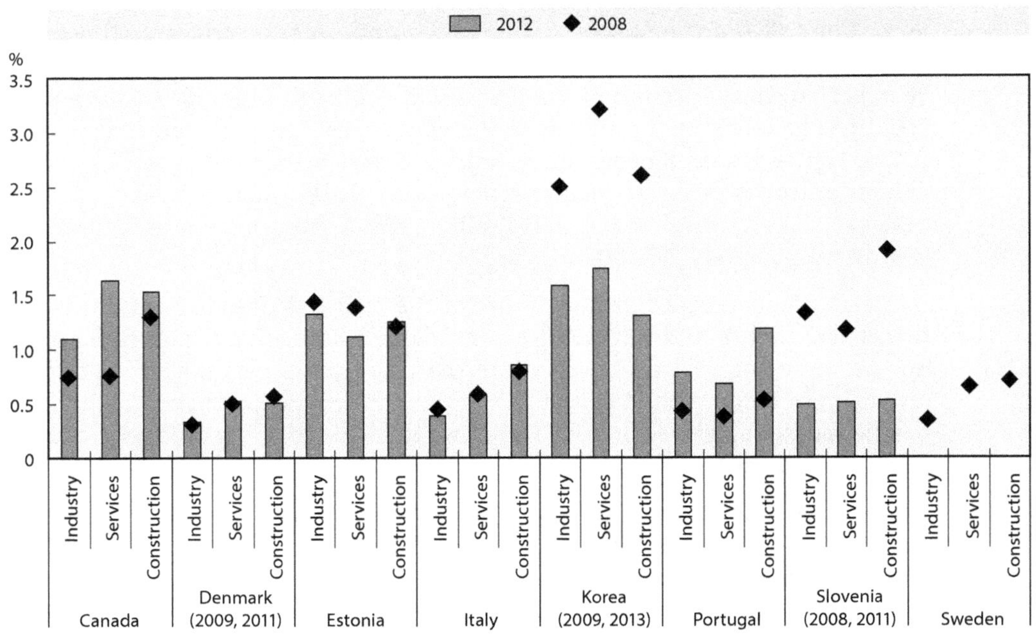

Source: OECD (2015), *Entrepreneurship at a Glance 2015*, http://dx.doi.org/10.1787/entrepreneur_aag-2015-en.

Why support start-ups?

Founding and growing innovative start-ups helps sustain innovation in the economy and vitalise the productivity and resilience of the economic system (OECD, 2010, 2011a, 2011b; Stangler, 2010; Endeavor-GEM, 2011; InnoGrips, 2011; UNCTAD, 2012). There is a strong correlation between advanced economies, a solid base of innovative entrepreneurs, greater leverage of the scientific and technological base, and productivity growth (OECD, 2005). New start-ups bring many benefits:

- Start-ups help to change the structure of the economy by introducing new, knowledge-intensive products and services and supporting innovation. They can help to redefine business models, as is happening with transport services and in the hotel and catering industry, and they can create synergies with the open-innovation strategies of large companies. In emerging countries, start-ups can transform societies by providing flexible solutions to the country's specific social development problems and challenges.
- Start-ups are dynamic, modern, open and innovative and are run by younger people, who inject these values into the business community. The launch of innovative start-ups generates positive externalities in the economic system by spreading a culture of experimentation and learning, which changes mindsets and increases acceptance of business risk by entrepreneurs and investors alike.
- Some countries benefit from the intangible value of start-up clusters, which improve the image of the cities or regions where they are located. Examples include Medellín in Colombia, Bangalore in India and Detroit in the United States.
- Start-ups can also create jobs, although very few start-ups become industry giants. They usually create good-quality jobs and help to activate demand for advanced skills in science, technology and business management.

Start-ups do not, however, emerge spontaneously; certain basic conditions must be met. Often, the private sector itself must assume the cost of creating these companies and the experimentation that takes place, because creating and expanding start-ups is very risky, with a high failure rate, but also potentially high returns. The willingness of entrepreneurs and investors is therefore essential for such enterprises to emerge and flourish. There are, however, areas in which public investment is justified.

Successful start-up ecosystems do not develop automatically. Public policies, in conjunction with private initiatives, can play a key role in fostering their emergence. Start-ups face specific challenges, not faced by traditional companies, during their founding, their growth and their expansion. These challenges are linked to the high risk and uncertainty of their business operations, particularly during the early stages of development. Specifically, there are six major barriers to the founding and growth of start-ups:

- An embryonic or basic science, technology, and innovation system in which very few science and technology institutes are training human resources with specific knowledge in areas that might generate ideas that could become businesses (e.g. engineering, electronics and medicine, as well as social sciences such as design and urban design), and in which connections and linkages between disciplines are scant.
- Little tradition for business and innovation. Some societies are more hostile to business risk than others. In such societies, there is a general distrust towards business and its positive impact for entrepreneurs and for the region or country as a whole.
- The funding gap between the entrepreneur's initial resources, including any received from public agencies or corporate funding to research and develop an idea with commercial potential, and the financial and infrastructure investment needed to turn that idea into an industrial prototype. A financial system able to dialogue with innovative entrepreneurs in their various stages of development is key to supporting the growth of these enterprises.
- Information asymmetry between the entrepreneur-innovator, investors and customers. The innovator knows what is technically feasible; the investor knows how to introduce and leverage new products in the marketplace and track consumer demand. For an invention to become an innovation, it requires a business plan that resolves issues related to the functionality, quality and feasibility of production and distribution. Often, innovators lack the business skills (management, negotiation, finance, marketing, etc.) needed to launch an enterprise. Start-uppers, meanwhile, do not possess information on distribution channels, positioning strategies and protection of intellectual property in their target market. A dynamic business environment with strong confidence among entrepreneurs, investors and consumers is a decisive factor in the process of starting a business and facilitates the flow of information. The quality and density of the innovation system and the institutions governing formal and informal transactions affect the dynamics and success of start-ups.
- A gap between start-uppers and their target market and a shortage of demand to activate and sustain production and the business model.
- Legal and administrative barriers that make it difficult to start, grow and wind up businesses; specific regulations and standards in several industries that make it difficult for start-ups to grow and scale up; and a lack of pro-innovation tax incentives.

The gaps in these six areas cannot be closed through market actions alone, and the experience of various countries shows that state intervention (through different forms and channels) is crucial to create the necessary conditions for start-ups to flourish and grow (OECD, 2013a). Furthermore, pro-startup policies require smaller budgets than other production and innovation development policies and can have a greater impact in a shorter space of time. As such, they are an important addition to countries' transformation strategies, which take much longer to bear fruit. With Start-Up Chile, for instance, as of May 2016, the businesses that were among the first seven generations of beneficiaries were valued at five times the amount invested by the government in the programme, according to data from Chile's Production Development Corporation, CORFO.

How to support start-ups?

Start-ups operate in dense, creative ecosystems with science and technology skills, investors, and physical and digital infrastructure. Several stakeholders act concurrently to create a suitable system for start-ups to emerge and expand.

The role of the private sector is growing, not only in terms of financing and investment, but also in terms of the provision of infrastructure for innovative start-ups. Large companies, especially those in the ICT and technology-intensive industries, are stepping up their investment in founding start-ups by adopting open-innovation strategies to increase opportunities to innovate by drawing on the talent of young people and learning more about consumer preferences. Today, large companies support start-ups through a wide range of measures. Those based on corporate venture capital are increasingly accompanied by the provision of seed capital and incubation services as part of open-innovation strategies. One such example is that of Telefónica's Wayra initiative in Peru, which seeks to tap into the country's innovative talent. Now operating worldwide, Wayra provides infrastructure, digital access, mentoring and seed capital to young people selected through an applications procedure.

Corporate venture capital for investment in innovative start-ups with high growth potential has been playing an increasingly important role in the open-innovation strategies of large companies (Gompers and Lerner, 1998; MacMillan et al., 2008). Corporate venture capital differs from the traditional kind in that it seeks not only a return on investment, but more importantly new solutions and innovations that will benefit the company (Dushnitsky and Lenox, 2005 and 2006; MacMillan et al., 2008; Weber and Weber, 2007). It therefore seems that corporate venture capital investments tend to bolster the investing company's innovativeness, increase its market value and improve its financial performance (Wadhwa and Kotha, 2006; Dushnitsky and Lenox, 2006; Allen and Hevert, 2007; Wadhwa et al., 2016). Innovative start-ups, meanwhile, benefit from the investing company's financial support and its commercial experience and network of contacts.

Since its introduction in the 1960s, corporate venture capital has grown rapidly, reaching 9% of the US venture-capital industry in 2015 and showing annual growth of 28%. In recent years, corporate venture capital strategies have expanded to other regions of the world. In the People's Republic of China, for instance, it represented 5% of total venture capital in 2015 (Boston Consulting Group, 2016). Furthermore, large companies are broadening their set of support tools, providing services such as incubation, acceleration and innovation laboratories. In 2010, only 1% of large companies had corporate venture capital shares, but by 2016 this figure had risen to 44%. An estimated 750 large firms have units dedicated to corporate venture capital, including Intel, Microsoft, General Electric and Google (Boston Consulting Group, 2012; Chesbrough, 2002; Dushnitsky and Lenox, 2005). Corporate venture capital funds invest mainly in the technology-intensive industries, including pharmaceutical, biotechnology, telecommunications and semi-conductors (MacMillan et al., 2008) (see Figure 1.2).

Figure 1.2. **Large firms involved in corporate venture capital by sector, 2010-12 and 2013-15**

(investments by the 30 leading corporate venture capital companies in each industry)

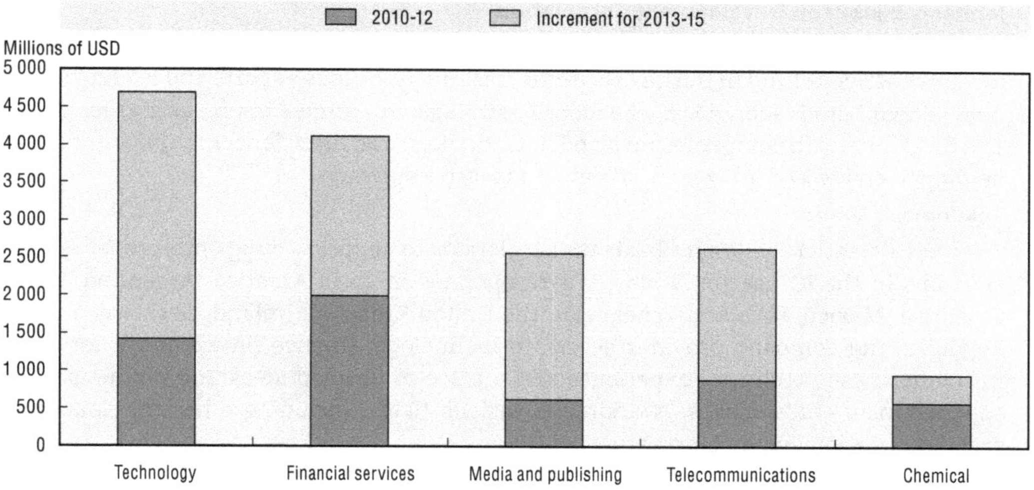

Source: Authors' work based on Boston Consulting Group (2016), *Corporate Venturing Shifts Gears.*

In addition to receiving support from large companies, start-ups also receive it from communities and networks through experience-sharing platforms and not-for-profit linkages, as well as from the people who participate in crowdfunding and support the creation of innovative start-ups based on their growth potential, their innovation intensity and their capacity to solve problems that are specific to certain places or that respond to certain challenges.

Traditional supporters of start-ups – i.e. national governments, universities, research centres, and more recently, regional and local government – also operate in this context (Figure 1.3) under different schemes, often with different objectives and incentives. Governments, for instance, seek to maximise the impact on intergenerational welfare. Communities, meanwhile, often seek solutions to specific short- and medium-term problems. Finally, private-sector investors often look for potential returns in the medium term. The fact that the various parties involved each have different priorities makes co-ordination and dialogue among them all the more important.

Figure 1.3. **Main stakeholders involved in the promotion of start-ups**

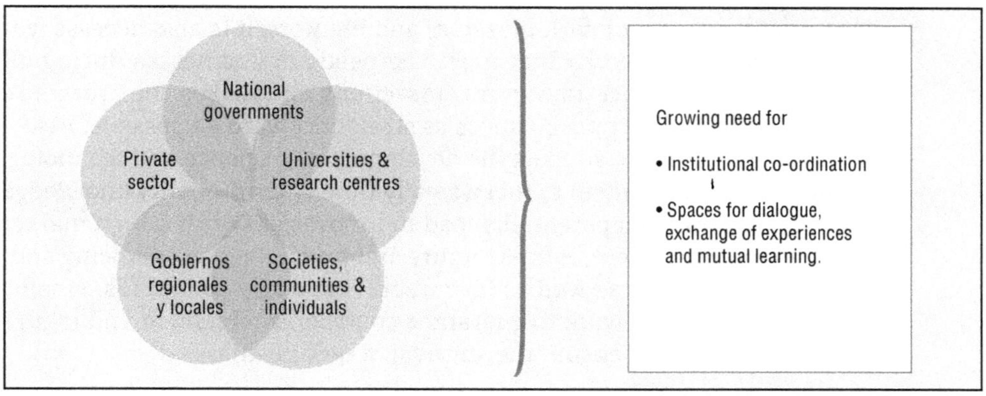

Source: Authors' work.

Box 1.1. Large companies actively promoting start-ups: Some examples

Johnson & Johnson Development Corporation

Since its inception in 1973, this venture-capital fund created by Johnson & Johnson has become a major investment fund in the health sector. It is run by various experts and leading figures in the field of health and technology, who identify strategic investment opportunities for the company. The fund invests in companies involved in technology and life sciences in the area of health care, helping to create and grow spin-offs and innovative start-ups.

Telefónica's Wayra

Telefónica created the Wayra business accelerator to support young entrepreneurs in founding start-ups in the ICT sector. Today, Wayra operates in Latin America (Argentina, Brazil, Chile, Colombia, Mexico, Peru and Venezuela), the United Kingdom, Ireland, Germany and the Czech Republic. The company provides access to technology, finance (in exchange for a 10% stake in the business), technical experience and a place to develop ideas and products. Currently it supports new entrepreneurs working in various fields, including e-health, cloud computing, social innovation and e-commerce.

Google for Entrepreneurs

Google for Entrepreneurs was launched in 2011 and has built Google Campus support spaces in several cities, including London, Madrid, Seoul, Warsaw, Tel Aviv and São Paulo. These campuses give start-ups access to Google's experience and mentoring. They also have a worldwide line of financial support aimed at coworking spaces, incubators and networking events. Google for Entrepreneurs promotes initiatives like Start Up Weekend, Techstars high-impact incubators, and Startup Grind contests.

BBVA Innovation Center

The BBVA bank supports start-ups in the financial technology, or fintech sector, including with big data, insurance, financial inclusion and online payments and transfers. The bank's Open Talent initiative rewards the best ideas in these fields, with the three regional winners (Europe, Latin America, and the United States and the rest of the world) each receiving EUR 30 000. There is also an accompaniment programme that provides mentoring and training to selected start-ups.

Source: OECD (2013a), *Start-up Latin America: Promoting Innovation in the Region*, http://dx.doi.org/10.1787/9789264202306-en; Johnson & Johnson (2016); Telefónica (2016); Google (2016); BBVA (2016).

Start-ups do not work in a vacuum. They need an environment that provides opportunities for technical education and that creates skills in specific areas (software programming, biotechnology, nanotechnology, materials, design, architecture, etc.), as well as frontline digital infrastructure and institutions that help to bring potential start-uppers in contact with investors and mentors. It is also necessary to have simple, flexible legal frameworks that meet the needs of businesses during all their growth stages, minimises uncertainty in transactions and makes the procedures for starting, running and winding up a business as straightforward as possible. Also, there needs to be a system in place to support the development of science and technology and improve the business environment to fuel a steady flow of good-quality knowledge, technologies and linkages that can potentially lead to innovations with a high market impact. Such a system requires talent, infrastructure and private-sector financing and investment in R&D and innovation, as well as favourable regulatory conditions. A stable institutional and regulatory framework to guarantee contract enforcement and regulate bankruptcy procedures is vital to ensure the survival of new businesses.

Public policies support start-ups both directly and indirectly. Indirect measures are essential because they shape the socio-economic environment in which start-uppers operate. They include policies related to science, technology and innovation, education, production development, and physical and digital infrastructure. Since the 1990s, several countries, including Chile, Finland, France, Israel, Italy and Mexico, have stepped up direct action to support start-ups by identifying the potentialities unlocked by the spread of ICTs. They have done so for two reasons: to try to emulate Silicon Valley's success (even though that success cannot be replicated), and to jumpstart stagnant growth and reinvigorate the business community.

Like start-ups themselves, direct actions to support them do not operate in a vacuum. They require indirect action to create the right conditions and environment for start-up ecosystems. Nevertheless, when they are designed and implemented properly, direct pro-startup policies play a vital role in driving the start-up of innovative businesses and creating spaces for experimentation and innovation. Without these policies, such spaces would remain silent. There is no single, optimal formula for promoting start-ups. Each ecosystem develops its own focus based on the country's features, development vision, and science, technology and production system. Direct policies to support start-ups (the focus of this report) reduce the main barriers to founding and growing start-ups. Such policies benefit start-ups, but also intermediary institutions, universities and stakeholders in the financial system (Table 1.2).

Table 1.2. **Gaps that shape direct policies to promote start-ups**

Funding gap	Programmes to improve access to seed capital and borrowing for start-ups, as well as incentives for the financial sector to work with start-ups, such as the promotion of venture capital, angel investors, etc.
Information asymmetry	Services for start-uppers through platforms, mentoring networks and collaborative spaces, and to support intermediary institutions such as incubators and accelerators.
Absence of demand	New public procurement programmes for start-ups and initiatives that challenge start-ups to provide innovative solutions.
Little tradition for business and innovation	Actions to raise awareness about start-ups (including prizes and events).
Legal and administrative barriers	Legal and administrative reforms to suit the needs of start-ups, such as easier procedures for starting and winding up a business.

Source: Authors' work.

Each country has a different blend of policies, depending on its institutional and regional structure and how developed its science and production is (OECD, 2013a; Primi, 2013). Institutional governance includes bodies responsible for innovation policy, production development and competitiveness and the public and private institutions that focus on supporting innovative start-ups, such as incubators, technology parks, angel-investor networks, incubators and accelerators, and more recently, development banks and start-up programmes set up by large companies. Based on the experiences of the OECD and Latin American countries that have most actively supported innovative entrepreneurship, a taxonomy can be drawn up in which the various instruments are classified according to the businesses' stage of development (seed, start-up, growth and expansion) (see Figure 1.4). When start-ups are founded, they are more than just young businesses; by their very essence, they are much more closely connected to their founder and his or her idea than a conventional business. As start-ups develop, they begin to take shape as companies and their needs change in terms of finance, services and regulations. The instruments vary according to the gap they serve to close, be it funding, information, demand, culture or the regulatory framework (Figure 1.4). A recent trend has been to combine financing services in new programmes that offer integrated support to simplify pro-startup schemes and respond better to the needs of start-ups.

Figure 1.4. **Policy mix to support start-ups**

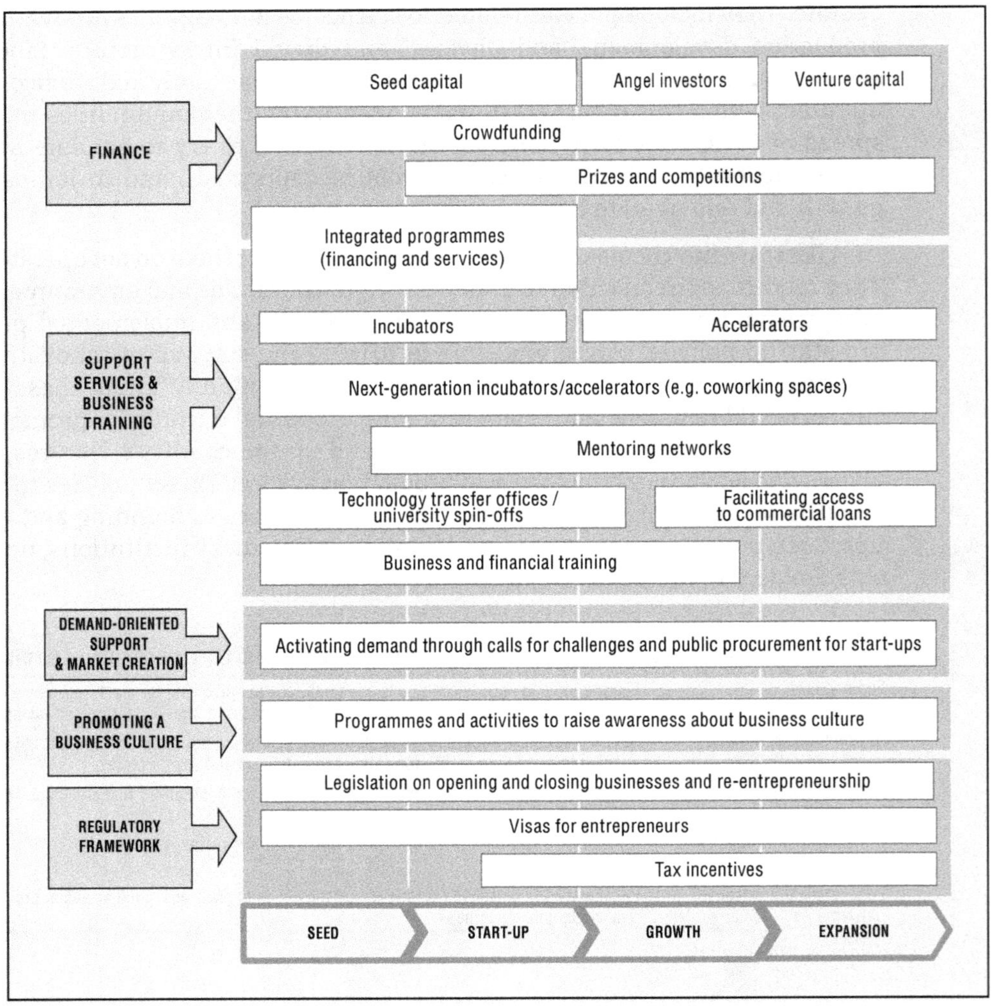

Source: OECD (2013a), *Start-up Latin America: Promoting Innovation in the Region*, updated and expanded.

The following sections describe the main features of the instruments for each area of action.

Closing the funding gap

Access to finance is a key factor in a company's creation, survival and expansion. It is even more critical for start-ups, given the greater risks and uncertainty that are inherent in the innovation process, and given that it is difficult for banks and investors to forecast how successful an innovation might become. Most financing comes from three sources: i) debt; ii) grants and government support; and iii) capital contributions (see Box 1.2). More recently, another form of financing has emerged, called crowdfunding. Different combinations of financing are used, depending on the company's stage of development (seed, start-up, growth and expansion). In the early stages, personal resources, family and friends, and bank debt (via loans and credit lines or cards) are the main sources of capital, sometimes supplemented by soft loans and subsidies. According to Branscomb and Auerswald (2002), the main sources of funding to early-stage technology development in the United States are funds from large corporations to promote spin-offs and to outsource R&D (32% of cases); federal and state government programmes (30%); angel investors (28%); venture capital (8%) and universities (3%). In the expansion stage, depending on the size and scope of the start-up, entrepreneurs will seek other sources of capital, such as angel investors and venture capital, which act as bridges before successful companies can enter the capital markets.

Public policy plays an important role in ensuring there are resources and financial options in the form of seed capital and in the form of incentives for the development of the industry through angel investors and venture capital (Table 1.3). In Finland, for instance, Veraventure Ltd., a subsidiary of the state-owned agency Finnvera, invests in regional venture-capital funds and manages the angel-investor network InvestorExtra. The Scottish Co-Investment Fund provides contributions of up to 50% to private equity funds that have invested in new businesses. Many countries, including France, Israel and Portugal, offer tax incentives for venture capital. Others, such as Australia, also promote foreign investment in local funds. In recent years, crowdfunding schemes have become important sources of financing for start-ups. In some countries, the public sector supports the creation of crowdfunding platforms. One such example is the "Accelerating the Crowdfunding Ecosystem" project developed by Mexico in partnership with the Multilateral Investment Fund, with a focus on social entrepreneurship.

Table 1.3. **Examples of programmes for financing start-ups in OECD countries**

Financing instruments		Key features	Policy examples
Direct financing	Grants and subsidies	Used as seed and early-stage funding for innovative start-ups in most countries, filling the financing gap between innovators and investors. Funds are used for feasibility studies, prototypes and proofs of concept. Awards are generally granted on a competitive basis.	Single Business Service (Australia); EXIST (Germany); Repayable Grants for Start-Ups (New Zealand); START (Russia); Small Business Research Initiative (United Kingdom); Small Business Innovation Research (United States).
	Venture capital	Public venture capital provides strategic funds designed to accelerate entrepreneurial activities at the early stages. Private venture capital focuses on companies scaling up at later, less risky stages.	Clean Energy Finance Corporation (Australia); Seed Fund Vera (Finland); Investment Grant for Business Angels (Germany); FSI France Investissement 2020 (France); Seed & Venture Capital Scheme (Ireland); Innovation Bridge and ALMI Invest (Sweden).
	Loans / loan guarantees	Loans are one of the most common forms of access to finance for start-ups. Governments offer reduced interest rates or make loans repayable only if the project succeeds. Governments can also act as guarantors for commercial loans to start-ups when they lack collateral or a track record.	Credit Guarantee Scheme for SMEs (Hungary); Vækstfonden (Denmark); Loans Service for R&I (European Union); Loan Fund for Start-ups (Poland); Enterprise Finance Guarantee (United Kingdom); the TTGV soft-loan programme (Turkey).
Third-party financing	Crowdfunding	Collective fund-raising tools enabled by advances in ICTs and social networks. These fast-growing platforms engage communities with innovation and start-ups. Challenges include the lack of regulation, cyber fraud and the need for scientific integrity.	More than 700 platforms exist around the world, including Kickstarter, CrowdCube, RocketHub, IndiGoGo: JOBS Act (United States); University of Utah's Technology Commercialization Office (TCO).

Source: Selected examples from OECD (2014b), *Science, Technology and Industry Outlook 2014*, http://dx.doi.org/10.1787/sti_outlook-2014-en.

Box 1.2. **Forms of financing for start-ups**

Debt financing

In addition to the initial capital provided by the founder, bank debt is one of the main sources of finance, both in the early stages of technology-based businesses and in their expansion stage. In the United States, bank debt represents 15% to 30% of the start-up capital of high-growth, knowledge-intensive firms (Wadhwa et al., 2009; Robb and Robinson, 2008; Robb and Robinson, 2014).

Grants

National and regional government agencies offer direct financing in the form of subsidies. Sometimes they require the beneficiaries to put up an equal amount in a matching-funds programme. Government support covers feasibility studies, proofs of concept, business-plan development, and procedures to start a business. This government contribution is essential in the seed and start-up stages, and accounts for about 30% of capital for new technology-based firms. This initial financing of innovative entrepreneurship is in addition to the funding available from other government programmes that promote collaborative R&D as well as the transfer and commercialisation of technologies from universities and research centres.

Capital contributions

Most of the resources used in founding and launching these companies comes from the personal assets of the "three Fs": friends, family and fools. These personal contributions generally cover 40% to 70% of the total investment and are acquired through personal networking, often for relatively small amounts. Note that due to their informal, familial nature, these capital contributions are particularly hard to measure.

Figure 1.5. **Percentage of the population aged 18-64 that contributed personal funds to an enterprise founded by another individual over the three years up to 2014**

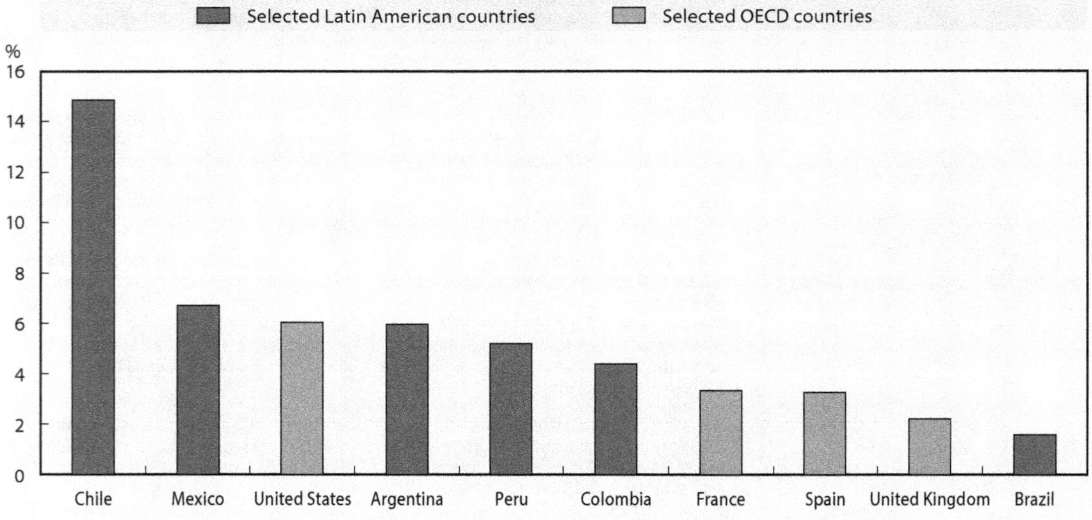

Source: GEM (2015), *Global Entrepreneurship: 2015/16 Global Report*.

Angel investors

Angel investors are typically entrepreneurs or businesspeople who, besides capital, bring their experience and their contact networks to the business (hence the term "smart money") at an early stage of its development. These investors operate on the middle ground between the informal capital provided by founders, friends and family on the one hand, and formal, venture capital on the other. They generally invest between USD 25 000 and USD 500 000 per company. Angel investors have greater flexibility in terms of maturity horizons and expected return on investment. They are less risk-averse in early stages and in innovative start-ups. Broadly speaking, they contribute capital to young enterprises that are not yet ready to attract venture-capital investment.

Box 1.2. Forms of financing for start-ups *(cont.)*

They play a key role by advising entrepreneurs and helping them to improve the quality of their investment proposals (design, business model, presentation). Recently, angel investors have begun to form groups and networks to allow them to share the risks and make larger investments. Most of these groups and networks are in the United States and the European Union, where they have tripled in number since the 2000s (OECD, 2011a; GEM, 2010).

Venture-capital funds

Venture capital refers to specialised or "professional" formal investment funds that provide capital for high-growth innovative enterprises in intermediate or expansion stages, before they enter the capital markets. In some advanced economies, such as the United Kingdom, the United States and Israel, a variety of organisations are devoted to these funds: independent organisations, bodies affiliated with financial institutions, government organisations, and angel-investor networks (Teubal and Luukkonen, 2006). Venture-capital funds make investments of around USD 3 million to USD 5 million per company (though these figures vary considerably from country to country and over time). From 1998 to 2005, for instance, the per-investment average fluctuated between USD 6 million and USD 13 million in the United States, between USD 1 million and USD 1.5 million in Europe, and between USD 2 million and USD 6 million in Israel (Ben Ari and Vonortas, 2007). In the United States, venture capital and angel investors tend to account for 20% to 50% of the start-up capital of new, high-growth, knowledge-based enterprises (Wadhwa et al., 2009). Venture capital is a subset of private equity, as is growth capital, which focuses on financing medium-sized and large firms before they begin public trading (or accepting government funds).

Venture capital is a major source of funding in the intermediate stages of the development of young, knowledge-intensive enterprises. This type of capital contribution has been vital in industries such as ICTs, biotechnology and life sciences. More recently, green venture-capital funds have been created to finance the emerging green-technology industry. Venture capital provides more than just financing: it supports the management and growth of innovative enterprises, playing an active role in their boards of directors, advising them on recruitment, and facilitating networking. However, since investment must be diversified to reduce risk, a critical mass is needed (Branscomb and Auerswald, 2002; Ben Ari and Vonortas, 2007; OECD, 2011b). According to estimates, on average, 65% of a venture-capital fund's investment generates only 3.8% of returns, whereas 4% of the investment generates more than 60% of returns (OECD, 2011b). To be effective, the venture-capital industry therefore needs the right environment, a minimum threshold of early-stage innovative entrepreneurship, a solid scientific and technological base, and a relatively mature innovation system.

Crowdfunding

Crowdfunding uses the Internet as a platform to obtain many small capital contributions, but raising capital is not the only benefit, as crowdfunding can also be used to assess market demand and for communication and marketing. Crowdfunding requires a stable Internet connection, regulations to ensure secure online bank payments, and regulations to prevent fraud and ensure the protection of personal data (OECD, 2015b). Some countries have begun setting up a system to ensure that crowdfunding runs smoothly. Mexico, for instance, created AFICO (Asociación de Plataformas de Fondeo Colectivo), an association for crowdfunding platforms that works alongside the National Banking and Securities Commission (CNBV). Crowdfunding provides relatively cheap access to seed capital. Funders are rewarded for their contribution. The rewards range from special offers on the goods or services to acknowledgement for their contribution to the project. This financing model, however, needs to offer rewards that are attractive enough to investors. Equity crowdfunding, by contrast, lets funders recoup their initial investments or share in the future profits of the enterprises being founded. Given their preliminary nature and potential to mobilise resources while minimising investment risk, this type of finance is becoming an important part of the funding model adopted by innovative start-ups.

Source: OECD (2013a), *Startup Latin America: Promoting Innovation in the Region*, http://dx.doi.org/10.1787/9789264202306-en; and OECD (2014), *OECD Science, Technology and Industry Outlook 2014*, http://dx.doi.org/10.1787/sti_outlook-2014-en.

Facilitating linkages and providing services

Various studies highlight that entrepreneurs' prior experience is a significant indicator of their success in future start-ups (Endeavor-GEM, 2011; IDB, 2009; Wadhwa et al., 2009). Entrepreneurship is a learning process involving trial and error. Through start-up, expansion and re-entrepreneurship, entrepreneurs build their skills, know-how and experience and thus improve their performance. Business skills are acquired through cumulative learning processes and require hands-on experience (learning by doing), but there are support mechanisms to help with learning and skills acquisition. In many countries, central and local governments provide various services to help firms in the seed and growth stages, including specialist consultancy services to close the gap between innovative ideas and the transformation of those ideas into a business. Such services include access to networking and the promotion of intermediary institutions operated by start-uppers. For instance, incubators, accelerators and university technology transfer offices provide support to students and researchers starting a business. Technology transfer offices provide integrated services to potential entrepreneurs and support the commercial exploitation of research findings. They provide technical consultancy and management services and facilitate access to seed capital.

Under the traditional incubator model, physical spaces are made available for a set period of time, usually between two and five years, during which the enterprises have access to infrastructure and services such as intellectual-property management, the commercialisation of technologies, and sometimes financing. Recently, however, there has been a shift towards more flexible systems involving collaborative workspaces and mentoring networks formed by people with specific knowledge in the various areas of activity of start-ups. Although it is still far too early to assess the impact of mentors on the performance of start-ups, some pioneering studies have found them to have a positive impact in New York (Endeavor Insight, 2015) and Chile (Gonzalez-Uribe and Leatherbee, 2015). Experience in the management of incubators has shown that they need to include results-based management incentives such as the market value or turnover of start-ups or the patents they have obtained. If results-based factors are not included, intermediary institutions may be rewarded more for the quantity of start-ups they support than for the quality. Accelerators, meanwhile, support start-ups that have a high growth potential as they internationalise and scale up their business model. They also facilitate access to venture capital for expansion and provide contacts and technical support.

Even if several large companies are actively promoting start-ups, potential linkages between established firms and start-ups may be missed. Public policy can encourage such linkages to be established through platforms. The European Union's Startup Europe Partnership, for instance, connects innovative start-ups with large corporations to help them scale up their businesses. The platform holds competitions to select the most promising start-ups and assists with business dealings between companies, strategic investments, and where appropriate, acquisitions. Each year it produces a ranking of Europe's "25 Corporate Startup Stars", which contains the 25 start-ups that collaborate most actively with large enterprises.

Creating markets

A recent trend in some countries is to use the innovative potential of start-ups to identify solutions to emerging problems. These include open calls for challenges focused on new enterprises, usually run by public-private partnerships. Examples include municipality and city initiatives such as Barcelona's "cities for consumers" project and similar projects by Helsinki and others. In 2014, Barcelona City Council launched the BCN|Open Challenge programme. The programme put forward six challenges related to various matters of interest to the city, including public transport, social inclusion and preserving cultural property. This led to the birth of 12 new businesses that were awarded public procurement contracts. Implementing these kinds of programmes often requires legislative reforms to allow start-ups to take part in the selection procedures for challenges that require innovative, flexible solutions to specific problems. In India, for instance, as part of the Make in India and Startup India campaign, since 2015 at least 20% of public procurement must be from micro and small enterprises. Within this framework, public procurement regulations have been reformed based on the experience of previous public procurements, sales and billing to enable new businesses to tender for contracts.

It is not easy to ensure that start-ups submit tenders, and there is no guarantee that they will do so, since they often face legal barriers, or are too small for the scale of the contracts. However, if experiments to open up markets to start-ups continue, start-ups will benefit from guaranteed access to a market, and countries will benefit from the discovery of innovative, effective solutions to problems associated with the management and delivery of products and services.

Transforming mindsets

Transforming mindsets is a long-term process that cannot be achieved solely through government programmes. In emerging and developing countries, however, promoting an entrepreneurial culture is a major part of public policy actions to create a better environment for innovation and for starting a business. Public policy actions can boost the ecosystem and transform cultures and mindsets, shaping the preferences of young people and future generations in particular. Examples include policies to promote the image of a country or city as a place for entrepreneurship, as recently introduced in Chile and Medellín, initiatives to work with the press and with radio and television broadcasters to raise public awareness, as in Panama and Argentina, and measures that demonstrate strong political leadership in promoting entrepreneurs, such as Mexico's decision to create a national entrepreneurship institute (INADEM). All countries are faced with the challenge of promoting a shift towards an innovative business culture nationwide and generating awareness among public and private entities, but each country responds to that challenge using its own model. Some countries respond to the challenges through public-private partnerships. In France, meanwhile, central and local government work on many initiatives in partnership with universities, while Colombia and South Africa – the first African host of the Global Entrepreneurship Network's Global Entrepreneurship Congress (GEC) – have citizenship programmes to position themselves in global networks.

Reforming legal frameworks

Various national, regional and local regulatory and administrative measures influence business start-up costs and barriers, affect start-up growth and determine the conditions for winding up and re-entrepreneurship. Business-friendly reforms include simplifying and harmonising administrative procedures, providing provisional initial permits, creating softer tax regimes specifically for start-ups, reducing the requirements to shut down a firm or declare bankruptcy (non-fraudulent) and streamlining the process of doing so, and providing financial support for the orderly closure of bankrupt firms to reduce the financial cost and the time needed. Another way of encouraging the growth of innovative enterprises is through legislation governing the listing of innovative start-ups on the stock market and mergers and acquisitions, for instance by reducing the cost of submitting the necessary information. Measures regulating the transfer and exploitation of the knowledge and technology generated by research projects also play an important role in encouraging innovative entrepreneurship. Such measures include intellectual-property management schemes, regulations setting the conditions for disseminating the results of publicly funded R&D projects and agreements on sharing out the profits generated when the results of R&D projects are exploited commercially. Defining these kinds of rules is important so that more private-sector resources are channelled towards creating technology-based enterprises.

Most countries have legal barriers to the development of start-ups and simplifying procedures is a common challenge. Some countries have made the regulatory framework simpler by introducing one-stop shops for start-ups or allowing them to register on line. Indonesia, for instance, introduced the One Stop Shop in 2006, a programme that incorporates the agencies one must go through to obtain a business licence and register the business. This initiative reduced the time needed to complete the formalities from 20-30 days to just ten days. Korea introduced the Start-Biz Online system in 2010, a one-stop shop to allow new businesses to register and pay taxes by entering their details only once on a web site. Chile in 2015 and Mexico in 2016 introduced laws so that a business can be started in a single day over the Internet.

In addition to legal frameworks that are friendly towards starting, expanding and winding up businesses, today's pro-startup legislation also includes special measures for the issuing of visas to investors, entrepreneurs and skilled workers, allowing countries to increase their global networks by attracting foreign talent. France, for instance, seeks to attract international business talent through the so-called "Talent Passport", which offers a simplified procedure for entrepreneurs and their families to obtain renewable four-year visas. Beneficiaries must operate in one of the seven areas identified as essential for the French economy. Startup Canada issues residency permits to entrepreneurs who have received an investment of at least USD 200 000 from a venture-capital fund or USD 75 000 from angel investors. Other countries, including Austria, Australia, Germany and Italy, grant visas to start-uppers who develop innovations that have a positive impact on their economies.

Lessons learned: Promote start-ups, but avoid start-up fever

Entrepreneurs and successful start-ups drive innovation by bringing new products, services, processes and technologies onto the market or improving those that already exist. Innovative start-ups improve productivity, increase innovation and create good-quality jobs, making them a major source of long-term growth in today's economies. Start-ups spread knowledge and use ideas commercially. They often grasp opportunities discarded by large firms, bridging the gap between research centres and knowledge markets.

However, they face major barriers during the seed and growth stages, so institutions, incentives and regulatory frameworks are needed to enable people to found and grow these businesses. Today, promoting start-ups is a task shared by various stakeholders (private, public and social), making it essential to ensure co-ordination and identify synergies among the various actions. Public policies can play an important role in providing incentives, such as seed capital to found and expand start-ups, and encouraging the private sector to invest in developing finance mechanisms to help start-ups expand, such as angel-investor networks and venture capital. Public policies can also create the right conditions for start-ups to grow by providing direct incentives for entrepreneurial capacity-building, services and infrastructure and by creating helpful regulatory frameworks. They can also create new forms of public-private partnership to forge synergies with new market trends such as corporate venture capital and new open-innovation models.

With the world's economy slowing, globalisation being redefined and the digital economy spreading, it comes as no surprise that other places want to emulate Silicon

Valley's success and find ways to create the same impact, so pro-startup programmes have proliferated in almost the entire world in recent years. Startup America, StartUp Britain, Start-Up Chile, Start-Up Russia, StartUp Perú and Startup Poland are just some examples. Meanwhile, collaborative workspaces and incubators are sprouting up in various African countries (The Economist, 2014a; UNCTAD, 2015; World Bank, 2016; Disrupt Africa, 2016). In the United States, cities and regions outside Silicon Valley have invested in building dynamic ecosystems for start-ups. They have created many support spaces and programmes, including seed-capital funds, accelerators, incubators, contests for entrepreneurs, venture-capital funds, entrepreneurship marathons and capacity-building programmes. These experiments are positive, especially for emerging countries such as those in Latin America analysed in this report, because they have reinvigorated stagnant production systems and given new opportunities to entrepreneurs and young people. It is important, however, not to fall into the trap referred to by Stangler (2016) as "startup fever", i.e. too much emphasis on building ecosystems without understanding their true impact on the success of start-ups.

There is no one correct formula for promoting start-ups and there is no recipe for an optimum start-up policy. Nevertheless, several lessons can be drawn from the experiences of countries that are implementing public programmes for start-ups. If countries adapt those lessons to their specific circumstances, they can draft and implement better policies (Box 1.3):

- **Analyse the environment and forge alliances.** Countries should identify existing stakeholders that have action programmes for the various stages of development of start-ups, learn from their experiences, forge alliances and direct their support towards closing existing gaps and creating incentives for the private sector to play a leading role.
- **Recognise and assess the specificities of each context.** Many lessons can be drawn from the experiences of others in promoting start-ups. Like in all areas of public policy, these lessons are vital to make swifter progress in learning how to manage policy. However, in addition to looking outside, countries also need to carefully analyse their own system and the specificities of their ecosystem to find niches and value-added and avoid what has been called a "start-up monoculture" (Ortmans, 2015; Stangler, 2016). Instruments that are successful in one region might not be appropriate for another, where the context for start-uppers may be different. Entrepreneurship is a process that involves experimenting, so standardising support instruments can be counterproductive. It is therefore vital to understand the situation of the start-ups in question when designing instruments to support them.
- **Plan for the short, medium and long term.** The history of start-ups contains many stories of failure and failed attempts. Seldom do start-ups become successful and scale up. When they do succeed, however, they do so very quickly, and the system needs to be ready to meet the needs of these emerging enterprises. As launching a start-up becomes easier, more accessible and cheaper, the complexities increase in the acceleration stages (The Economist, 2014b). It is important to consider what needs start-ups may have in the future if they are successful in order to get the necessary mechanisms up and running in terms of financing and regulation. For example, if a country wants to support biotech start-ups, it must analyse legislation on clinical trials and other factors that might not be ready for companies to operate using global standards. The European Union, for instance, has a strategy for creating a barrier-free, single digital market allowing purchases and sales throughout Europe thanks to the benefits of digitisation.

- **Monitor the implementation of programmes, gather evidence and use it to fine-tune policies.** Monitoring and measuring impact are important to design well-informed policies. Generating data on the situation of start-ups, start-up performance and the impact of public policy remains a challenge in most countries, partly because start-ups are a new phenomenon, and partly because a wide range of definitions are used across the various support programmes. Several countries are experimenting with ways to close these information gaps. For example, in 2016 the European Commission introduced the European Startup Monitor to monitor the progress of start-ups, draw up a profile of their founders and identify challenges and opportunities for policies. The first edition in 2016 recorded more than 2 300 start-ups in 28 member states and includes information on the sectors, financing methods and employee numbers of start-ups and on the profile of start-uppers, including their age, gender and training. In Poland, Startup Poland issued the "Polish Startups Report 2015", which provides the first mapping of digital start-ups in the country and includes related information on the nature of start-ups, including business models, capital structure, turnover, employees and innovation (Startup Poland, 2015). Italia Startup conducted a study in 2015 on the profile of Italian entrepreneurs, which revealed that successful start-uppers have extensive prior experience and are aged over 40 (Italy Startup, 2015).
- **Include performance conditions in instruments and create exit mechanisms.** Incentives work best when there are clear performance conditions. For instance, start-ups obtaining a second line of financing in order to grow may have to establish their company in the country, or the amount of public financing assigned to incubators may be proportional to some kind of performance indicator for the start-ups themselves, rather than to the number of start-ups. At the same time, measures to support the venture-capital industry are much more effective when exit timeframes and conditions for the support are clearly established beforehand, as happens in Israel (OECD, 2013a).

Box 1.3. **Promoting start-ups in the United States: Five lessons learned**

Recent studies by the Kauffman Foundation identified the following five lessons learned from the management of pro-startup programmes in the United States:

1. There is little evidence that incubators lead to successful start-ups (Fletsch, 2015). Public support can have a greater impact if it focuses on collaborative spaces that encourage beneficial practices for start-ups, such as knowledge sharing and networking.
2. Start-uppers benefit from networking events that allow them to meet other start-uppers, as well as mentors and investors. The Startup Weekend hosted by Google Entrepreneurs, for instance, meets in several cities, bringing together start-uppers, potential investors, partners and sponsors. Start-uppers also benefit from mentoring networks such as Pipeline in the Midwest of the United States, which provides mentoring to high-impact start-ups throughout the different stages of their business cycle.
3. Creating public venture-capital funds presents major challenges, since public agencies often lack the expertise to assess whether investments will be profitable or not.
4. Strict regulations and administrative burdens are barriers to the founding of innovative start-ups. In the United States, for instance, an occupational licence is required to perform certain professional activities, mainly those requiring skilled labour. This type of administrative barrier requiring outlays may hinder the introduction of innovative products or new organisational setups. Furthermore, simplifying the system for paying taxes encourages businesses to register formally.
5. To facilitate the learning process in public policies to support start-ups, it is necessary to generate data that will measure the impact of policies and identify the conditions for and indicators of successful start-ups.

Note: Set up in the mid-1960s, the Ewing Marion Kauffman Foundation supports start-up hubs in US metropolitan areas and conducts research on entrepreneurs, start-ups and ecosystems in the United States.
Source: Authors' work based on Stangler, D. and J. Wiens (2015), *The Dos and Don'ts of Local Entrepreneurship Promotion.*

References

Allen, S.A. and K.T. Hevert (2007), "Venture capital investing by information technology companies: Did it pay?", *Journal of Business Venturing*, Vol. 22, pp. 262-282.

Bayrasli, E. (2015), *From the Other Side of the World: Extraordinary Entrepreneurs, Unlikely Places*, Public Affairs, New York.

BBVA (2016), BBVA Innovation Center website, http://www.centrodeinnovacionbbva.com/ (accessed in July 2016).

Ben Ari, G. and N. Vonortas (2007), *Risk Financing for Knowledge-Based Enterprises: Mechanisms and Policy Options*, Center for International Science and Technology Policy, George Washington University, Washington, DC.

Boston Consulting Group (2016), *Corporate Venturing Shifts Gears*, The Boston Consulting Group, https://www.bcgperspectives.com/Images/BCG-Corporate-Venturing-Shifts-Gears-Apr-2016_tcm80-208404.pdf.

Boston Consulting Group (2012), *Corporate Venture Capital: Avoid the Risk, Miss the Rewards*, The Boston Consulting Group, http://www.bcgsea.com/documents/file120517.pdf.

Branscomb, L. and P. Auerswald (2002), *Between Invention and Innovation: An Analysis of Funding for Early-Stage Technology Development*, NIST, Dept. of Commerce.

Business Insider (2014), *This is the Definitive Definition of a Startup*, http://www.businessinsider.com/what-is-a-startup-definition-2014-12.

Calvino, F. et al. (2016), "No country for young firms?: Start-up dynamics and national policies", *OECD Science, Technology and Industry Policy Papers*, No. 29, OECD Publishing, Paris, http://dx.doi.org/10.1787/5jm22p40c8mw-en.

Chesbrough, H. (2002), "Making sense of corporate venture capital", *Harvard Business Review*, https://hbr.org/2002/03/making-sense-of-corporate-venture-capital.

Disrupt Africa (2016), Disrupt Africa website, http://disrupt-africa.com/, accessed in July 2016.

Dushnitsky, G. and M.J. Lenox (2006), "When does corporate venture capital investment create firm value?", *Journal of Business Venturing*, Vol. 21, pp. 753-772.

Dushnitsky, G. and M.J. Lenox (2005), "Corporate venture capital and incumbent firm innovation rates", *Research Policy*, Vol. 34(5), pp. 615-639.

Endeavor Insight (2015), *Creando el ecosistema de emprendimiento en el sector Tech de Medellín*, Endeavor Global, New York.

Endeavor-GEM (2011), *High-Impact Entrepreneurship Global Report*, http://www.gemconsortium.org/report/47124.

European Digital Forum (2016), *The 2016 Startup Nation Scoreboard*, European Digital Forum, Lisbon.

European Startup Monitor (2015), *European Startup Monitor 2015*, http://europeanstartupmonitor.com/fileadmin/presse/download/esm_2015.pdf.

Fletsch, E. (2015), "Are incubators beneficial to emerging businesses?", *Growthology Kauffmann Foundation Blog*, http://www.kauffman.org/blogs/growthology/2015/03/are-incubators-beneficial-to-emerging-businesses.

Fortune (2016), The Unicorn List, http://fortune.com/unicorns/, accessed in July 2016.

GEM (2015), *GEM 2015/2016 Global Report*, Global Entrepreneurship Research Association, London.

GEM (2010), *Global Entrepreneurship Monitor: 2010 Global Report*, Babson College and Universidad del Desarrollo.

Gompers, P.A. and J. Lerner (1998), "The determinants of corporate venture capital success: organizational structure, incentives and complementarities", *NBER Working Paper* No. 6725.

Gonzalez-Uribe, J. and M. Leatherbee (2015), *Business Accelerators and New-Venture Performance: Evidence from Startup Chile*, London School of Economics, mimeo.

Google (2016), Google for Entrepreneurs website, https://www.googleforentrepreneurs.com, accessed in July 2016.

IDB (2009), *High Growth SMEs, Innovation, Entrepreneurship and Intellectual Assets. Study of High Growth SMEs in Brazil, Chile and Mexico*, Multilateral Investment Fund Science & Technology Division, Inter-American Development Bank, Washington, DC.

InnoGrips (2011), "Policies in support of high-growth innovative SMEs", *INNO-Grips Policy Brief* No. 2, June 2011.

Italia Startup (2015), *Identikit dello Startupper Italiano*, (Italian start-upper's identity kit), https://s3.amazonaws.com/iprs/files/attachments/20159/387f6113-738d-4e25-97f7-a227a7cd944c_O.pdf, accessed in July 2016.

Johnson & Johnson (2016), *Johnson & Johnson Development Corporation*, www.jjdevcorp.com, accessed in July 2016.

Kantis, H. et al. (2015), *Condiciones sistémicas para el emprendimiento dinámico: América Latina en el nuevo escenario global*, PRODEM.

Kantis, H. and J. Federico (2012), "Entrepreneurship policy in Latin America: Trends and challenges", in R. Blackburn and M. Schaper (2012), *Government, SMEs and Entrepreneurship Development: Policy, Practice and Challenges*, Routledge, London and New York.

MacMillan, I. et al. (2008), *Corporate Venture Capital (CVC): Seeking Innovation and Strategic Growth*, National Institute of Standards and Technology, U.S. Department of Commerce, Washington, DC.

Ministry of Commerce and Industry of India (2016), *Startup India Action Plan*, Government of India, http://startupindia.gov.in/actionplan.php accessed in July 2016.

OECD (2015a), *Entrepreneurship at a Glance 2015*, OECD Publishing, Paris, http://dx.doi.org/10.1787/entrepreneur_aag-2015-en.

OECD (2015b), *New Approaches to SME and Entrepreneurship Financing: Broadening the Range of Instruments*, OECD Publishing, Paris.

OECD (2014), *OECD Science, Technology and Industry Outlook 2014*, OECD Publishing, Paris, http://dx.doi.org/10.1787/sti_outlook-2014-en.

OECD (2013a), *Start-up Latin America: Promoting Innovation in the Region*, Development Centre Studies, OECD Publishing, Paris, http://dx.doi.org/10.1787/9789264202306-en.

OECD (2013b), *Perspectives on Global Development 2013: Industrial Policies in a Changing World*, OECD Publishing, Paris, http://dx.doi.org/10.1787/persp_glob_dev-2013-en.

OECD (2011a), *Financing High-Growth Firms: The Role of Angel Investors*, OECD Publishing, Paris, http://dx.doi.org/10.1787/9789264118782-en.

OECD (2011b), *Entrepreneurship at a Glance 2011*, OECD Publishing, Paris, http://dx.doi.org/10.1787/9789264097711-en.

OECD (2010), *SMEs, Entrepreneurship and Innovation*, OECD Publishing, Paris, http://dx.doi.org/10.1787/9789264080355-en

OECD (2005), "Micro-policies for growth and productivity: Final report", OECD, Paris, www.oecd.org/sti/ind//34941809.pdf.

Ortmans, J. (2015), *Avoiding a Startup Monoculture*, Kauffman Foundation, Kansas City, MO http://www.kauffman.org/blogs/policy-dialogue/2015/april/avoiding-a-startup-monoculture.

Primi, A. (2013), "The evolving geography of innovation: A territorial perspective", in Cornell University, INSEAD and WIPO (2013), *The Global Innovation Index 2013: The Local Dynamics of Innovation*, Geneva, Ithaca and Fontainebleau.

Ries, E. (2010), "What is a startup?", *Startup Lessons Learned*, blog, www.startuplessonslearned.com/2010/06/what-is-startup.html.

Robb, A.M. and D.T. Robinson (2014), "The capital structure decisions of new firms", *Review of Financial Studies*, Oxford Journals, Vol. 27(1), pp. 153-179.

Robb, A.M. and D.T. Robinson (2008), *The Capital Structure Decisions of New Firms*, Kauffman Foundation, http://www.kauffman.org/what-we-do/research/kauffman-firm-survey-series/the-capital-structure-decisions-of-new-firms, accessed in September 2012.

Stangler, D. (2016), "The ecosystem trap", *Growthology Kauffmann Foundation Blog*, Kansas City, MO, http://www.kauffman.org/blogs/growthology/2016/04/the-ecosystem-trap.

Stangler, D. (2010), *High-Growth Firms and the Future of the American Economy*, Kauffman Foundation, Kansas City, MO, http://www.kauffman.org/what-we-do/research/firm-formation-and-growth-series/highgrowth-firms-and-the-future-of-the-american-economy.

Stangler, D. and J. Wiens (2015), *The Dos and Don'ts of Local Entrepreneurship Promotion*, Kauffmann Foundation, Kansas City, MO http://www.kauffman.org/what-we-do/resources/entrepreneurship-policy-digest/the-dos-and-donts-of-local-entrepreneurship-promotion.

Startup Poland (2015), *Polish Startups Report 2015*, Startup Poland, Warsaw, http://startuppoland.org/wp-content/uploads/2015/10/Startup-Poland-raport-ENG-01.pdf.

Telefónica (2016), Wayra website, http://wayra.org/, accessed in July 2016.

Teubal, M. and T. Luukkonen (2006), "Venture capital industries and policies: Some cross-country comparisons", *Discussion Papers* No. 1006, The Research Institute of the Finnish Economy, Helsinki.

The Economist (2014a), *Startup Fever*, www.economist.com/news/britain/21618837-boom-new-businesses-may-not-help-economy-much-startup-fever.

The Economist (2014b), *The Startup Explosion*, www.economist.com/blogs/economist-explains/2014/03/economist-explains-25.

UNCTAD (2015), "Promoting entrepreneurship for development", note by the UNCTAD secretariat prepared for the seventh session of the Enterprise and Development Commission, 20–24 April 2015, Geneva, http://unctad.org/meetings/en/SessionalDocuments/ciid29_en.pdf.

UNCTAD (2012), *Entrepreneurship Policy Framework and Implementation Guidance*, United Nations, New York and Geneva.

UNECE (2012), *Fostering Innovative Entrepreneurship: Challenges and Policy Options*, New York and Geneva.

Wadhwa, A. et al. (2016), "Corporate venture capital portfolios and firm innovation", *Journal of Business Venturing*, Elsevier, Vol. 31(1), pp. 95-112.

Wadhwa, A. and S.B. Kotha (2006), "Knowledge creation through external venturing: Evidence from the telecommunications equipment manufacturing industry", *Academy of Management Journal*, Vol. 49(4), pp. 819-835.

Wadhwa, V. et al. (2009), *The Anatomy of an Entrepreneur: Making of a Successful Entrepreneur (sic)*, Kauffman Foundation for Entrepreneurship.

Weber, B. and C. Weber (2007), "Corporate venture capital as a means of radical innovation: Relational fit, social capital, and knowledge transfer", *Journal of Engineering and Technology Management*, Vol. 24 (1/2), pp. 11–35.

World Bank (2016), *World Development Report 2016: Digital Dividends*, World Bank, Washington, DC, http://dx.doi.org/10.1596/978-1-4648-0671-1.

Chapter 2

Promoting start-ups in Latin America: Progress made and open challenges

This chapter presents an overview of policies to support start-ups in Latin America, based on the experiences of Chile, Colombia, Mexico and Peru. It is an update of the first report on start-up policies in the region (OECD, 2013). The chapter identifies lessons, results and challenges for the future. Since 2012, the concept of start-ups has attracted growing attention from many stakeholders in Latin America, from media and innovation experts to investors and policy makers. During that time, several countries have adopted policies to support start-ups. Unlike more traditional methods to support innovation and competitiveness, these policies have evolved rapidly. In just a few years, they have improved their design, focus and structure. Results are beginning to emerge, especially regarding people's perceptions of the region and its image as a place for innovative entrepreneurship.

The statistical data for Israel are supplied by and under the responsibility of the relevant Israeli authorities. The use of such data by the OECD is without prejudice to the status of the Golan Heights, East Jerusalem and Israeli settlements in the West Bank under the terms of international law.

Introduction

Start-ups are no longer associated only with Silicon Valley. Today, many countries have start-up ecosystems and a growing entrepreneurial culture, and Latin America is one of the emerging regions in this area. Governments, the private sector and universities have begun to support the creation of start-ups, as they become increasingly aware of the potential of these enterprises to transform the region's economies.

Since 2010, the concept of start-ups has attracted growing attention from many stakeholders in Latin America, from the media and innovation experts to investors and policy makers. Several countries have adopted policies to support start-ups. Chile has been the pioneer, thanks to a more structured policy that it is currently building upon and strengthening, while Mexico has made the most progress in the last five years. Unlike more traditional methods to support innovation and competitiveness, these policies have evolved rapidly. In just a few years, they have improved their design, focus and structure. Results are beginning to emerge, especially regarding people's perceptions of the region and its image as a place for innovative entrepreneurship.

This chapter presents an overview of policies to support start-ups in Latin America based on the experiences of Chile, Colombia, Mexico and Peru. It is an update of the first report on start-up policies in the region (OECD, 2013). The chapter identifies lessons, results and challenges for the future. The first section briefly describes the context in which start-ups have been emerging in Latin American countries and presents data that are beginning to paint a picture of the region's start-up scene. The second section compares pro-startup policies in the four countries over time. The third and final section identifies challenges for the future and provides policy recommendations.

Despite the barriers they face, start-ups are shaking Latin America

This section briefly introduces the regional context in which the incipient Latin American start-up ecosystems are operating. Although the section makes it clear that there are insufficient comparable data to measure the size of the start-up scene and its impact on the region, it presents emerging evidence based on new data that are outlining the situation of start-ups and their ecosystems in the countries of Latin America.

A sluggish regional economy and major global uncertainty

Latin America faces a complex situation. Although the global economy has made some progress in finding new sources of growth, it needs to do more. The global outlook is not promising for the countries in the region as they try to overcome their structural gaps in terms of skills, productivity and innovation. Sluggish growth and global uncertainty have exacerbated the region's structural weaknesses. Following a five-year slowdown, the region went into recession in 2015, a trend set to continue in 2016, with the economy projected to contract between 0.5% and 1% before recovering slightly in 2017 (OECD/CAF/ECLAC, forthcoming 2016). With commodity prices plateauing, the Chinese economy slowing and the global economy becoming uncertain due to disruptive technological changes, the region's economies have been left with gaps in productivity, skills and technology that make it difficult for them to escape their current plight (OECD/CAF/ECLAC, forthcoming 2016). Three features of the region's economies are making them more vulnerable to the global slowdown in growth and international trade: their specialisation in national resources, their poorly diversified export baskets and their dependence on imports for high-tech goods (Figure 2.1; ECLAC, 2015a).

Figure 2.1. **Latin America and the Caribbean in the global economy, 2015**

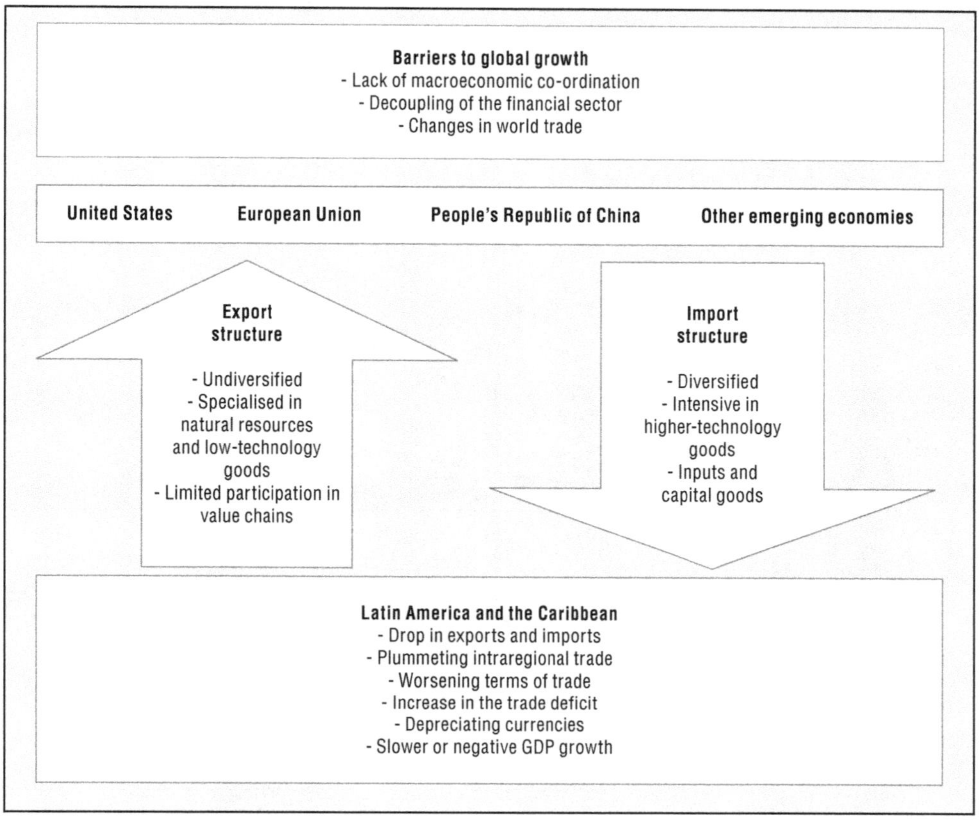

Source: ECLAC (2015a), *Latin America and the Caribbean in the World Economy 2015. The regional trade crisis: assessment and outlook.*

The digital economy has made inroads, but the innovation gap remains

Latin American countries continue to invest little in science, technology and innovation (Table 2.1). Their investment in research and development (R&D) grew from 0.63% of GDP in 2009 to 0.74% in 2014, but this figure remains well below the average for OECD countries (2.3% in 2014) (Figure 2.2; OECD, 2015b; RICYT, 2014). The dynamics of the boom period have not yet led to the kind of structural change and additional innovation that would have raised local value-added in more sectors and economic activities. Substantially higher private investment in R&D along with greater and better public-sector support is necessary to boost innovation. Latin American countries need new incentives and policies to encourage private-sector investment in innovation, including measures to support the creation of start-ups. The countries of the region have still not introduced measures to support the kind of innovation and industrial development that will capitalise on the opportunities offered by global knowledge economies (ECLAC, 2015b).

Figure 2.2. The challenge for Latin America: Mobilising public and private investment in R&D

A. Investment in R&D and private-sector contribution, selected countries, 2014

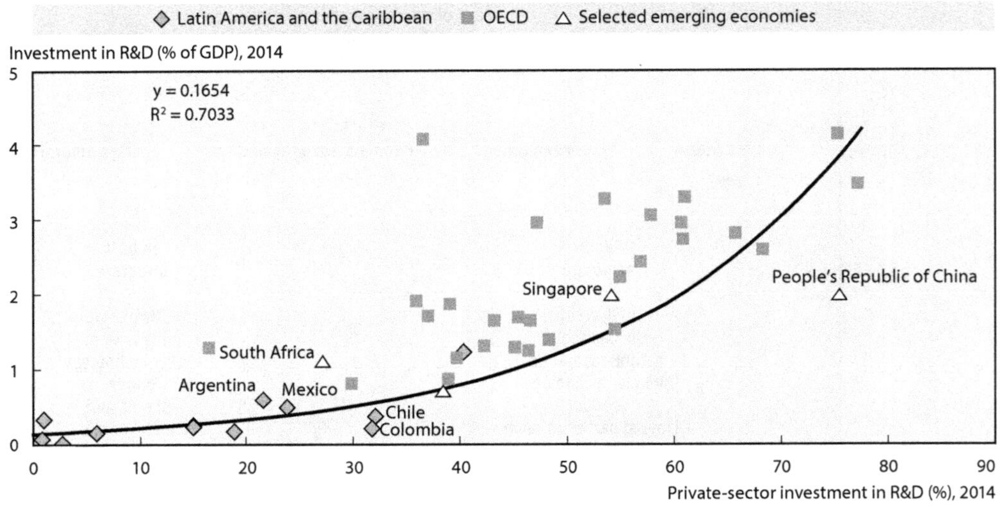

Note: "Latin America and the Caribbean" refers to Argentina, Bolivia, Brazil, Chile, Colombia, Cuba, Ecuador, El Salvador, Mexico, Panama, Paraguay and Uruguay. "Selected emerging economies" refers to China, Russia, Singapore and South Africa.

B. Investment in R&D (% of GDP), selected countries, 2014

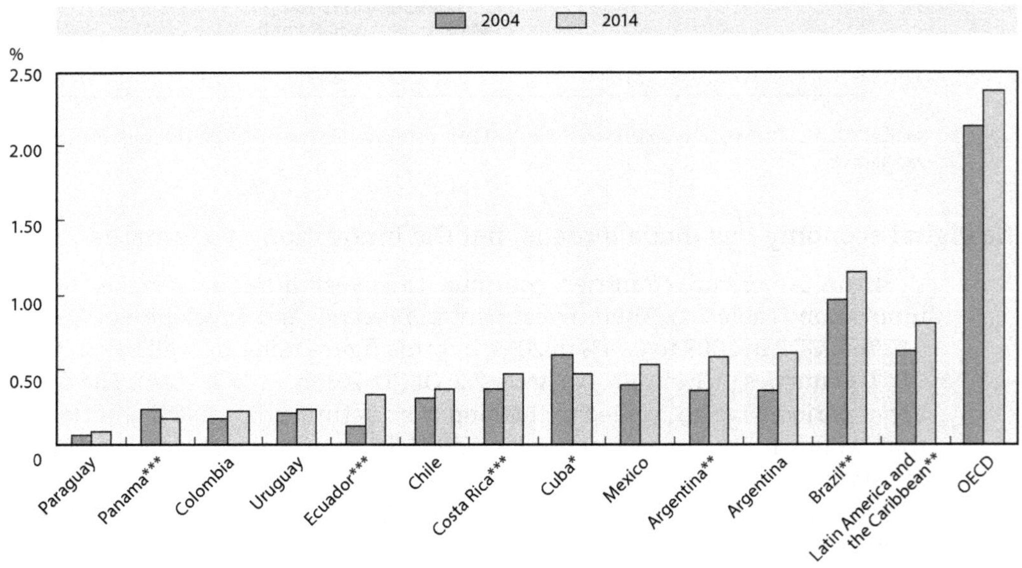

Note: Data marked with a single asterisk (*) are for 2013, those with a double asterisk (**) are for 2012, and those with a triple asterisk (***) are for 2011.

Source: Based on data from the United Nations Educational, Scientific and Cultural Organization (UNESCO); *Red de Indicadores de Ciencia y Tecnología Iberoamericana e Interamericana* (RICYT); the OECD's Main Science and Technology Indicators (MSTI) database (www.oecd.org/sti/msti.htm); Brazil's Ministry of Science and Technology; Mexico's National Institute of Statistics and Geography (INEGI); Chile's Ministry of Economy, Development and Tourism; the World Bank database; and Cuba's National Office for Statistics.

Table 2.1. **Innovation indicators, OECD countries and Latin America, 2014**

Country	R&D (% of GDP)	Private-sector investment in R&D (%)	Researchers per 1 000 employees	Number of scientific publications (2013)	Number of patents granted by the United States Patent and Trademark Office in 2012-14	High-tech exports (% of manufacturing exports in 2014)
Argentina	0.61	21.44	2.64	8 053	217	2.11
Brazil	1.15*	40.35	1.35*	48 622	878	4.15
Chile	0.39	31.96	0.9	5 157	153	0.63
Colombia	0.23	31.71	0.34*	4 455	62	1.53
Mexico	0.5	23.76	0.78	13 112	555	17.21
Peru	0.2*			647	9	0.41
Australia	2.11	61.91	8.59*	47 805	5 718	3.14
United States	2.74*	60.85	8.34*	412 541	329 613	12.78
Finland	3.17	53.53	14.18	10 156	3 815	10.9
Israel	4.11	36.54	17.62*	11 300	8 393	25.11

Note: Data marked with an asterisk (*) are the most recent available.
Source: Authors' work based on data from the United Nations Educational, Scientific and Cultural Organization (UNESCO); Red de Indicadores de Ciencia y Tecnología Iberoamericana e Interamericana (RICYT, www.ricyt.org); the OECD's Main Science and Technology Indicators (MSTI) database (www.oecd.org/sti/msti.htm); World Bank indicators (http://databank.bancomundial.org/data/home.aspx); USPTO (2014), *United States Patent and Trademark Office Performance and Accountability Report 2014*; and the UN Comtrade database (http://comtrade.un.org).

In the age of the digital economy, connectivity and access to information and communication technologies (ICTs) are basic essentials for business development. Digital infrastructure, access to ICTs and cyber-security are essential components for creating and operating start-ups, both for the businesses and for consumers. In addition to contributing to the creation of start-ups in sectors directly related to the digital age, such as the mobile apps and software development sector, ICTs also have an impact on various aspects related to the process of founding and expanding start-ups (OECD, 2015c; ECLAC, 2013; 2015b). The aspects include:

1. *Operating and managing e-commerce.* E-commerce is expanding rapidly and there are excellent opportunities for businesses in developing countries to take advantage of its lower transaction costs and global reach (ECLAC, 2013, 2015b; UNCTAD, 2015c). For start-ups to benefit from e-commerce platforms, countries need to have trustworthy online payment systems that guarantee data protection and prevent fraud. Businesses need high-quality connectivity and broadband to reach suppliers and customers.
2. *Faster procedures and access to public and private services.* By adopting ICTs, public administrations make the procedures required to start a business and pay taxes faster and more flexible. E-signatures, for instance, allowed Chile and Mexico to pass legislation that removed procedures and enabled people to start a business in a single day. Connectivity, high-quality digital infrastructure and data protection are essential to make this possible.
3. *Access to new forms of platform capitalism and crowdfunding.* One of the salient features of start-ups today is that they operate in networks and target a global market. ICTs need to be accessible and designed for productive use in order for start-ups in emerging and developing countries to operate effectively. The spread of ICTs also enables the development of new forms of service and financing for start-ups, such as crowdfunding platforms. These new forms of financing require widespread access to ICTs and the Internet, and regulations on cyber-security and data protection.

ICT uptake has grown over the last decade, but there remains a large gap with the OECD countries (ECLAC, 2013). The ICT Development Index (IDI) shows that ICT infrastructure, access and use improved in almost all of the region's economies between 2002 and 2011 (Figure 2.3). However, there are vast differences in connectivity and ICT use from one country to another in the region, as well as between urban and rural areas within countries. Fast, reliable broadband is crucial for start-ups to be able to do online transactions and participate in the digital economy, but in most of Latin America, connections are much slower than in more advanced countries. The average broadband download speed at the end of 2014 was 7.3 Mbps, compared with an average of 32.2 Mbps among OECD countries. Download speeds in Brazil, Chile, Mexico and Uruguay were faster than the regional average (ECLAC, 2015b) (Figure 2.4).

Figure 2.3. **ICT Development Index: Selected Latin American and Caribbean countries and OECD average, 2002-11**

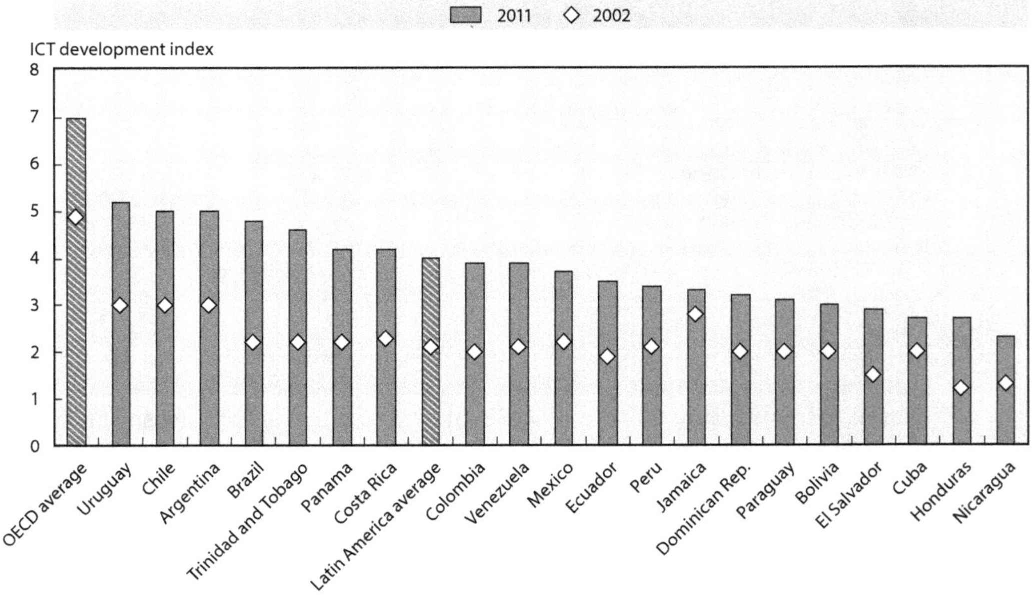

Note: ICT Development Index (ITI) by the United Nations International Telecommunication Union. A composite index based on ICT readiness (number of fixed-telephone subscriptions per 100 inhabitants, mobile-cellular telephone subscriptions per 100 inhabitants, international Internet bandwidth per user, percentage of households with a computer, percentage of households with Internet access), ICT intensity and usage (percentage of individual using the Internet, fixed-broadband subscriptions per 100 inhabitants, wireless broadband subscriptions per 100 inhabitants), and skills to use ICTs effectively (adult literacy rate, secondary-education gross enrolment ratio, tertiary-education gross enrolment ratio).
Source: ECLAC (2013), *Entre mitos y realidades. TIC, políticas públicas y desarrollo productivo en América Latina*, which uses data from the ITU's World Telecommunication/ICT Indicators database.

Figure 2.4. **Broadband download speeds, selected countries, 2014**
(megabits per second)

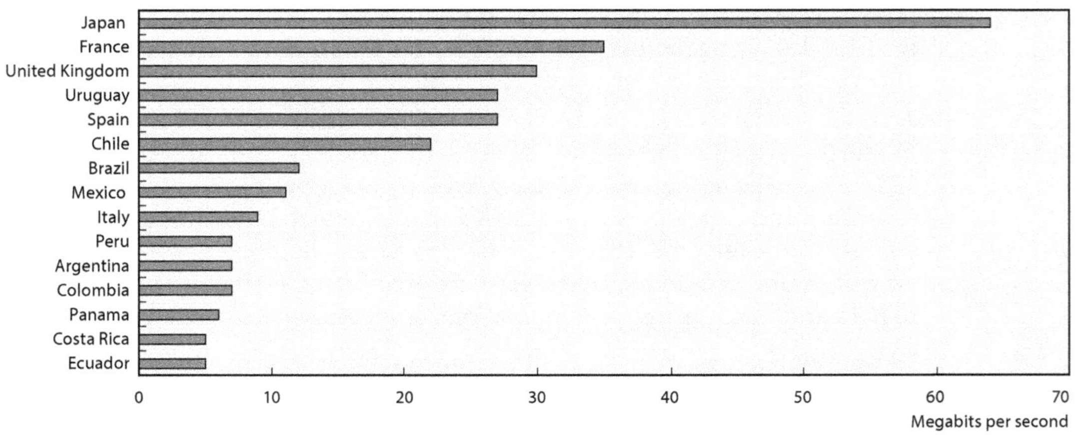

Source: ECLAC (2015b), *The new digital revolution: From the consumer Internet to the industrial Internet*, which uses data from the Regional Broadband Observatory (ORBA) based on the Ookla database.

In recent years, most countries in the region have implemented policies to promote ICT uptake and have updated their legislation. The purpose of most of these policies has been to strengthen infrastructure and provide training to businesses and users (ECLAC, 2015b). Nevertheless, countries need to improve infrastructure and skills for ICT uptake by businesses and individuals, close digital gaps between different territories within countries, regulate cyber-security, and adopt data protection and anti-fraud policies.

The venture-capital industry is expanding in the region

In addition to the innovation gaps, the region faces low levels of financial inclusion, especially for new firms. In the manufacturing sector, for instance, ECLAC estimates that 70% of large firms have access to the formal financial system, but that figure falls to just 40% for small businesses (ECLAC, 2015b). The lack of financial inclusion limits the ability of new businesses to grow and innovate. This is especially true of start-ups. The venture-capital industry has made a number of improvements in this area.

In Latin America, the venture-capital industry began to develop in the mid-1990s, supported by the Inter-American Development Bank and some public bodies such as the Production Development Corporation (CORFO) in Chile, the Brazilian Development Bank (BNDES), the Nacional Financiera (NAFINSA) development bank in Mexico, and the Bancóldex development bank in Colombia. Private-sector investment in investment funds traditionally comes from family offices and high-net-worth individuals (Miranda, 2012).

Although Latin America's venture-capital industry is still far smaller than that of the OECD countries (Figure 2.5), it is expanding. The industry's investments doubled between 2011 and 2015 (Figures 2.6 and 2.7). Brazil dominates the industry in the region, providing 74% of total investment in 2014-15. In the last five years, the industry has taken off in Mexico, which now has the second largest volume of venture-capital investments (12% in 2014-15).

Figure 2.5. **Venture-capital investments as a percentage of GDP, 2014**
(the top five countries according to the OECD's *Entrepreneurship at a Glance* and estimates for Latin America)

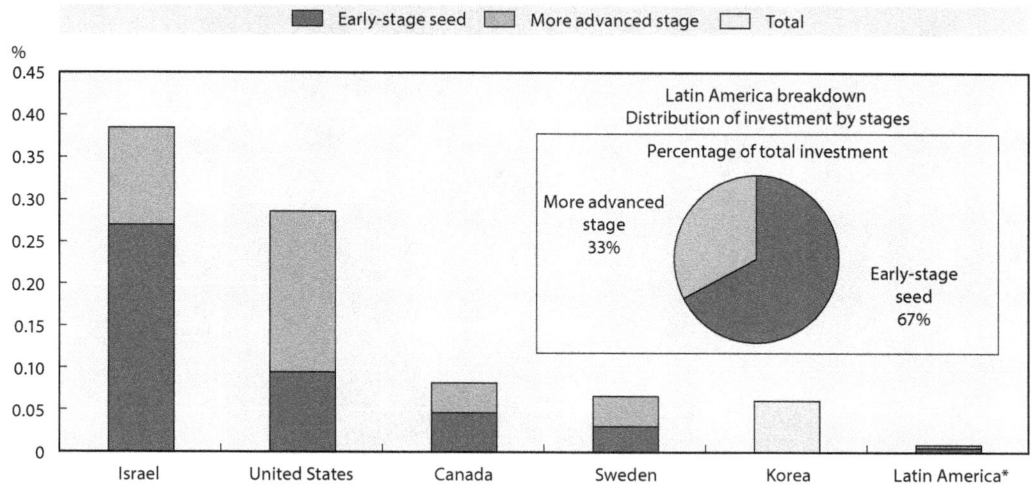

Note: * preliminary estimate.
Source: Figure 7.1 in OECD (2015b), *Entrepreneurship at a Glance 2015* for OECD countries. Data for Latin America are preliminary estimates based on data for investment in venture capital published in LAVCA (2016), *Latin America Venture Capital: Five Year Trends* and GDP data from the *World Bank Indicators* in US current 2014 dollars.

Figure 2.6. **Venture-capital investment in Latin America by country, 2011-12 and 2014-15**
(investment for each country in millions of USD and as a percentage of the total)

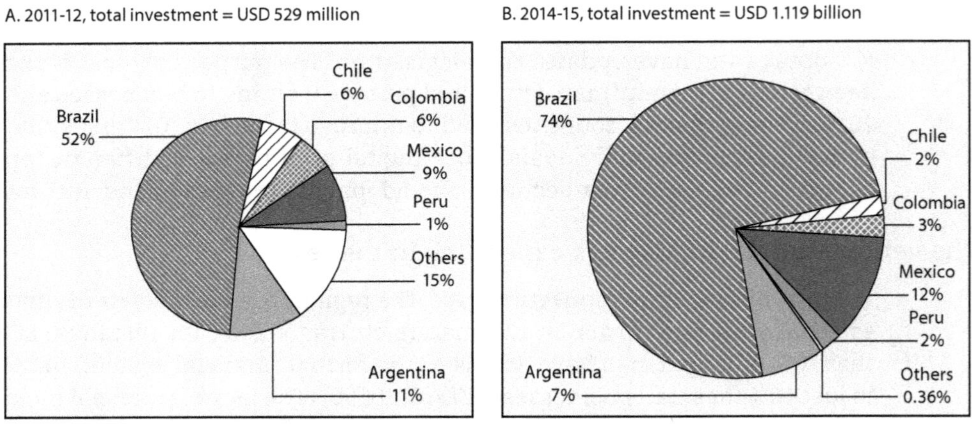

Source: LAVCA (2016), *Latin America Venture Capital: Five Year Trends*.

Figure 2.7. **Top venture-capital centres in Latin America, 2011-15**
(capital raised [USD] and number of fund closings)

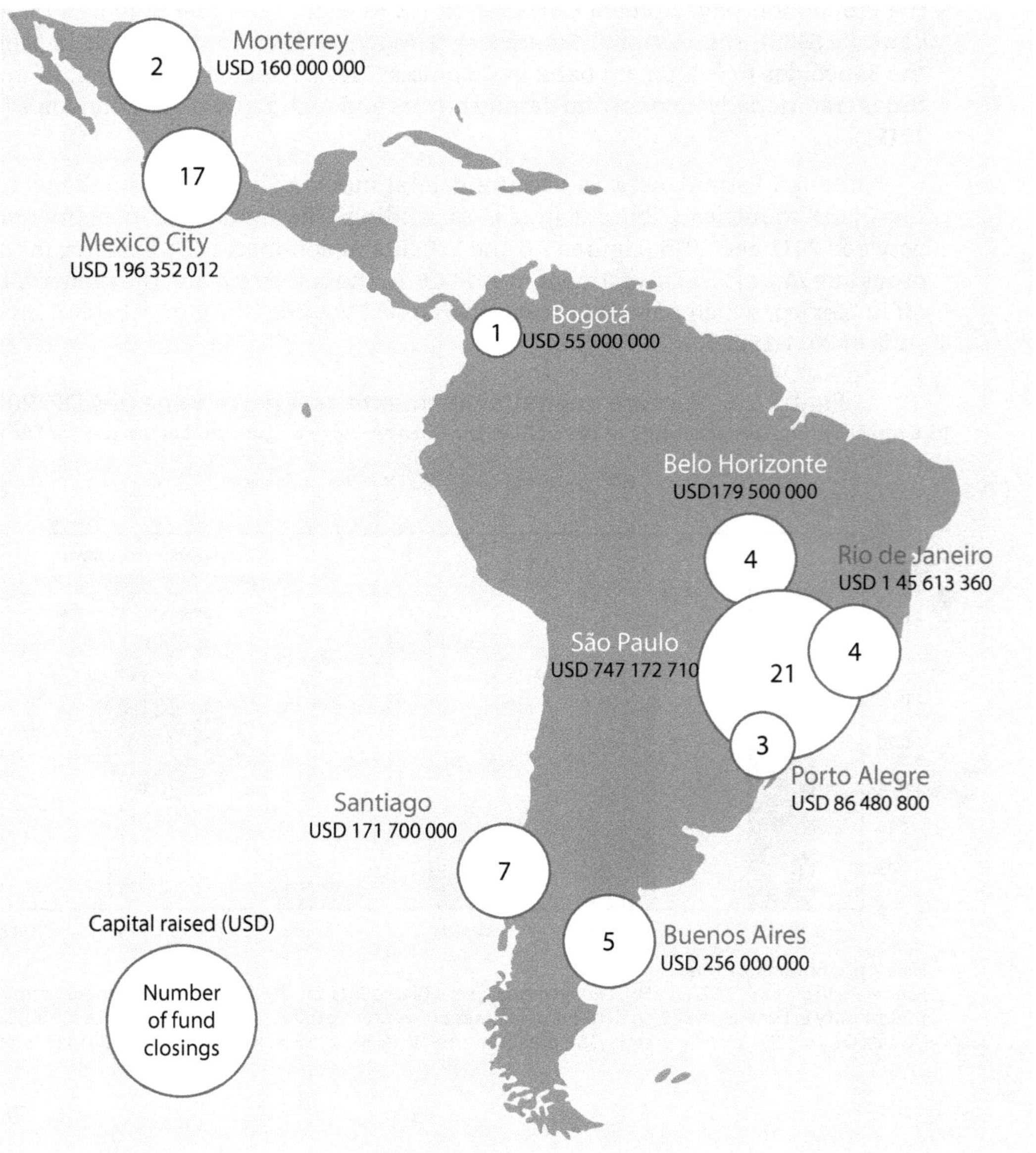

Source: LAVCA (2016), *Latin America Venture Capital: Five Year Trends*.

Historically, venture-capital funds have tended to invest in ICT-related industries, and more recently they have turned to biotech and renewable energies (OECD, 2011). In Latin America, investors have followed a similar pattern. The vast majority of investment has been in information technology (83% in 2014-15) (Figure 2.8), especially in financial technology and e-commerce. Over the last five years, financial services, renewable energies, health, life sciences, the media and entertainment have recorded increases in investment (LAVCA, 2016).

Figure 2.8. **Venture-capital investment in Latin America by sector, 2011-12 and 2014-15**

(millions of USD)

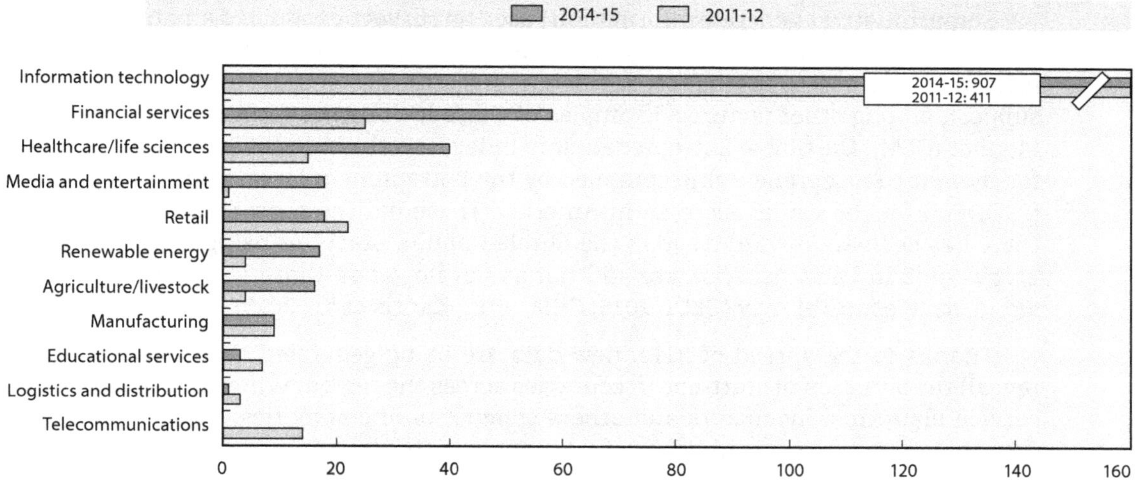

Source: LAVCA (2016), *Latin America Venture Capital: Five Year Trends*.

Start-ups reveal a different, more dynamic side of the region

The start-up landscape in Latin America shows a region that is moving forward, a dynamic region that is capable of creating ideas and innovative businesses, a region that is in much better shape than aggregate innovation indicators suggest. And this is despite technology and innovation systems that are not very dynamic, legal barriers that make it difficult to start and grow businesses, and a financial system that tends not to invest in start-ups. There is a palpable change of mindset in the region, a growing acceptance of a business culture, and a change in how people perceive the launch of innovative enterprises. Back in the early 2010s, start-ups were seen as something alien to the region's culture, but today, there is a sense that Latin American countries have the opportunities to create and grow new, innovative enterprises. Start-ups in the region still face the same major barriers to scale-up: limited resources from funds, little appetite for risk among investors, and legislation that is still often unfavourable and complex. But there is a real sense that something in the region is changing, and quickly. The region now has more start-uppers, more large firms with open-innovation strategies and new policies to support start-ups. It also has the opportunity to position itself in the new start-up landscape by developing its own ecosystems, rather than replicating the experience of Silicon Valley. In these ecosystems, start-ups may not be able to achieve the same market values as their Silicon Valley counterparts, but they can produce real technologies, products and services that solve emerging problems.

However, success stories and the perceptions of those operating in the region's ecosystems are the only indications of this forward momentum. Hard data comparing countries in the region with each other and with the rest of the world are lacking. Neither ministries, nor the agencies that design policies to support start-ups, nor national statistical institutes systematically monitor data in order to reveal the dynamics of this phenomenon. There are no official databases on start-ups, and the myriad of definitions of start-ups makes it difficult to measure them. Despite these difficulties, because public policies have recently begun to focus on promoting start-ups and because the region's ecosystems have begun to perform well, institutions are starting to test ways to generate new data to describe the business environment and the performance of start-ups in Latin America.

Some initiatives generate information based on surveys conducted among businesses and other stakeholders in the ecosystem. Their aim is to describe ecosystems in terms of infrastructure, access to finance, entrepreneurs' attitudes and the availability of public support, among other features. Examples of these include the Global Entrepreneurship Monitor (GEM), the Global Entrepreneurship Index, and the Index of Systemic Conditions for Dynamic Entrepreneurship compiled by the Entrepreneur Development Programme (PRODEM) for the countries of Latin America. These indices show that in recent years there has been an upward trend in the number of new start-ups being founded, but the ecosystems in Latin America are still not as developed as those in other parts of the world, such as in Tel Aviv (GEDI, 2016; GEM, 2015; Kantis et al., 2015).

Thanks to the spread of ICTs, new data are being generated that reveal (or could reveal) the situation of start-ups in countries across the region. When investors, support service platforms, incubators and others conduct online activities, they are gathering data that, if processed, could be useful to measure the dynamics of start-ups. AngelList – a database that investors often use to find basic information about start-ups before making investment decisions – shows that in Latin America, Brazil has the largest number of start-ups, followed by Mexico. Mexico has the least concentration in a single city, with only 32% of Mexican start-ups located in Mexico City. Chile has the highest concentration, with some 80% of start-ups located in the capital, Santiago (Figure 2.9). The Global Startup Ecosystem Ranking is based on data from surveys of experts, start-ups, investors, providers of services to start-ups and others. It combines these survey data with other sources of information and ranks the top 20 start-up ecosystems around the world according to several dimensions, including funding, talent, performance, market reach and start-up experience. As of 2016, only two Latin American ecosystems appear in the ranking: São Paulo (Brazil) and Santiago (Chile). Figure 2.10 illustrates the diversity among the ecosystems in terms of: number of start-ups (indicated by the size of the bubble), access to finance (measured as the number of months required to raise a financing round) and global market reach (measured as the number of languages in which the service or product is available).

Figure 2.9. **Start-ups in Latin America and their distribution by city, 2016**
(number of start-ups and their distribution by city according to 2016 data from AngelList)

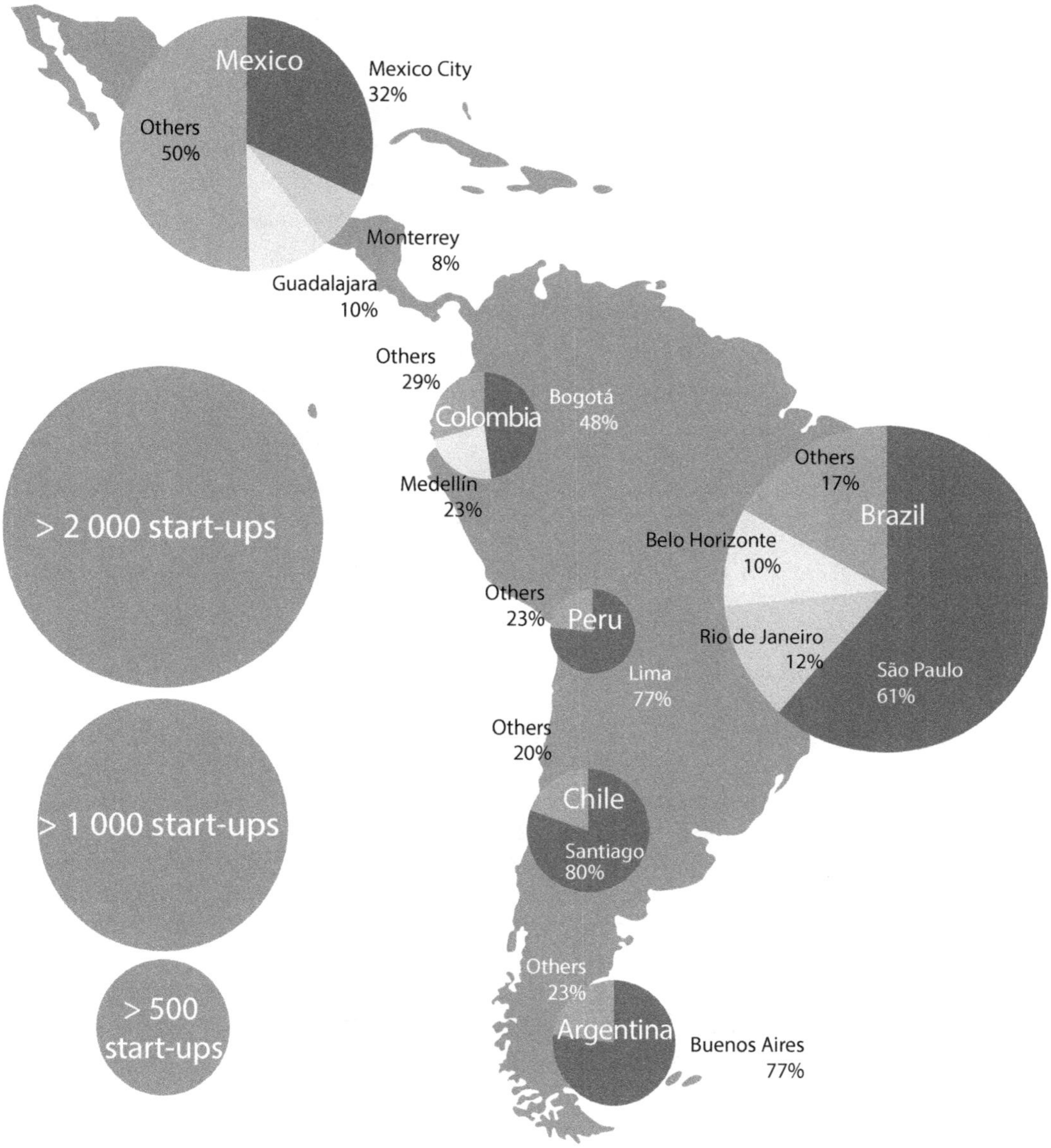

Source: Authors' work based on AngelList (2016).

Figure 2.10. **Features of selected start-up ecosystems, 2015**

(number of start-ups, months to raise a financing round, number of product/service languages)

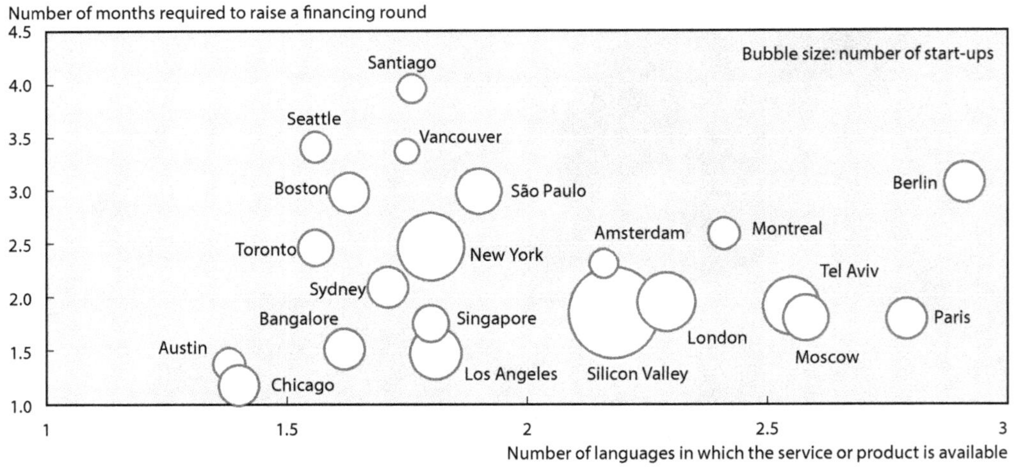

Note: The figure shows data for the 20 ecosystems that appear in *The Global Startup Ecosystem Ranking* (Compass, 2015) and for Santiago de Chile, the only other Latin American ecosystem for which data is available (Santiago de Chile).

Source: Authors' work based on Compass (2015), *The Global Startup Ecosystem Ranking* and data provided by Compass in 2016.

As countries in Latin America started to implement pro-startup policies, they have generated more data on start-ups and could reveal who the start-uppers are. For example, in 2015, CORFO estimated that Chile had 1 unicorn, 4 centaurs and 31 little ponies, while in 2016 the Mexican Association of PE & VC Funds indicated that Mexico had 1 centaur and 26 little ponies in 2016. These figures are in line with economies like Singapore, which has 2 unicorns, 12 centaurs and 27 little ponies among its 1 000 start-ups (CORFO, 2015). At the same time, the implementation of programmes to support start-ups is generating new data that could create a more accurate picture of start-ups in Latin America. For instance, in 2016, Start-Up Chile conducted a survey to show how many start-ups responded to the call for applications and how many were successful. It found that more than 80% of the beneficiaries were men and 75% were foreigners, mostly from the United States, Argentina, India and Brazil. The survey showed that the survival rate of businesses was higher among Chileans (55%) than among foreigners (less than 50%).

Structuring policies, reforming instruments and forging partnerships

Since 2010, policies to promote start-ups have started to become more prominent in Latin American countries' development and innovation strategies. Several countries have introduced programmes to support start-ups, including Argentina, Brazil, Chile, Colombia, Mexico, Panama, Peru and Uruguay (OECD, 2013, 2015a). This section compares current policies to promote start-ups in Chile, Colombia, Mexico and Peru based on the reviews of their experiences in chapters 3, 4, 5 and 6 of this report. The national governments of all four countries have stepped up their commitment to promoting the creation and expansion of start-ups, and some local governments have also committed to this end.

Each country has its own focus in its pro-startup policies, and each designs and manages its policies under a different institutional structure.

- When Chile introduced Start-Up Chile in 2010, it made promoting entrepreneurship a priority in its national production-development strategy. Chile then reformed the policy based on the results the monitoring and evaluation it conducted, and the country now prioritises retaining more talent and businesses in the country. Chile promotes the founding of start-ups in the regions outside Santiago and supports the founding of firms that either offer innovative solutions to social problems or operate in one of the country's strategic sectors (smart mining, the food industry and engineering, for instance). Today, public policy focuses on three areas: i) closing the early-stage funding gap; ii) modernising services to entrepreneurs by introducing more flexible mechanisms tailored to the needs of start-uppers, such as collaborative workspaces and mentoring networks; and iii) simplifying regulations for starting a business (a new law actually allows people to start a business in a single day).
- Colombia's pro-startup policies prioritise financial inclusion and create incentives for the financial markets to view start-ups as potential customers and beneficiaries. The country launched the iNNpulsa Colombia programme in 2012 to promote the creation of start-ups. Today, Colombia is reforming the programme by introducing a voucher scheme to give new businesses access to financing and services managed by accredited intermediary organisations. Colombian cities play an active role in promoting start-ups. Bogotá and Medellín, for instance, promote start-ups through public-private partnerships.
- Mexico is the country that has made the most progress in promoting start-ups between 2013 and 2016. The launch of the National Institute of Entrepreneurship (INADEM) in 2013 strengthened the institutional framework for start-ups. Meanwhile, the reintroduction of seed capital has closed the early-stage funding gap, thus achieving one of the challenges identified in the 2013 review (OCED, 2013). Mexico has also improved the financial inclusion of start-ups. Venture capital has taken off in the country, which now has the second most active industry in Latin America, behind Brazil (LAVCA, 2016). Mexico has reformed regulations to make it easier to start a business, the Express Companies Act being a notable example. It has also modernised services for entrepreneurs by launching mentoring networks and collective workspaces. Finally, Mexico has invested in promoting an entrepreneurial culture in the country and creating an image of Mexico as a place for entrepreneurship with a global impact.
- Peru introduced the Start Up Perú programme in 2012. Since then, it has improved the programme design and it has increased the budget for start-ups, which now receive resources from the innovation fund. The Start Up Perú programme has been expanded, and today it includes seed capital and support for angel-investor networks. Peru also promotes the founding of start-ups based on scientific research through a competition organised by the National Science and Technology Council (CONCYTEC). Universities and the private sector are actively promoting start-ups in Peru, and the development bank COFIDE has just made promoting start-ups one of its strategic lines of action. COFIDE is looking to promote venture capital and the financial inclusion of new enterprises.

There are differences among the countries in terms of priorities and the stage of development of pro-startup policies, but all four are making progress in learning about such policies and implementing them. Latin American countries have made progress in this area, with five key achievements (Figure 2.11a and b):

1. They have strengthened the institutional framework for supporting start-ups, especially Mexico, which created INADEM in 2013, and Chile, which has made policies to support start-ups part of its national production-development strategy and has opened a unit within CORFO devoted to start-ups. The region has also reformed its development banks, with measures to promote start-ups becoming priorities for Bancóldex in Colombia, NAFINSA in Mexico and COFIDE in Peru. Chile and Mexico have completed their experimental phase and are now incorporating their pro-startup policies into their national strategies. To institutionalise these policies in such a way, they need to find ways to make these bottom-up pro-startup schemes compatible with the more selective nature of production-development policies so that they can find potential synergies in priority areas, like the automotive sector in Mexico and smart mining in Chile.
2. The countries have prioritised social and regional inclusion in their pro-startup policies and have introduced measures to enable start-ups to develop in regions beyond the capital city. These measures aim to place start-ups in a better position to transform regional economies, taking into account the specific features of production ecosystems and societies in the regions. Mexico has the most ecosystems outside the capital city, followed by Colombia; Chile is the country that most needs to increase opportunities for founding start-ups in the region.
3. The countries recognise that it is important to invest in transforming mindsets and promoting a culture of entrepreneurship. Even today, risk aversion is high in Latin American societies, and relatively few people see entrepreneurs as key contributors to national development. Measures to promote a business culture are important in the region, since they help change people's mindsets. Start-Up Chile's media impact has helped to make Chile a talking point around the world and has inspired many young people to become entrepreneurs. In Mexico, meanwhile, the launch of INADEM has raised awareness of the crucial role that entrepreneurship plays in the country's development, inspiring the Mexican youth and the diaspora to create and open up new opportunities.
4. The countries have modernised support instruments, become more aware that instruments need to take all stages of start-up development into account (seed, start-up, growth and expansion), and introduced next-generation instruments that are more flexible and in keeping with global trends. All four countries have introduced new pro-startup schemes that are more modern, more comprehensive and better suited to the needs of start-uppers. Collaborative workspaces are one example. The countries have also reformed instruments to streamline new forms of financing, such as crowdfunding. In these areas, because governments have worked together with entrepreneurs and the private sector, they have reformed instruments and improved practices more quickly than in other areas. The range of instruments tends to provide integrated support, combining access to infrastructure, finance, services and contact networks. In addition, policy makers have worked in partnership with the private sector and with research and technology institutes, which has improved the capacity to respond to the needs of the people targeted by the policies.
5. The countries have been streamlining procedures and reforming legislation to make it easier to create and expand businesses. Chile and Mexico have passed legislation enabling people to start a business in a single day, but procedures are still complex and tax incentives for new, highly innovative businesses are still insufficient.

Latin American countries began promoting start-ups only recently, and in this short span of time they have had to learn how to organise institutions and design instruments. The main lessons they have learned are as follows:

1. **They need to fine-tune their eligibility criteria** to ensure that the programmes reach the people they target and to make the procedures for selecting beneficiaries simpler and better structured. Like OECD countries, not all Latin American countries define start-ups in exactly the same way. Countries normally define them based on age and performance (growth potential, turnover or jobs) or based on their innovation and technology intensity (Table 2.2). Chile adopts performance-based criteria, with instruments geared towards high-impact enterprises that meet certain conditions in terms of turnover, jobs or both. Some of its programmes, however, only take into account the age of the company and certain aspects of the business (whether it operates in a priority sector or is "innovative"). Mexico prioritises high-impact and innovative enterprises. Like in Chile, its instruments take into account the company's age and certain performance criteria. However, this multiplicity of definitions is not helpful to policy implementation, which needs to outline the scope of support, determine who is eligible and identify impact indicators.
2. **Make programmes more flexible and dynamic.** Windows of opportunity open and close much faster for start-ups than for traditional companies, so public policies need to develop new forms of support that are in keeping with the ever-changing needs of start-ups in order to attract candidates with the greatest potential for success. Should they fail to do so, they may end up selecting projects with poor prospects. New ways of selecting beneficiaries are also necessary, which means that public institutions need to take on new roles and forge new partnerships with intermediaries that are more in touch with the realities of start-ups. Institutions have learned lessons from their recent experience, which has taught them that start-ups need public policies that are specifically geared towards them. Policies should be more flexible and dynamic, and policy makers should engage in dialogue with investors and the private sector. Start-up policies target entrepreneurs with innovative ideas, whose needs are different from those of other businesses. Such policies have reinvigorated institutions that promote production development. The management teams have become more agile and the institutions themselves are now structured in such a way as to understand the needs of the business environment and respond to them quickly, without bureaucracy. Chile and Mexico actually have specialised institutions for start-ups.
3. **Building partnerships with the private sector and internationally.** Public policies to support start-ups operate best when they create synergies with the private sector. Examples of these synergies are Telefónica's Wayra and Open Future initiatives, which are boosting the business environment in Latin America and creating opportunities to increase the scope and impact of public policies. Meanwhile, the growing importance of start-ups has led to the creation of private associations that are giving voice to the needs and visions of entrepreneurs in the region and enabling policy makers to observe the needs of new entrepreneurs in real-time. One such organisation is the Association of Latin American Entrepreneurs (ASELA), which was formed in 2013 within the context of the Pacific Alliance. Today, the entrepreneur associations of Argentina, Chile, Colombia, Mexico and Peru are members of ASELA (Box 2.1).

Table 2.2. Definitions of start-ups used by public policy in Chile, Colombia, Mexico and Peru, 2016

Chile						
	Two-year turnover > USD 1 million	**Potential turnover growth > 20% in 3 years**	**Innovative / technological content**	**Global target market**	**Age**	**Programmes/ Tools**
Dynamic start-up	✓	✓	---	---	---	PRAE, Seed Capital (CORFO)
Early-stage start-up (seed)	✓	✓	✓	✓	---	Startup Chile Seed (CORFO)
Scale-up stage start-up (Scale)	✓	✓	✓	✓	< 6 years	Startup Chile Scale (CORFO)
Colombia						
	Market validation / proven product momentum	**Unique market product**	**Innovative content (unique market product)**	**Technological/digital content**	**Age**	**Programmes/ Instruments**
Enterprise *(emprendimiento)*	✓	✓	✓	---	---	iNNpulsa Colombia programmes
Early-stage start-up *(etapa temprana)*	---	---	---	✓	---	Ideas APPS.co programme
Consolidation-stage start-up *(etapa consolidación)*	✓	---	---	✓	---	APPS.co Growth and Consolidation Programme
Mexico						
	Generating a new industry for the country	**High growth potential**	**Innovative content**	**Positive impacts (sectoral, societal, environmental, cultural) in its environment**	**Age**	**Programmes/ Tools**
High-impact enterprise (INADEM): Early-stage	---	✓	✓	✓	< 2 years	Support for high-impact enterprises (INADEM)
High-impact enterprise (INADEM): Scale-up stage	---	✓	✓	✓	> 2 years	Support for high-impact enterprises (INADEM)
High-impact enterprise (INADEM): Generating a new industry	✓	✓	✓	✓	> 2 years	Support for high-impact firms at the industrial and/ or commercial scale-up stage (INADEM)
	Pilot/research stage concluded successfully, with verifiable financial data (turnover). Innovation for global problems in which Mexico can become a leader. Entrepreneur with proven experience in the sector.					
Peru						
	Priority sectors	**Scientific/ technological content**	**Innovative content**	**Impact solutions for the country**	**Age**	**Programmes/ Tools**
Innovative entrepreneurs/ start-ups	---	---	✓	---	< 3 years	Start Up Perú
High-impact, dynamic enterprises	---	---	✓	---	1-5 years old	Start Up Perú
Technology-based firms	Health, agriculture or technological environment	✓	---	✓	---	Ideas Audaces (CONCYTEC)

Note: The table shows a non-exhaustive selection of the main programmes operating in 2016. PRAE refers to the Regional Pro-Entrepreneurship Programmes (*Programas Regionales de Apoyo al Emprendimiento*)

Source: Authors' work based on the analysis in chapters 3, 4, 5 and 6.

Box 2.1. Uniting entrepreneurs to improve policies: The Association of Latin American Entrepreneurs and Mujeres del Pacífico

ASELA

The Association of Latin American Entrepreneurs (ASELA) was formed in 2013. Its current members are the entrepreneur associations of Argentina, Chile, Colombia, Mexico and Peru. Created as part of regional co-operation in the Pacific Alliance, ASELA represents more than 35 000 entrepreneurs. Its aims are to be the effective representative of entrepreneurs, to promote the development of the entrepreneurial environment, to ensure gender equity, to create national and international networks for entrepreneurs, and to foster public policies to promote entrepreneurship.

Its impact objective is to increase the social capital of entrepreneurs in the region, in the sense of building linkages between people and organisations that could be financially valuable and could drive the growth of businesses. To achieve this, ASELA plans to build a new E2E (entrepreneur-to-entrepreneur) partnership model, taking advantage of online connections, which enable democratic, equitable participation at a lower cost to entrepreneurs.

In terms of its impact on businesses, ASELA hopes that as firms join entrepreneur networks, early-stage mortality will fall and consolidated micro, small and medium-sized enterprises – especially those run by women – will grow more easily. Through these measures, ASELA aims to impact 200 000 entrepreneurs in the region. Its achievements to date include:

- reforms and pro-enterprise policies in Chile (six laws) and Mexico (Express Companies Act)
- collaboration with the four Pacific Alliance countries in developing their entrepreneurship agenda
- the introduction of legal assistance for entrepreneurs in three countries, with more than 10 000 users
- the acquisition of information. In 2016, ASELA conducted a study on the profile of entrepreneurs in Chile. It intends to replicate that study in Colombia, Mexico and Peru.

Mujeres del Pacífico (Women of the Pacific)

The Women of the Pacific network has promoted and supported women entrepreneurs in Pacific Alliance countries (Chile, Colombia, Mexico and Peru) since 2013. The network organises several types of activities to create regional synergies and generate information. One such activity is the "female entrepreneurship tours", which promotes learning through exchanges among the four countries. The participating women entrepreneurs exchange knowledge and share their success stories with each other. The network has its own studies centre that focuses on generating statistics related to female entrepreneurship. Through this centre, the network works in partnership with ASELA on mapping female entrepreneurship. The network is also working in partnership with the Production Development Corporation (CORFO) on a qualitative study of 1 500 female entrepreneurs in seven of Chile's regions. Mujeres del Pacífico offers acceleration services to start-ups run by women and has an e-commerce platform called hAb America.

Source: Official ASELA information in 2016.

Figure 2.11. **Direct support for innovative start-ups in Latin America: A comparison of different countries, 2012-16**

A. 2012

Operational | Developing | Need to be created or reformed | Recently created

Categoría	Instrument	Chile	Colombia	Mexico	Peru
Financing	Seed capital	Operational	Recently created	Need to be created or reformed	Recently created
	Angel investors	Developing	Recently created	Need to be created or reformed	Need to be created or reformed
	Venture capital	Operational	Recently created	Developing	Need to be created or reformed
Business services and entrepreneurial training	Incubators	Operational	Developing	Developing	Recently created
	Accelerators	Developing	Need to be created or reformed	Developing	Need to be created or reformed
	Corporate spin-offs	Need to be created or reformed	Need to be created or reformed	Need to be created or reformed	Need to be created or reformed
	Technology transfer and university spin-offs	Developing	Need to be created or reformed	Operational	Need to be created or reformed
	Business and financial training	Operational	Developing	Developing	Developing
Regulatory framework	Legal framework for starting, expanding and winding up businesses	Developing	Developing	Developing	Developing
	Tax incentives and special taxes	Developing	Need to be created or reformed	Developing	Need to be created or reformed

B. 2016

Operational | Developing | Non-operational | Recently created

Category	Instrument	Chile	Colombia	Mexico	Peru
Financing	Seed capital	Operational	Developing	Operational	Developing
	Crowdfunding	Developing	Recently created	Recently created	Recently created
	Angel investors	Non-operational	Recently created	Operational	Recently created
	Venture capital	Operational	Developing	Operational	Recently created
	Prizes	Developing	Non-operational	Operational	Recently created
Integrated support	Integrated public/private programmes (financing and services)	Operational	Developing	Developing	Developing
Support services and business training	Incubators	Operational	Operational	Operational	Developing
	Accelerators	Operational	Operational	Operational	Developing
	Next-generation incubators and accelerators (coworking)	Recently created	Recently created	Recently created	Recently created
	Mentoring networks	Developing	Recently created	Developing	Recently created
	Support for developing commercial loans for startups	Non-operational	Developing	Non-operational	Non-operational
	Technology transfer and university spin-offs	Developing	Recently created	Operational	Recently created
	Business and financial training	Operational	Operational	Operational	Operational
Demand-oriented support & market creation	Public procurement and other	Recently created	Developing	Developing	Non-operational
Promoting a business culture	Raising awareness about the innovative business culture	Developing	Operational	Operational	Developing
Regulatory framework	Legal framework for starting, expanding and closing businesses	Operational	Developing	Developing	Developing
	Tax incentives and special taxes	Operational	Operational	Developing	Recently created
	Special visas for start-ups	Operational	Non-operational	Non-operational	Non-operational

Note: This table is not intended to classify the countries. The 2012 table is taken from OECD (2013), *Start-up Latin America: Promoting Innovation in the Region*, while the 2016 table is is based on qualitative information gathered from the country case studies presented in chapters 3 to 6 of this report. The purpose of the table is to offer an overview of the range of instruments to support start-ups, indicating what stage of development each instrument is at in each country in the region.
Source: OECD (2013), *Start-up Latin America: Promoting Innovation in the Region* for panel a (2012), and authors' work based on case studies of the countries presented in chapters 3, 4, 5 and 6 of this report for panel b (2016).

Conclusions and challenges for the future

Start-ups will not be the ultimate solution for development in the region, but creating a startup-friendly environment, channelling public investment (especially in the early stages) and private investment (at the expansion stage) towards start-ups and creating flexible, modern services for new entrepreneurs are essential parts of the transformation strategies in Latin American countries. Policies to promote start-ups do not so much need huge sums of public investment (see chapters 3, 5 and 6 of this report for data on Chile, Mexico and Peru) as they need careful thought and a flexible design. They also require simple, rapid instruments, as well as partnerships and co-operation with financial and investment institutions and with universities and technology centres.

Start-ups do not operate in a vacuum: the production and innovation ecosystem determine how likely start-ups are to succeed. For start-ups to emerge there needs to be a system of dynamic innovation, a solid base in science and technology, good skills and education, and access to good-quality ICTs. The impact of start-up policies therefore depends not only on their design and the structure of the various instruments, but also on overall co-ordination with other areas of public policy.

The current climate is marked by sluggish growth and the depletion of traditional sources of growth due to low commodity prices and low external demand, which in recent years has been driven mainly by the People's Republic of China. Diversifying production, joining the new digital economy and ensuring a bright future for manufacturing are therefore urgent objectives for the region so that it can overcome gaps and structural stagnation. If Latin American countries can achieve these objectives, they will be able to make the necessary strides towards more inclusive, long-term growth to meet the growing demands of their societies, especially young people. It is therefore important and urgent to capitalise on experiences in promoting start-ups, to strengthen the instruments and programmes that work, and to reform those that are not producing the desired results (Table 2.3). To do this, the countries in the region need to tackle several challenges, of which the following are most urgent:

1. **Map start-ups and measure their impact.** Start-ups are a recent phenomenon in the region. As countries consolidate their pro-startup programmes, they are tweaking the criteria they use to determine which enterprises are eligible to benefit from public programmes and their role in the national innovation system. It is important for countries to improve official company registries and use the broad scope of such records to generate data on the performance of start-ups, which they could then use to analyse the features of businesses that fail or cease trading. Countries could obtain additional data on the nature and behaviour of start-ups that import and export goods by combining the information in official company registries with the statistical records of customs agencies. Meanwhile, information and communication technologies, the platform economy and new policy tools provide opportunities to generate new data and to map the development of the start-up scene in Latin American countries. It is important for countries to monitor the implementation of programmes and conduct impact assessments at a reasonably early stage to ensure that they use their resources efficiently. Data from new sources, such as the platform economy, could also be used to map the profile of start-uppers in the region. These sources would reveal what impact the profile of entrepreneurs (gender, age and education) and the environment in which they operate have on the founding and expansion of start-ups, and indirect pro-startup policies would therefore be better informed. Countries could also explore to what extent start-up policies change the organisational structure of traditional policies to support innovation and production development. Programmes to support start-ups might also be modernising and invigorating traditional systems by introducing new ways of planning, managing and implementing public policies and by requiring changes to the profiles of the people in charge.

2. **Simplify and consolidate support programmes and bring them more in line with the needs of the target population.** Although initial experimentation with different programmes and mechanisms are helping to determine what works best in each context, if there are too many instruments, they are not effective for defining a policy that is easy for entrepreneurs to use.
3. **Facilitate productive investment.** Although the situation has improved in recent years, the region still adopts a conservative approach and is averse to the risks associated with productive investment. Financial institutions, private investors and investment funds could help boost investment in the region, but countries will need to reform legislation and create tax incentives to enable and facilitate productive investment. They also need to change mindsets and focus on investment.
4. **Increase regional co-operation.** The countries in the region can increase the impact of start-up development through greater regional co-operation. By co-operating with each other, countries can speed up the learning process and the transfer of best practices, as well as help regional initiatives to achieve critical masses for market opportunities and financing. The community that supports start-ups in Latin America is young, and it already meets together and co-ordinates more than traditional areas of public policy. Countries could speed up learning processes and create good practices by improving the structure of these spaces for dialogue and by introducing peer review. Regional co-operation could also help to close funding gaps and attract larger levels of investment, which would respond to the challenges that the countries face in terms of finance and target markets. Regional funds like the Pacific Alliance initiatives to promote start-ups and entrepreneurship are therefore important, and countries should do more to encourage such initiatives.

Table 2.3. **Promoting start-ups in Latin America: Progress made and open challenges**

Recommendations made in OECD (2013) to improve the design and implementation of support for innovative start-ups in Latin America	The situation in 2016 compared with 2012
Increase co-ordination between support programmes for start-ups and innovation and production-development policies.	↑
Provide incentives to promote the development of an entrepreneurial culture and mindset, especially among young people.	✓
Ensure there are financing schemes at all stages of development of new enterprises.	↑
Take advantage of the new trends of "open innovation" and corporate venture capital that are emerging in the private sector.	↑
Introduce results-oriented management criteria in incubators and in the agencies that facilitate access to public programmes to promote start-ups.	↑
Design increasingly integrated instruments that simultaneously offer financing options, consultancy services and capacity-building.	✓
Simplify the legal framework for starting a business.	↑
Invest in generating new and better indicators to improve how the dynamics of start-up creation and growth are measured.	✓
Evaluate programmes regularly and ensure there are feedback mechanisms between evaluation results and design reviews for programmes and incentives.	=
Create synergies with private initiatives to promote start-ups.	✓
Identify modalities for international and regional co-operation to enhance the impact of support for start-ups and create synergies among entrepreneurial ecosystems, taking advantage of new, region-wide spaces.	→
Identify opportunities for synergies between the potential of start-ups and the priority areas for production development in each country, and identify ways to ensure there is balance between bottom-up support and support focused on sectors prioritised in the country's diversification strategy.	→
Make progress in implementing tax incentives that are friendly towards innovation and innovative entrepreneurship.	→
Simplify the management of pro-startup programmes to make them more attractive to the private sector and to ensure they can be managed quickly, in keeping with the fast-moving nature of the markets.	→
Boost the region's image as a place for innovation.	→
Identify forms of regional co-operation.	→

Legend: = Progress has been made, but it remains a priority.
✓ The indicated reforms have been made.
↑ Improvements made between 2012 and 2016.
✓ Remains a priority objective.
→ New challenges for the future.

Source: Authors' work based on OECD (2013), *Start-up Latin America: Promoting Innovation in the Region* and on the chapters on specific countries in this report.

Box 2.2. **Boosting investment across Latin America**

Recently, some private initiatives have emerged for start-ups looking to take advantage of the benefits of operating throughout the Latin America region.

NXTP Labs investment funds. Launched in 2011, this investment fund targets businesses throughout Latin America, focusing its financing on early-stage tech start-ups. NXTP Labs provides USD 25 000 of capital in exchange for a 2-10% shareholding and an acceleration programme. In 2016, it had a portfolio of 170 start-ups in Argentina, Brazil, Chile, Colombia and Mexico in the Internet, software, e-commerce and technology for agribusiness sectors, among others.

Pacific Alliance Venture Capital Fund. In 2016, the Pacific Alliance reached an agreement with the Inter-American Development Bank (IDB) to create the venture-capital fund. The purpose of the fund is to provide capital and mentoring to high-impact start-ups that are at the early stages of development or at the scale-up stage. Managed by Angel Ventures, the fund received an initial joint investment of USD 100 million from the Inter-American Investment Bank Multilateral Investment Fund (MIF), the National Institute of Entrepreneurship (INADEM) and Bancóldex for investment in 25 growing start-ups or businesses that operate in the fintech, health, biotech or ICT sector, among others, and that have the potential to grow in the Pacific Alliance countries.

Angel investment with a region-wide focus. In 2013, Chile Global Angels, Peru Capital Network, Angel Ventures Mexico and the Capitalia Colombia Angel Investors Network formed the Ángeles del Pacífico (Angels of the Pacific) network to combine efforts and pool resources for region-wide operations. Angel Ventures was launched in 2009, and five years later it launched Angel Ventures Peru to take advantage of the growing dynamism of Peru's start-up ecosystem. The Peruvian organisation benefits from the founding partner, which transfers knowledge to Angel Ventures Peru and makes its investment portfolio and network of angel investors available to it. Finally, in 2014, with support from the MIF and the University of Montevideo's IEEM Business School, the Xcala regional initiative was launched to support angel-investor networks. Xcala offers financial support, provides training to networks and monitors angel investment in Latin America.

References

Compass (2015), *The Global Startup Ecosystem Ranking 2015*, The Startup Ecosystem Report Series, http://www.businesslocationcenter.de/imperia/md/blc/service/download/content/the_global_startup_ecosystem_report_2015.pdf.

CORFO (2015), "The Chilean Experience in Developing a Global Entrepreneurship Hub", presentation by E. Bitrán in October 2015, mimeo.

ECLAC (2015a), *Latin America and the Caribbean in the World Economy: Continuing Crisis in the Centre and New Opportunities for Developing Economies*, Economic Commission for Latin America and the Caribbean, United Nations, Santiago, Chile.

ECLAC (2015b), *The New Digital Revolution: From the Consumer Internet to the Industrial Internet*, Economic Commission for Latin America and the Caribbean, United Nations, Santiago, Chile.

ECLAC (2013), *Entre mitos y realidades. TIC, políticas públicas y desarrollo productivo en América Latina*, Economic Commission for Latin America and the Caribbean, United Nations, Santiago, Chile.

GEDI (2016), *Global Entrepreneurship Index, 2016*, The Global Entrepreneurship and Development Institute, Washington, DC.

GEM (2015), *GEM 2015/2016 Global Report*, Global Entrepreneurship Research Association, London.

Kantis, H. et al. (2015), *Condiciones sistémicas para el emprendimiento dinámico. América Latina en el nuevo escenario global*, PRODEM.

LAVCA (2016), *Latin America Venture Capital: Five Year Trends*, Latin American Private Equity & Venture Capital Association, http://lavca.org/2016/07/15/new-vc-latin-america-venture-capital-five-year-trends/.

Miranda, G. (2012), "Venture Capital in Latin America: Connecting Opportunities", *Kauffman Fellows Report*, Vol. 4, Kauffman Fellows Press, http://www.kauffmanfellows.org/journal_posts/venture-capital-in-latin-america-connecting-opportunities/.

OECD (2015a), *Innovation Policy in Panama: Design, Implementation and Evaluation*, Development Centre Studies, OECD Publishing, Paris, http://dx.doi.org/10.1787/9789264233447-en.

OECD (2015b), *Entrepreneurship at a Glance 2015*, OECD Publishing, Paris, http://dx.doi.org/10.1787/entrepreneur_aag-2015-en.

OECD (2015c), *OECD Digital Economy Outlook 2015*, OECD Publishing, Paris, http://dx.doi.org/10.1787/9789264232440-en.

OECD (2013), *Start-up Latin America: Promoting Innovation in the Region*, Development Centre Studies, OECD Publishing, Paris, http://dx.doi.org/10.1787/9789264202306-en.

OECD (2011), *Financing High-Growth Firms: The Role of Angel Investors*, OECD Publishing, Paris, http://dx.doi.org/10.1787/9789264118782-en.

OECD/CAF/ECLAC (forthcoming 2016), *Latin American Economic Outlook 2017: Youth, Skills and Entrepreneurship*, OECD Publishing, Paris, http://dx.doi.org/10.1787/leo-2017-en.

UNCTAD (2015), *Information Economy Report 2015: Unlocking the Potential of E-commerce for Developing Countries*, United Nations, New York and Geneva.

USPTO (2014), *United States Patent and Trademark Office Performance and Accountability Report 2014*, Alexandria.

Chapter 3

Promoting start-ups in Chile

This chapter presents an overview of policies to promote start-ups in Chile. Support for start-ups has shifted from a pilot phase to a more structured one in co-ordination with the national transformation strategy. Chile is strengthening the financing chain for start-ups, especially in early stages and is introducing new support services to entrepreneurs, including mentoring networks and collaborative workspaces. The country has also introduced conditionalities and incentives to encourage entrepreneurship in the regions within the country, to attract citizens who have studied abroad to return to Chile to do business, and to support social inclusion through entrepreneurship. It has taken steps to improve the legal framework for starting businesses, including a law to enable people to start a business in one day.

Introduction

Chile's experience in supporting start-ups goes back to the 1990s, when it introduced incentives to bolster venture capital in the country. Since then, its policy approach has shifted as the country seeks to complete the financing chain at the start-up and growth stages. In 2010, the launch of the Start-Up Chile programme marked a milestone in policies to promote start-ups in the country, and in the region. The programme's media coverage helped to establish Chile's position in the global debate on start-ups. The implementation of the programme also provided valuable lessons regarding policy design and management (OECD, 2013). When Start-Up Chile was introduced, creating and promoting the growth of start-ups was an objective, an aspiration for the country (OECD, 2013). Chile has yet to fully map out the start-up scene in the country, but there has been a change in the country's image, and start-ups are emerging and expanding nationwide. Between 2010 and 2016, Chile has refined its pro-startup policies and instruments. In 2014, the country's strategy to promote start-ups moved from a pilot phase to a more structured one, under the 2014-18 entrepreneurship policy.

This chapter presents an overview of policies to support start-ups in Chile, focusing on changes that have taken place between 2012 and 2016 and identifying challenges for the future.

Start-ups in Chile: The current situation

Chile's science and innovation performance remains below the OECD average (OECD, 2014; Figure 3.1), and start-ups are not emerging and growing naturally. In addition to the barriers they would face in any country, start-ups in Chile and Latin America face systemic difficulties resulting from the low propensity for business risk within society and among investors, the low density of the science and technology system, and barriers related to logistics, regulations and standards. All these factors hinder the emergence and growth of start-ups. However, Chile's market-oriented, innovative start-ups give a very different, more dynamic picture of the country. Although start-ups are a new phenomenon and Chile's business ecosystem is not nearly as dynamic as those of the world's most advanced countries, they are a reality, and one that is growing.

It is not easy to gauge the size and dynamism of Chile's start-ups, for want of comparable data across countries. Since 2010, however, public policy has prioritised start-ups, which has helped generate data on them. According to end-2015 estimates by the Production Development Corporation (CORFO), Chilean start-ups included one unicorn (i.e. a start-up worth at least USD 1 billion), four centaurs (worth between USD 100 million and USD 1 billion) and 36 little ponies (worth between USD 10 and 100 million) (Figure 3.2). These figures are comparable with those of more developed start-up ecosystems, such as that of Singapore, which has around 1 000 start-ups, including 2 unicorns, 12 centaurs and 27 little ponies (CORFO, 2015a). Chilean start-ups operate in various areas. Several have emerged in the field of technologies applied to education, some of which have been successful and have internationalised and recorded large turnovers (Gal&Leo, Puntaje Nacional, Papinotas, Poliglota, Musiglota and U-Planner). Other areas in Chile with a large number of start-ups are financial technology, the sharing economy, agribusiness and biotechnologies (Box 3.1).

Figure 3.1. **Comparison of science and innovation performance in Chile, 2014**
(normalised performance index relative to median OECD values)
(OECD median = 100).

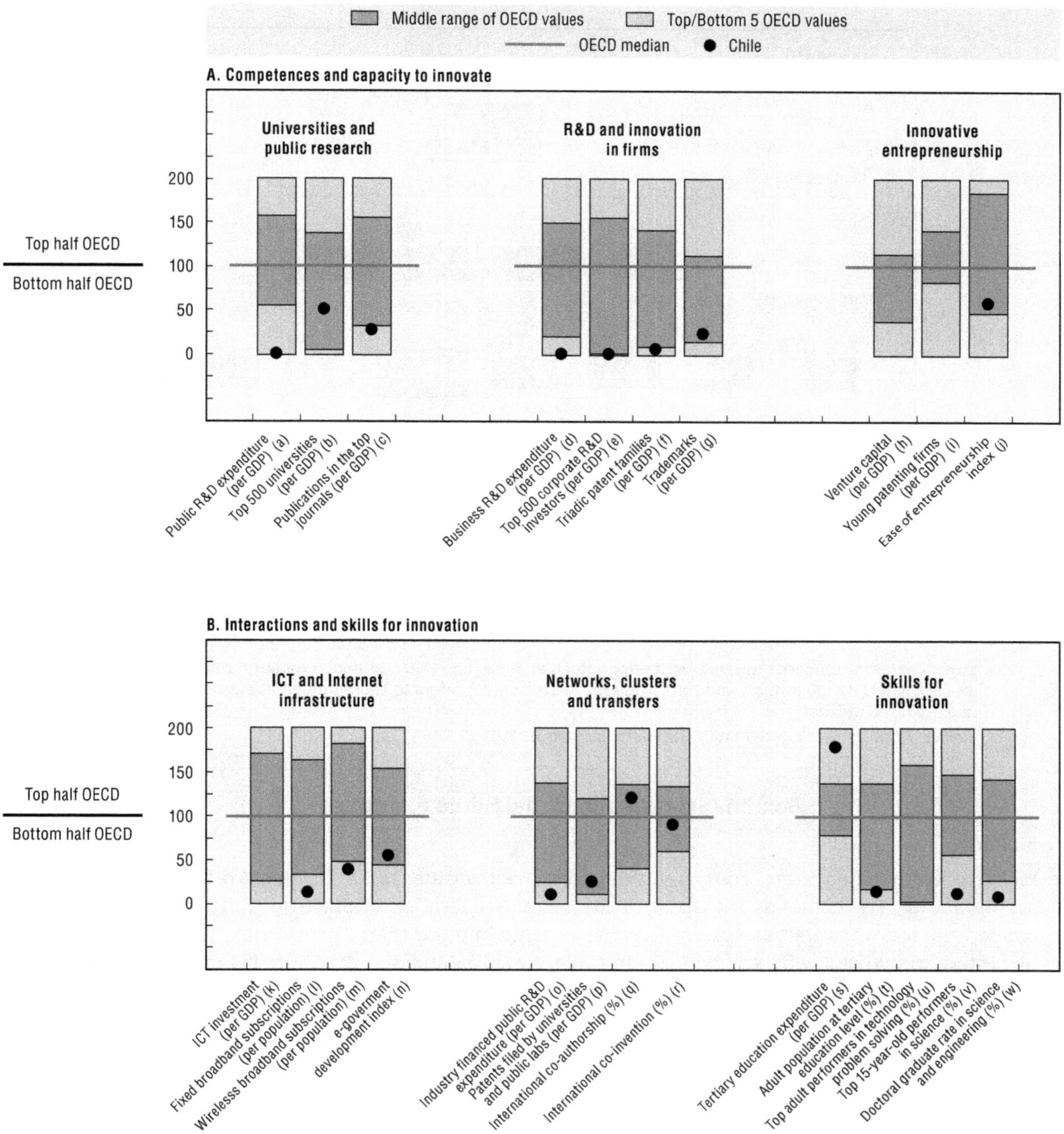

Note: The indicators are adjusted to the size of the country (GDP or population size). The values for Chile are compared with the median value for OECD countries, i.e. the middle-ranked country of all the OECD countries for which data is available. For more details on the methodology used, see the STI country profiles in OECD (2014).

Source: OECD (2014) *Science, Technology and Industry Outlook 2014*, http://dx.doi.org/10.1787/sti_outlook-2014-en, based on OECD (2014), *Main Science and Technology Indicators (MSTI) Database*, June, www.oecd.org/sti/msti.htm.

Figure 3.2. **Unicorns, centaurs and little ponies in Chile, 2015**

(estimated figures as of end-2015)

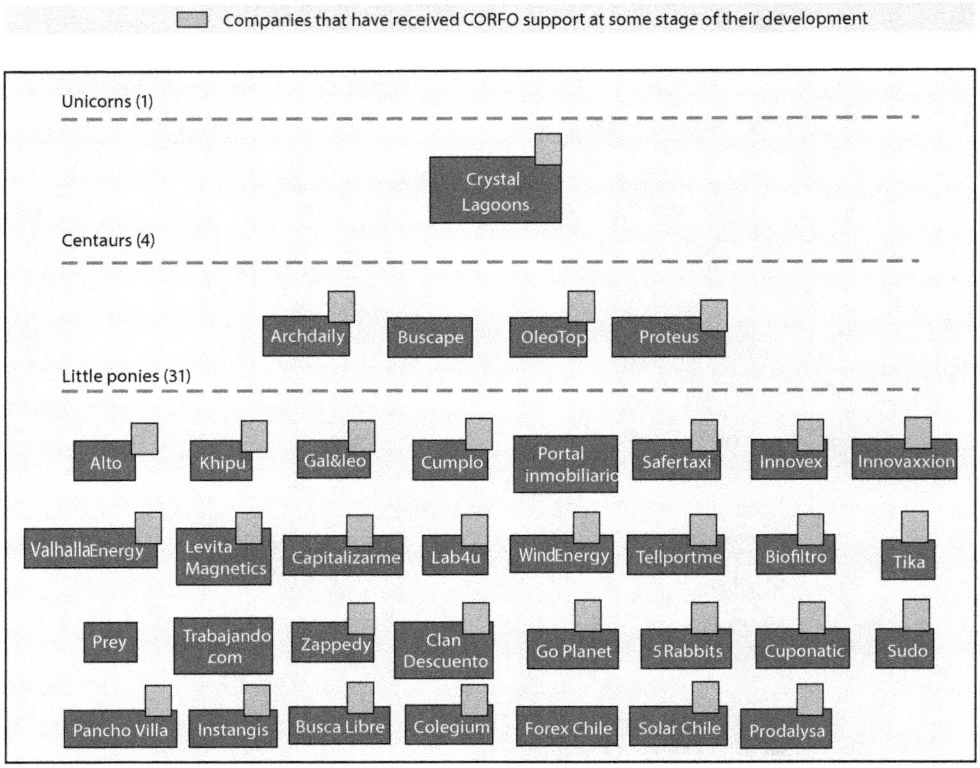

Note: The term "unicorns" refers to start-ups valued at more than USD 1 billion; "centaurs" refers to those valued at between USD 100 million and USD 1 billion; "little ponies" refers to those valued at between USD 10 million and USD 100 million.

Source: Authors' work based on CORFO data (November 2015).

Box 3.1. **Start-ups in Chile: Some examples**

BioFiltro

BioFiltro is an innovative company that treats wastewater and develops technology for sustainability. The company took part in the second-generation of Start-Up Chile in 2012 and created the innovative BIDA® system that has patents in more than 35 countries. The company has internationalised, with subsidiaries in Chile, New Zealand and the United States and more than 130 plants around the world.

Proteus

This pharmaceutical start-up developed the first anaesthesia in Chile following the discovery of an essential microalga for producing the anaesthetic neosaxitoxin. Proteus obtained its first patent in 2008 thanks to financing from Chile's Production Development Corporation (CORFO). The company's market value places it in the centaur category, and it has contracts with major companies, including German firm Grünenthal.

Karün

Founded in 2012, this start-up designs and manufactures spectacles using plastic recycled from fishing nets, which provides a flexible but sturdy material. The company combines craftsmanship and laser cutting technology to produce original products. Karün has received the international B-CORP certification for its sustainability work and has raised around USD 500 000 from investors and USD 175 000 from crowdfunding in Chile.

Source: Authors' work based on the companies' websites.

Chile is structuring and strengthening its policy for start-ups

Chile's experience in supporting the creation of companies with high growth potential goes back to 1998, when CORFO took the strategic decision to promote the forming of private venture-capital funds through the F1 credit facility (on a 1:1 basis with private-sector contributions, a ratio that increased to 2:1 for the F2 lines and 3:1 for the F3 lines). In 2000, it introduced a fund to support incubators, and since then it has reformed the fund several times based on performance assessments. In 2004, it created the first seed-capital fund for new enterprises in order to close the early-stage funding gaps (OECD, 2013).

In 2010, the government launched Start-Up Chile. The programme had an immediate impact. It was a key turning point in the country's support for start-ups and led to the structuring of start-up policy as part of the country's production development strategy. Start-Up Chile's initial objectives were as follows: i) to position Chile as a benchmark in innovation and entrepreneurship in Latin America; ii) to promote a culture of entrepreneurship; iii) to place greater emphasis on innovative entrepreneurship; and iv) to create a critical mass of new entrepreneurs in Chile in order to attract foreign talent to open new businesses in the country. To achieve these goals, the programme provided non-repayable seed capital of USD 40 000 to new entrepreneurs, access to basic infrastructure for initial operations, and simpler visa procedures for foreign beneficiaries. The programme also provided training activities and opportunities to network with investors and local entrepreneurs.

In 2012, Chile began to redefine the criteria for supporting start-ups, gradually replacing experimental initiatives with a more structured, integrated approach to national production-development policy. Also in 2012, CORFO created an Entrepreneurship Division to structure and monitor support for start-ups. The country has also identified new priorities for start-up promotion under the 2014-18 entrepreneurship policy (which has been included as one of CORFOs' five strategic lines of action) and has allocated resources for policy implementation. Chile's support for start-ups had therefore moved from a pilot phase to a more structured phase in 2014. CORFO has increased the share of its budget allocated to supporting dynamic enterprises (i.e. businesses that could achieve turnover of at least USD 1 million in two years and could grow at rates above 20% in the following three years) from 10.5% in 2012 to 13% in 2016. Investment and financing was the budget line that increased the most in its share of the total budget (from 4.3% in 2012 to 30.6% in 2016) (Figure 3.3).

CORFO monitors and assesses programmes and applies the lessons learned to its policies to support start-ups (Box 3.2). One of the main lessons learned from the first assessments of Start-Up Chile was that programmes to support innovative entrepreneurship must take regional factors into consideration. If Chile designs and implements national policies without taking the regions into account, it may not fully mobilise the entrepreneurial talent living outside the capital. From 2016, in line with the national development goal of supporting inclusive growth, the new instruments and conditions seek to create the right environment for start-ups and innovation opportunities to emerge in the regions beyond Santiago's metropolitan area.

Figure 3.3. **CORFO budget by strategic line, 2012-16**
(percentage of the total innovative-entrepreneurship budget, by strategic line)

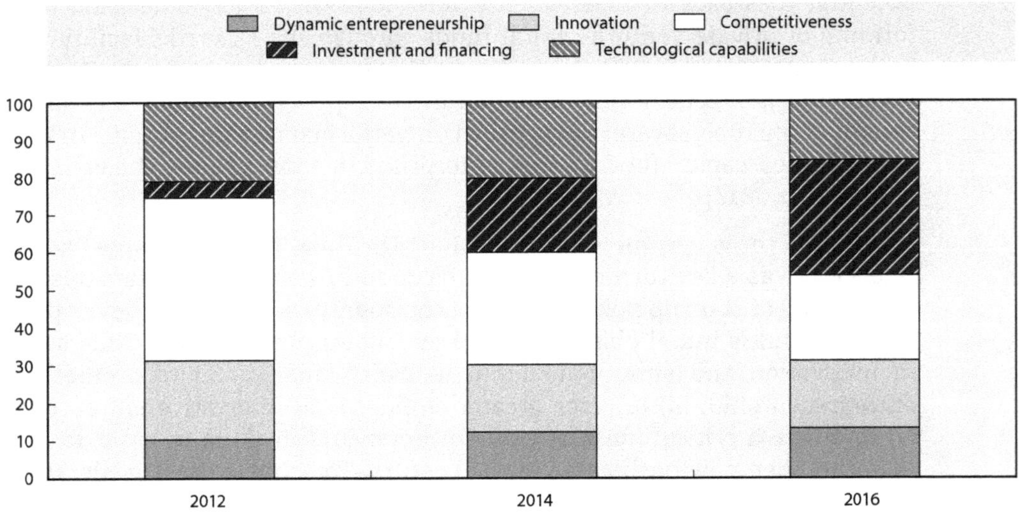

Note: "Investment and financing" includes support for venture capital.
Source: Authors' work based on official CORFO data updated in 2016.

Box 3.2. **Conducting assessments to draw lessons and reform policies: Chile's experience**

Chile's experience in promoting innovative entrepreneurship dates back to the late 1990s. The country has learned how to manage policy implementation through monitoring and evaluation. Assessments are effective when they are part of the policy cycle and when there are existing mechanisms to incorporate the results of assessments into future programme design and management. In 2007, for instance, CORFO assessed the seed-capital programmes it introduced in 2004. The assessment revealed that it is not efficient to have two financing lines: one for founding start-ups and one for growing them. CORFO therefore decided to reform the instrument to create a single system with two phases, called the Subsidio Semilla de Asignación Flexible (SSAF), or Flexible Seed Grant.

In 2011, CORFO also assessed the support programmes for the venture-capital industry. These assessments led to the creation of the Early Stages Fund and the Development and Growth Fund, thus distinguishing between the different operating mechanisms according to the phase of development.

In late 2015, CORFO carried out an assessment of the Start-Up Chile programme. Based on the weaknesses it found, CORFO changed the programme's objectives and launched new lines of support. As a result, in 2016, Start-Up Chile created incentives for start-ups to maintain their operations in Chile, introduced measures to support start-ups established outside Santiago's metropolitan area, and created two new lines: joint investment for start-ups in the growth phase and pre-incubation for female entrepreneurs.

Source: OECD (2013), *Start-up Latin America: Promoting Innovation in the Region*, http://dx.doi.org/10.1787/9789264202306-en and CORFO data for 2016.

Chile is modernising its policy mix for start-ups

By structuring start-up promotion policies, Chile is modernising and expanding its policy mix. The 2014-18 entrepreneurship policy is formulated in four main branches, in line with the national production-development strategy (Figure 3.4):

- financing for start-ups, which was allocated 61% of the total budget for entrepreneurship in 2016
- promotion of the development of ecosystems (25% of the total 2016 budget)
- support based on technology intensity (8% of the total 2016 budget)
- support for entrepreneurship for social inclusion (6% of the total 2016 budget).

The first review of policies to support start-ups in Latin America highlighted that Chile was seeking to expand the financing available to cover all stages of a business's development, from seed to expansion (OECD, 2013). Today, one of Chile's strengths is that it has instruments designed for each stage of a start-up's development (Figures 3.5a and b and Table 3.1). Between 2012 and 2016, Chile has introduced the following main changes:

1. It has bolstered the chain of financing, especially in the early stages, but venture capital and angel investors are still weak links in the financing chain.
2. It has introduced new instruments in its services to entrepreneurs, including mentoring networks and collaborative workspaces. It has also reformed support for intermediaries (incubators and accelerators) to make it more flexible and results-oriented.
3. It has included conditionalities and incentives to encourage the creation of start-ups in the regions, to attract Chileans who have studied abroad back to the country to do business, and to support social inclusion through entrepreneurship.
4. It has taken steps to improve the legal framework for starting businesses, including a law to enable people to start a business in one day.

Figure 3.4. **Budget for start-ups, CORFO 2016**

(percentage assigned to each instrument)

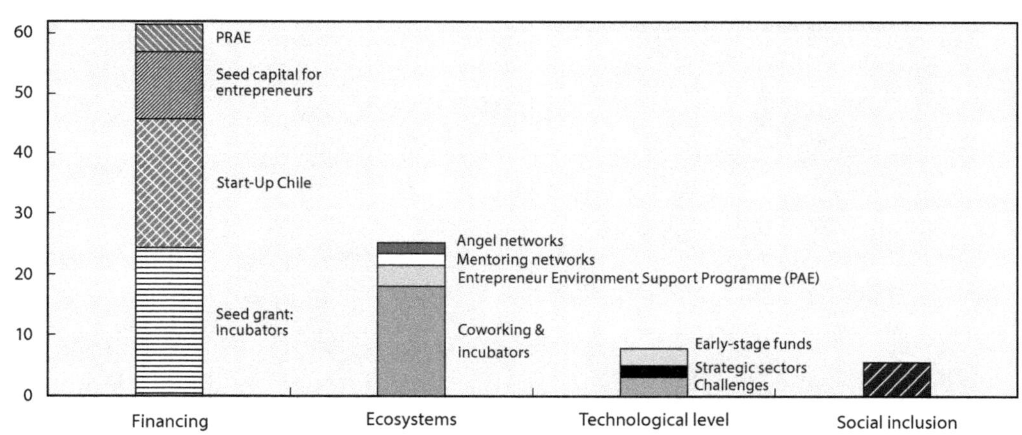

Notes: Start-Up Chile includes The S Factory (TSF). "Social inclusion" includes support for the development of social and inclusive enterprises and funds from the SSAF scheme for social enterprises. PRAE (Programas Regionales de Apoyo al Emprendimiento) refers to regional entrepreneurship support programmes. "Technological level" means instruments to create technological developments, attract global talent and connect with university R&D.

Source: Official CORFO data in 2015.

Figure 3.5. **Policy mix to support start-ups in Chile, 2012 and 2016**

A. 2012

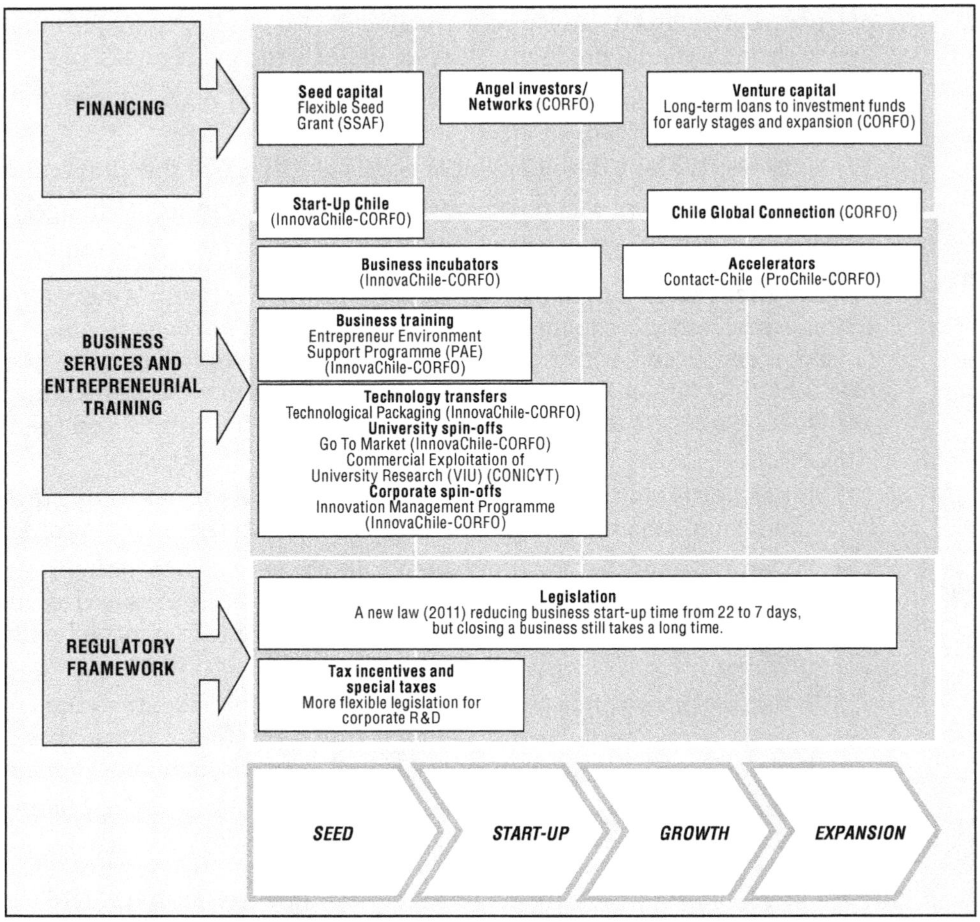

Source: OECD (2013), *Start-up Latin America: Promoting Innovation in the Region*, http://dx.doi.org/10.1787/9789264202306-en.

Figure 3.5. **Policy mix to support start-ups in Chile, 2012 and 2016** *(cont.)*

B. 2016

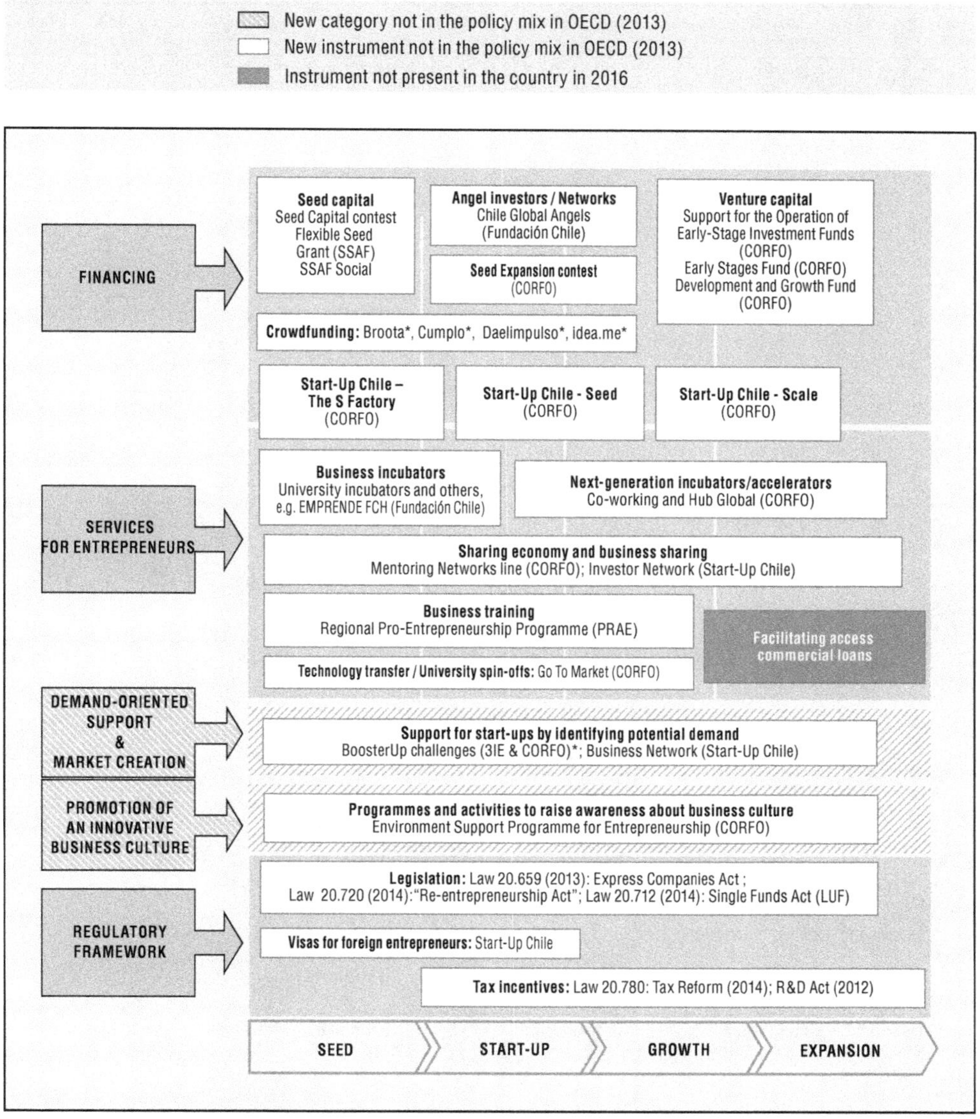

Note: Items marked with an asterisk (*) are private initiatives. The diagram shows information available on some programmes as of May 2016.

Source: OECD (2013), updated and expanded based on official information from Chile in May 2016.

Table 3.1. **Selected instruments to support start-ups in Chile, 2016**

Instruments		Beneficiaries	Type of support		Maximum amount of support	Introduced in
FINANCING FOR ENTREPRENEURS						
Seed Capital contest		Early-stage dynamic start-ups	Seed capital co-financing	75% of the total cost	Up to CLP 25 million	2010
Seed Capital Expansion contest		Expanding enterprises		70% of the total cost	Up to CLP 100 million	2014
Regional Pro-Entrepreneurship Programmes (PRAEs)		Enterprises in priority sectors in the regions		75% of the total cost	Up to CLP 25 million	2010
Start-Up Chile	The Startup Factory (TSF)	Start-ups led by women, at the idea or prototype stage	Integrated (co-financing, training, mentoring and linkages)	90% of the total cost	Up to CLP 10 million	2015
	Seed	Early-stage start-ups (at least a prototype or minimum viable product)	Integrated (co-financing, training, mentoring and linkages)	90% of the total cost	Up to CLP 20 million	2010
	Scale	Expanding start-ups	Integrated (co-financing, training, mentoring and linkages)	70% of the total cost	Up to CLP 60 million	2015
SUPPORT FOR THE ECOSYSTEM AND SERVICES						
National incubators programme		Incubators	Co-financing	Line 1- Launch: 75% of the total cost. Line 2- Operation: 65% of the total cost. Line 3- Operation: 55% of the total cost	Up to CLP 200 million per line	2014
Co-working support		Co-working spaces	Co-financing	75% of the total cost	Co-working line: up to CLP 164 million Hub Global line: up to CLP 200 million.	2015
Support for mentoring networks		Mentoring networks	Co-financing	75% of the total cost	Up to CLP 164 million	2014
SUPPORT FOR PRIVATE CAPITAL						
Early-Stage Fund / Early-Stage Technology Fund		Investment funds for early-stage businesses	Credit line available for investment funds	200% of the fund's completed and pledged investments.	---	2012
Development and Growth Funds		Fund managers / investment funds for expansion-stage businesses	Credit line available for investment funds	100% of the fund's completed and pledged investments.	---	2012
Support for the Operation of Early-Stage Investment Funds		Fund managers	Co-financing	75% of the project's total cost	Up to CLP 80 million	2015

Note: CORFO is the institution in charge of all the above programmes.
Source: Authors' work based on CORFO data updated in 2016.

Although it is too early to fully assess the impact of the various programmes to support start-ups, the country is visibly more buoyant than it was in 2012. As of early 2016, the Chilean ecosystem for start-ups included more than 1 000 start-ups supported by public policy and 34 facilities across the country specialising in start-ups (co-working spaces, incubators and accelerators). According to CORFO data, the first five years of the Start-Up Chile programme saw the mobilisation of capital amounting to USD 420 million and the creation of more than 5 000 jobs.

By structuring public policy and fine-tuning the policy mix, Chile has also made progress in how it defines and identifies start-ups for the purpose of public policy. Chile prioritises dynamic enterprises, i.e. those with high growth potential, and adapts its instruments to the age and nature of businesses (Figure 3.6).

Figure 3.6. **Definitions of start-ups for public policy in Chile, 2016**

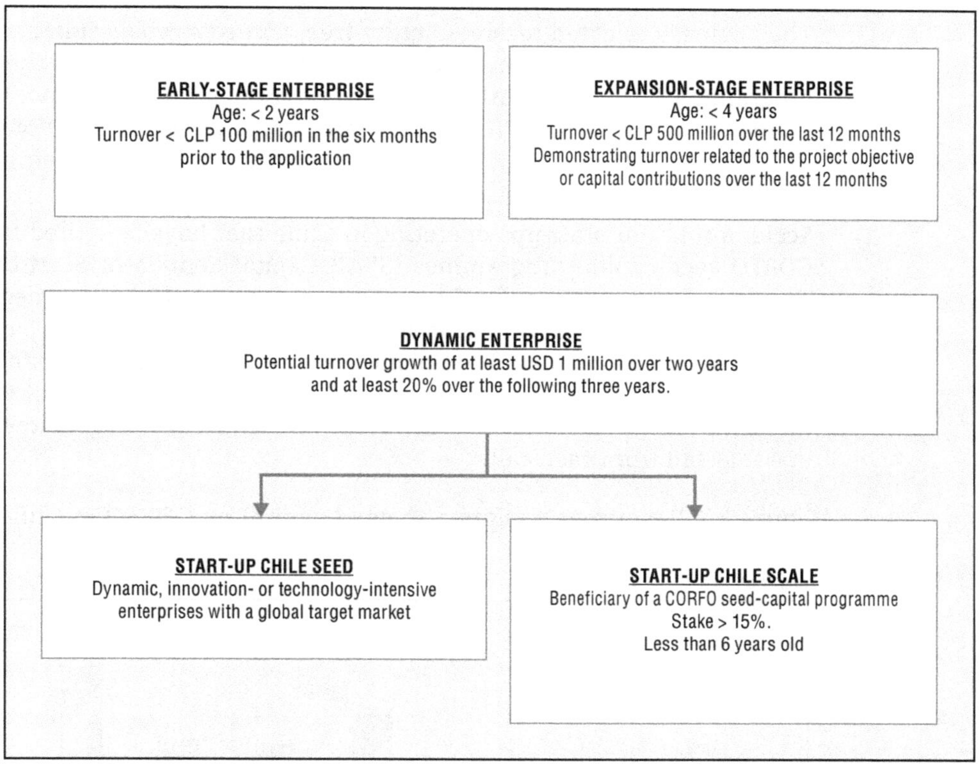

Source: Authors' work based on CORFO data, updated in 2016.

The following sections describe the main changes in the policy mix to promote start-ups in Chile, with special emphasis on the most recent reforms. The changes described are grouped into five action areas: i) closing the funding gap; ii) facilitating linkages and providing services; iii) creating markets; iv) transforming mindsets; and v) reforming legal frameworks. Of particular note are the reforms made to financing and services to meet the needs of entrepreneurs in the regions.

Chile is strengthening the financing chain and focusing on expanding early-stage financing

Over the years, Chile has sought to complete the financing chain so that it extends from the seed to the expansion stage of start-ups. It has also stepped up support at the seed stage, and the country has various seed-capital instruments as part of Start-Up Chile and other programmes (Figure 3.7). Since 2010, the Capital Semilla (Seed Capital) contest has been supporting the founding of companies with a high growth potential. The programme co-finances the implementation of projects for up to CLP 25 million (Chilean pesos, about USD 35 000), or 75% of the total cost of the project. The Flexible Seed Grant (SSAF) scheme also includes a category for supporting start-ups. The SSAF is an indirect support instrument introduced in 2013 that assigns resources to new entrepreneurs through certified incubators acting as intermediaries.

Start-Up Chile operates with a similar setup and currently runs three financing lines:

- **The S Factory (TSF):** a pre-acceleration line for teams with at least one woman founder. TSF's main aim is to support technology firms owned by women. Participating businesses receive support to transform an idea or concept into a prototype or a minimum viable product in three months of pre-acceleration. They receive non-repayable co-funding for up to CLP 10 million (about USD 14 000) or up to 90% of the total project cost. TSF makes two calls for applications every year, with 20 to 30 start-ups selected from each call.

- **Seed:** an acceleration line for start-ups that already have a functional prototype. The business selected receives equity-free, non-repayable capital contributions to the tune of CLP 20 million (about US 30 000) for up to 90% of the total cost.The programme lasts six months and has two annual calls for applications, with 80 to 100 start-ups selected from each call. It also offers an additional incentive of CLP 5 million (about USD 7 600) to beneficiaries who expand their businesses into the regions and to Chilean students studying abroad.
- **Scale:** a fund for start-ups operating in Chile that have benefited from one of the CORFO seed-capital programmes (SSAF, Capital Semilla or Start-Up Chile Seed). The focus is on start-ups in the expansion phase that have momentum (increase in turnover, clients, investment) and are seeking to scale up in Latin America or further afield. The selected companies receive non-repayable capital contributions to the tune of CLP 60 million (about USD 90 000), equal to 70% of the co-funding. Two calls for applications are made every year under the programme, with 15 start-ups selected from each call.

Figure 3.7. **Resources assigned to seed capital by CORFO in Chile, 2007-16**
(millions of USD)

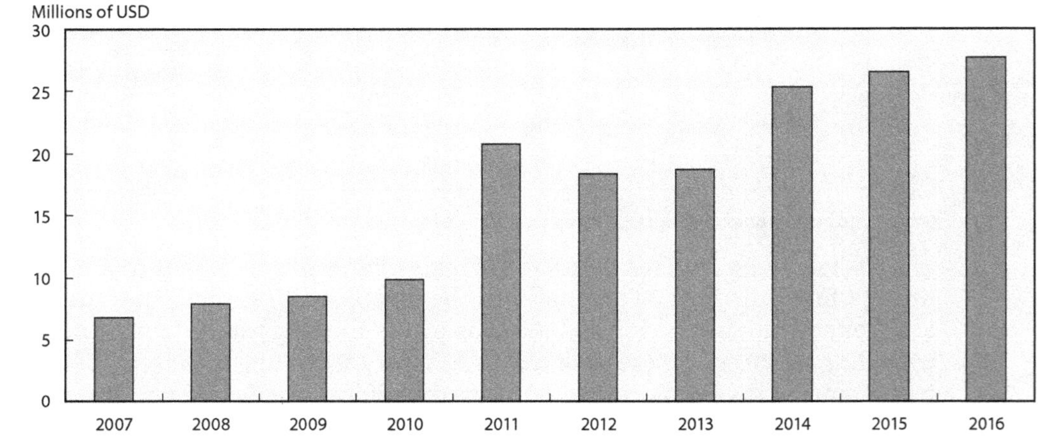

Note: Total seed capital comprises all programmes active each year. Since 2010, the figures also include the Start-Up Chile line.

Source: OECD (2013), *Start-up Latin America: Promoting Innovation in the Region*, http://dx.doi.org/10.1787/9789264202306-en, updated; and CORFO data for 2016.

Since it was introduced in 2010, Start-Up Chile has become a comprehensive, integrated programme to promote start-ups, providing financing and services to entrepreneurs. Initially, Start-Up Chile sought to change the country's entrepreneurship mindset from a traditional one to a technology-based approach, geared towards the international market and a global impact. To achieve this objective, it worked to increase the number of start-ups in the country attracting foreign entrepreneurial talent. Start-Up Chile provided seed capital for the founding of new start-ups, access to basic infrastructure for initial operations, and simpler visa procedures for foreign beneficiaries. By monitoring Start-Up Chile's implementation, CORFO has been able to identify the programme's strengths and weaknesses and use that information to improve its design. Between 2010 and 2015, Start-Up Chile received more than 10 000 applications and supported 1 309 start-ups in 77 countries (mainly in Chile, the United States, Argentina, India and Brazil), more than half of which are still operating as of 2016. According to CORFO estimates, the start-ups that it supported that still operate have created more than 5 000 jobs (about five per start-up), while private co-investments have more than quintupled CORFO's initial investment. One of the major challenges that Chile has identified is the ability to hold on to talented entrepreneurs. More than 65% of the businesses that Start-Up

Chile has supported are located abroad, and those that begin in Chile tend to leave the country quickly. The monitoring of the programme's results found that the new goals for Start-Up Chile in 2016 include creating incentives for the development of the regions, attracting Chilean entrepreneurs who have studied abroad and retaining successful foreign entrepreneurs who have received support from Start-Up Chile.

Crowdfunding is still in its infancy in Chile. As of 2015 there were five platforms in the country: debt-based platforms Cumplo and Becual, equity-based platform Broota, and rewards-based platforms Dale Impulso and Fondeadora. As of 2015, crowdfunding platforms had funded 1 500 projects (start-ups as well as artistic and social projects), raising around USD 55 million (MIF, 2015). Public policy faces the challenge of creating synergies with these new forms of financing and developing legislation to enable and regulate them.

Public policy has supported the development of the venture-capital industry in Chile since the late 1990s. CORFO has financed venture-capital funds in Chile since 1998, sometimes providing as much as three times the private sector's investment. In 2012, CORFO changed its lines of support for venture capital, differentiating between the capital it provides for investment funds operating in the early stages (on a 2:1 basis) and that which it provides for those in the expansion stage (on a 1:1 basis). In 2015, CORFO also introduced the Support for the Operation of Early-Stage Investment Funds programme, aimed at fund managers considering including activities related to business acceleration, such as collaborative workspaces. The programme provides up to CLP 160 million (around USD 221 000), with a fixed component equal to 75% of the project cost (up to a maximum of CLP 80 million) and a variable component for the second year of operation based on activities during the first year. CORFO also has other support programmes for the venture-capital industry. In 2012, it launched the CORFO Venture Capital for Innovative Firms programme to provide long-term loans to the managers of investment funds that invest in firms with high growth potential. The credit line is equal to 200% of the fund's investments. Since 2011, the Fénix Mining Exploration Fund has supported the mining industry by providing long-term loans to investment funds for investment in young exploration and mining firms. Also in 2011, CORFO launched its Venture Capital for Direct Investment in Investment Funds programme (K1) to encourage private investment in small and medium-sized enterprises that are less than seven years old and are registered as a corporation or joint-stock company.

Through its Investors Club formed in January 2016, Start-Up Chile aims to support the development of an ecosystem for early-stage investment (venture capital) and to support start-ups looking for capital. To date, the club has more than 70 members (angel investors, venture capital, family offices and private equity).

Despite these initiatives, the industry is still in its infancy in Chile, where there are still structural and cultural barriers holding back private investment in start-ups (OECD, 2013; Echecopar et al., 2015). As of 2014, CORFO was providing 74% of total investment. Data published by the Chilean Association of Investment Fund Administrators (ACAFI) shows that the venture-capital industry in Chile mobilises much smaller amounts of investment than in more advanced economies. In 2015, investments totalled USD 396.1 million, with the 33 funds averaging USD 12 million each. All the funds receive public support through CORFO. In 2014, Chilean investment funds invested around USD 60 million in 28 new enterprises, up 27% on the figure for 2013, and about five times more than they invested in 2004 (Figure 3.8). The venture-capital fund with the largest investment was Austral Capital (USD 32.8 million), followed by Negocios Regionales (USD 32 million) and Chiletech (USD 30.9 million) (ACAFI, 2015a). In terms of funds raised, between 2011 and 2015 Chile was ranked third in Latin America with USD 119 million, behind Brazil (USD 1.33 billion) and Mexico (USD 356 million) (LAVCA, 2016).

Figure 3.8. **Venture capital in Chile, 2014**

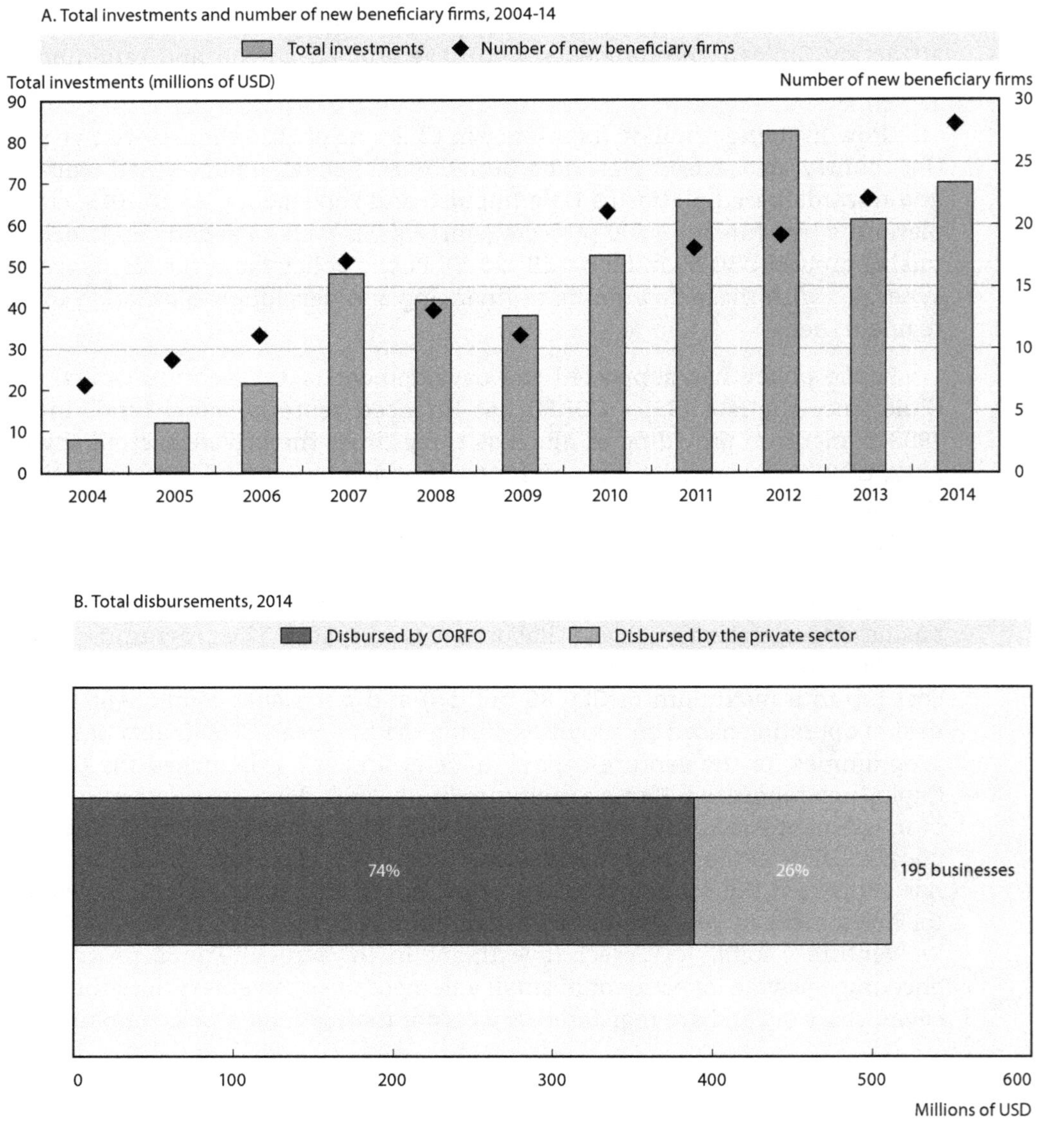

Note: Current USD for each year. 84% of the specified amounts invested is considered venture capital. The data include investments from four private-investment funds that are not considered venture capital (ACAFI, 2015b).
Source: Authors' work based on CORFO (2015b), *Informe Público de Capital de Riesgo. Resultados Acumulados al 31 de Diciembre de 2014*, and on ACAFI (2015b) *Anuario de Fondos de Inversión*, December 2014.

Angel investors remain a weak link in the financing chain for start-ups in Chile, and have lost ground since 2012. Of the seven networks that once existed, five no longer operate, and in 2013 CORFO suspended applications for the Support for Angel Capitalist Networks financing line. Nevertheless, some angel-investor networks remain active, including Fundación Chile's angel-investor network Chile Global Angels, which runs the "¡Despega!" (Launch!) initiative. Through this competition, angel investors in the Chile Global Angels network provide financing and mentoring services to the winning project. In 2015 the competition attracted more than 140 applications and was won by chemical firm Dentoxol, which produces an innovative medical product. Dentoxol received USD 22 000 from angel investors.

Chile is modernising its services for start-ups and is looking to tap into the sharing economy

As it seeks to support start-ups, Chile is modernising and improving its support services for entrepreneurs. It is reforming the system for incubators and accelerators, as well as experimenting with new mechanisms that are more flexible and dynamic and that require less paperwork in order to better respond to the needs of entrepreneurs. In 2015, for instance, Chile launched the Support for Operating Collaborative Workspaces for Entrepreneurship programme, which funds some of the operating expenses of collaborative workspaces up and down the country. Chile also began to co-fund mentoring networks in 2014 through non-repayable capital contributions covering 75% of the cost of building mentoring networks in the country. This programme is linked to the Seed Capital contest, in which applicants can opt for an additional non-repayable CLP 500 000 capital injection if they request the support of a mentor through one of the networks. Thanks to this initiative, as of November 2015 there were 500 mentoring networks in Chile spread across seven networks. By 2016, CORFO hopes to have 1 000 mentors so that no seed enterprise is without a mentor.

In 2014, the focus shifted away from the global impact – which had been the main criterion during the first phase of support for start-ups in 2010 – and towards the market impact of start-ups, irrespective of whether their impact is national, regional or global. This change overcomes the weakness of prioritising the acceleration phase over the creation phase (OECD, 2013). CORFO supports university tech spin-offs through the Go to Market programme. During the first phase, this programme provides financing for innovation workshops and covers the cost of presenting projects. During the second phase, it finances a one-month stay in the country or market chosen for the sale of the product, as well as the development of a practical programme in that country or market.

In recent years, Chilean universities have increasingly been supporting start-ups, with some university incubators receiving international recognition. Two appear in the University Business Incubator ranking, an annual list of the top 25 university incubators in the world produced by UBI Global, a consultancy that specialises in analysing university business incubators. The International Business Innovation Institute (3IE) at Universidad Técnica Federico Santa María is ranked 17th and Chrysalis at Pontífica Universidad Católica de Valparaíso is ranked 24th. At Pontífica Universidad Católica de Chile (UC), the science and technology research agency DICTUC focuses on the development of technological spin-offs. DICTUC created SIRVE, an anti-seismic technology firm, in 2003; it also created Eduinova, a company dedicated to research and development on educational innovation and technology, in 1995. Universidad de Santiago de Chile has the INNOVO centre, an incubator specialising in tech firms that has given rise to several successful spin-offs, including VoZE, a firm that began operating in 2013 and designed Chile's first prototype electric vehicle, the first series of which will be launched in 2016.

Chile is supporting regional and social inclusion through new conditionalities in its policy mix

Promoting equal opportunity is becoming a priority also in policies to support start-ups. This new focus comes from two main considerations. First, given the desire to strengthen the connection between actions to support start-ups and national production-development strategy, priorities have converged. Second, the policy to support start-ups in Chile, as outlined in the 2014-18 Chile Entrepreneurship Policy, is the result of a cumulative process of learning how to design and manage policies. Start-Up Chile's first assessments revealed the limits of a pro-startup policy that fails to take the regions into account (information published by CORFO in 2016). Start-ups in regions outside

Santiago's metropolitan area are faced with a wider gap in terms of access to funding and services. Furthermore, because there was not a regions-based approach, there was a disconnection between production development priorities in strategic industries (often located outside Santiago's metropolitan area) and pro-startup measures, which, at the user level, focus mainly on the capital.

In response to the need for greater inclusiveness, Chile introduced new incentives. The main reforms recently introduced involved the launch of four new programmes:

1. Regional Pro-Entrepreneurship Programmes (PRAEs). Introduced in 2014, the PRAEs co-finance start-ups with high growth potential, specifically, those with the potential to record growth above 20% during the first three years. CORFO provides non-repayable contributions covering up to 75% of the total cost of the project up to a maximum of CLP 25 million (USD 34 000). Applications are submitted via one of CORFO's approved sponsors.
2. The SSAF-Social programme. Introduced in 2014, SSAF-Social provides resources to new entrepreneurs through certified incubators with a proven experience in supporting social-innovation enterprises.
3. The S Factory (TSF) programme for gender inclusion. Created in 2015 as part of Start-Up Chile, TSF is a pre-accelerator for high-impact start-ups run by women. The programme provides entrepreneurial training, workspaces and mentoring services, as well as 90% co-financing for up to CLP 10 million (around USD 15 000) for each project.
4. The Environment Support Programme for Entrepreneurship and PAEI-Regional Innovation. Introduced in 2015, this programme aims to create a more business-oriented culture and raise business skills in the regions. It co-finances programmes that have a substantial regional impact and that promote entrepreneurship and innovation. CORFO subsidises up to 70% of the project costs, up to a maximum of CLP 50 million.

Start-Up Chile is also introducing reforms to improve regional inclusion. It has opened regional offices in Valparaíso and Concepción, and in 2015 it began to offer the Go-Regional incentive, which consists of a CLP 5 million (USD 6 800) non-repayable contribution – in addition to the CLP 20 million (USD 27 500) under the Start-Up Chile Seed programme – for start-ups to set up base in the regions (Go-Regional incentive). As of 2016, after two editions of Start-Up with this additional incentive, 23 start-ups have benefited from the Go-Regional incentive by moving into the regions: 15 in Valparaíso, 8 in Concepción.

The Support for Operating Collaborative Workspaces for Entrepreneurship programme also has a regional focus. Created in 2005, the programme supports the opening of collaborative workspaces – co-working spaces, laboratories and accelerators – in regions with few incubators or accelerators. It covers 75% of the project costs in the form of a non-repayable capital contribution, up to a maximum of CLP 200 million (USD 145 000). The first stage of the programme focused on turning the cities of Antofagasta, Valparaíso and Concepción into new innovation hubs. By the end of 2015, Chile had 30 collaborative workspaces for entrepreneurship in the regions. One example is the CoWork Espacio Atacama centre in Antofagasta, which was formed by a partnership between CORFO; Chrysalis; the Pontífica Universidad Católica's business incubator in Valparaíso in partnership with Fundación Mi Norte; Universidad Católica del Norte; and Corporación Incuba2. The centre has air-conditioned rooms for meetings and spaces for training, and it provides mentoring, training, legal and accounting services.

Policies to support the opening of regional start-up centres are beginning to bear fruit. It is still too early to assess their impact, since the instruments to support start-ups in the regions began operating only as recently as 2014, but there are signs that they have had positive results. According to CORFO estimates in 2015, the concentration of businesses located in Santiago (rather than in the regions) has fallen from 75% to around 50%. Temuco, for instance, is positioning itself as a dynamic cluster of tech enterprises. Start-Up Chile has 39 start-ups in the regions: 22 in Valparaíso, 15 in Concepción, 1 in Maule and 1 in the Los Lagos Region. Of these, 24 have benefited from the Go-Regional incentive introduced in 2015.

Chile is seeking to open up markets for start-ups

Start-Up Chile facilitates market access for start-ups by connecting large firms with its portfolio of start-ups through the Business Network programme (Red de Empresas). More than 70 organisations in Chile and abroad participate in the programme, which was launched in 2016. The Business Network establishes linkages between large firms and start-ups so that the start-ups can offer solutions to problems identified by large firms, thus benefiting both parties. Universidad Técnica Federico Santa María's International Business Innovation Institute (3IE) runs a programme to accelerate technology start-ups called Booster UP, which receives support from CORFO. The programme selects start-ups that propose innovative solutions to challenges put forward by the industry in the intelligent-expertise priority areas identified in the national production-diversification strategy (e.g. logistics, smart mining, and the winemaking industry). In the fourth edition of Booster UP, held in 2015, the winning start-ups put forward solutions in smart industries in various sectors: food and wine, mining, logistics and inventory, seismic technology and energy efficiency.

Chile is making it easier to start a business and is facilitating re-entrepreneurship

Chile has been reforming its regulatory framework for starting and winding up businesses. In 2014, the country introduced three reforms to deal with some of the weaknesses identified in the OECD study (2013):

1. Law 20 659/2014 (*Ley de Empresas en un Día*, or Express Companies Act) simplified procedures for incorporating, amending or dissolving commercial companies.
2. Law 20 720/2014 (*Ley de Re-emprendimiento*, or Re-entrepreneurship Act) facilitated swifter negotiations between creditors and debtors for unsuccessful enterprises and made it easier to start a new business thanks to the rapid discharge of the debtor.
3. Law 20 712/2014 (*Ley Única de Fondos*, or Single Funds Act) sought to make investment in the country's investment funds bigger and more diverse, introducing tax incentives for foreign investment in Chilean investment funds, creating a single tax, and simplifying tax payment procedures.

While it is too early to assess the impact of the reforms, these simplifications, alongside existing incentives such as Law 20 570/2012 (*Ley de Incentivos para la Innovación*, or Innovation Incentives Act), are expected to create a more business- and investment-friendly legal framework.

Conclusions and challenges for the future

Chile has a long tradition of promoting innovative entrepreneurship, having gradually learned how to design and co-ordinate better public policies. Since the country first introduced measures to promote innovative entrepreneurship in the late 1990s, it has learned the importance of having appropriate instruments to accompany businesses throughout the various stages of their development, from the transformation of an idea into a concrete project and the translation of that project into a business plan, to the eventual launch of the company. The need for the financing chain became apparent when Chile first tried to foster start-up development by supporting venture capital despite the lack of seed capital and the huge barriers that hindered the creation of new enterprises. Subsequent attempts to complete the financing chain have allowed Chile to develop a set of comprehensive measures to support entrepreneurship from the seed to the expansion stage. These attempts have also highlighted the importance of piloting new policies and monitoring their implementation to assess their impact in a timely manner.

Chile has shown its capacity to innovate and anticipate trends in the region. In the late 1990s it began to promote venture capital, and in 2010 it introduced the widely publicised Start-Up Chile programme, which helped transform the start-up scene, showing that start-ups also exist in Latin America. More recently, the country has focused on next-generation support instruments like crowdfunding, the sharing economy and mentoring networks. Chile has also shown that it can monitor programmes, assess outcomes, and react quickly to reform incentives. For example, based on its assessments of businesses supported under Start-Up Chile's first call for applications, Chile has included incentives to promote start-ups at the regional level.

As outlined in this chapter, Start-Up Chile is not the only instrument for start-up promotion in the country, but the programme and its communication strategy have been particularly significant, leading to greater optimism and an overhaul of public policies to pave the way for new types of businesses. Start-Up Chile has inspired many other countries, which have introduced programmes with similar strategies and objectives. Traditional production-development policies need a fresh approach if support for start-ups is to be successful. Start-ups are much more dynamic, fast-paced and changing, so policies must be agile and keep pace with market developments. For this reason, one of the under-acknowledged impacts of pro-startup policies is that they can contribute to the creation of dynamic, collaborative management practices in public institutions, and that this new mindset, geared towards short- and medium-term results, can have knock-on effects on other departments.

With traditional sources of growth based on natural resources being exhausted, Chile faces the challenge – today, more than ever – of diversifying its economy by transforming its productive structure and creating business-development opportunities centred around innovation, science and technology. Such opportunities are essential to transform growth and make it more inclusive and sustainable to respond to its citizens' expectations, especially those of young people. Support for start-ups is therefore an important component that Chile needs to build upon and appropriately structure in order to maximise results and impacts. Chile's main start-up policy challenges include:

- Creating an environment that is more attractive to productive investment and business development and, more importantly, mobilising private resources in addition to public investment, especially in the form of venture capital and investment funds.
- Consolidating and simplifying the policy mix to promote start-ups. Although trials are necessary to identify good practices, it is also important to simplify the system of incentives to make the policy more entrepreneur-oriented and easier to communicate so that it can be implemented more smoothly.
- Creating synergies between the national smart-specialisation strategy and the business ecosystem's potential across the country.

- Increasing the survival rate of start-ups and finding mechanisms to channel benefits towards Chile, even when companies need to operate in other countries because of the nature of their business.
- Structuring the monitoring and assessment processes to improve the quality of information used for decision-making, and introducing monitoring for start-ups that do not receive public support so that they can be used as control groups when assessing results.

References

ACAFI (2015a), "Informe 2014-2015. Reporte de venture capital y private equity: una mirada al mercado chileno y de la región", Asociación Chilena de Administradoras de Fondos de Inversión, Santiago, Chile.

ACAFI (2015b), "Anuario fondos de inversión. Diciembre 2014", Asociación Chilena de Administradoras de Fondos de Inversión, Santiago, Chile.

CORFO (2015a), "The Chilean Experience in Developing a Global Entrepreneurship Hub", presentation by E. Bitrán in October 2015, mimeo.

CORFO (2015b), "Informe público de capital de riesgo: Resultados acumulados al 31 de diciembre de 2014", Corporación de Fomento de la Producción, Santiago, Chile.

Echecopar G. et al. (2015), *Learning From Outliers: A Revisionist Perspective of the Role of Institutions in Venture Capital Market Creation*, mimeo.

MIF (2015), *Creating a Crowdfunding Ecosystem in Chile*, Multilateral Investment Fund, Inter-American Development Bank, Washington, DC, http://www.fomin.org/en-us/Home/Knowledge/Publications/idPublication/142687.aspx.

LAVCA (2016), *Latin America Venture Capital: Five Year Trends*, Latin American Private Equity & Venture Capital Association, http://lavca.org/2016/07/15/new-vc-latin-america-venture-capital-five-year-trends/.

OECD (2014), *OECD Science, Technology and Industry Outlook 2014*, OECD Publishing, Paris, http://dx.doi.org/10.1787/sti_outlook-2014-en.

OECD (2013), *Start-up Latin America: Promoting Innovation in the Region*, Development Centre Studies, OECD Publishing, Paris, http://dx.doi.org/10.1787/9789264202306-en.

Chapter 4

Promoting start-ups in Colombia

This chapter presents an overview of policies to support start-ups in Colombia, focusing on changes that have taken place between 2012 and 2016. Like in other Latin American countries, the promotion of start-ups is an emerging and evolving topic in Colombia. In 2012, Colombia launched the iNNpulsa programme to promote entrepreneurship. Colombia's pro-startup policy seeks to attract investment from financial institutions in start-ups, as well as to promote a business culture in the country. One prominent feature in the country is the growth of start-ups in cities like Bogotá and Medellín, which are looking to become hubs for start-ups in the country and in Latin America.

Introduction

Like other countries in the region, Colombia is focusing on start-ups and on designing policies and instruments to promote the creation of innovative enterprises. Promoting innovative entrepreneurship only recently became a priority for the country. The 2010-14 National Development Plan, entitled "Prosperity for All", introduced the idea, which received fresh impetus when the 2014-18 National Development Plan, entitled "Everybody for a New Country", included it in the country's transformation strategy.

This chapter presents an overview of Colombia's policies to support start-ups, focusing on changes that have taken place between 2012 and 2016 and identifying challenges for the future.

Start-ups in Colombia: The current situation

Colombia's science, technology and innovation system performs well below the levels observed in OECD countries. Investment in research and development and private-sector investment in innovation is lower than in more advanced countries. Although access to information and communication technologies (ICTs) has increased and more people are using them, the gaps with emerging and developed countries remain wide (OECD, 2014; Figure 4.1).

However, there is a growing entrepreneurial culture, with more and more start-ups emerging and expanding (Box 4.1). Start-ups in Colombia operate in different sectors. Some successful ones are in high-tech sectors, such as the aeronautical firm NEDIAR, which began operating in 2011 and has provided technology to the country's main airline, Avianca, since 2014.

Figure 4.1. **Comparison of science and innovation performance in Colombia and the OECD, 2014**

(normalised performance index relative to median OECD values)

(OECD median = 100)

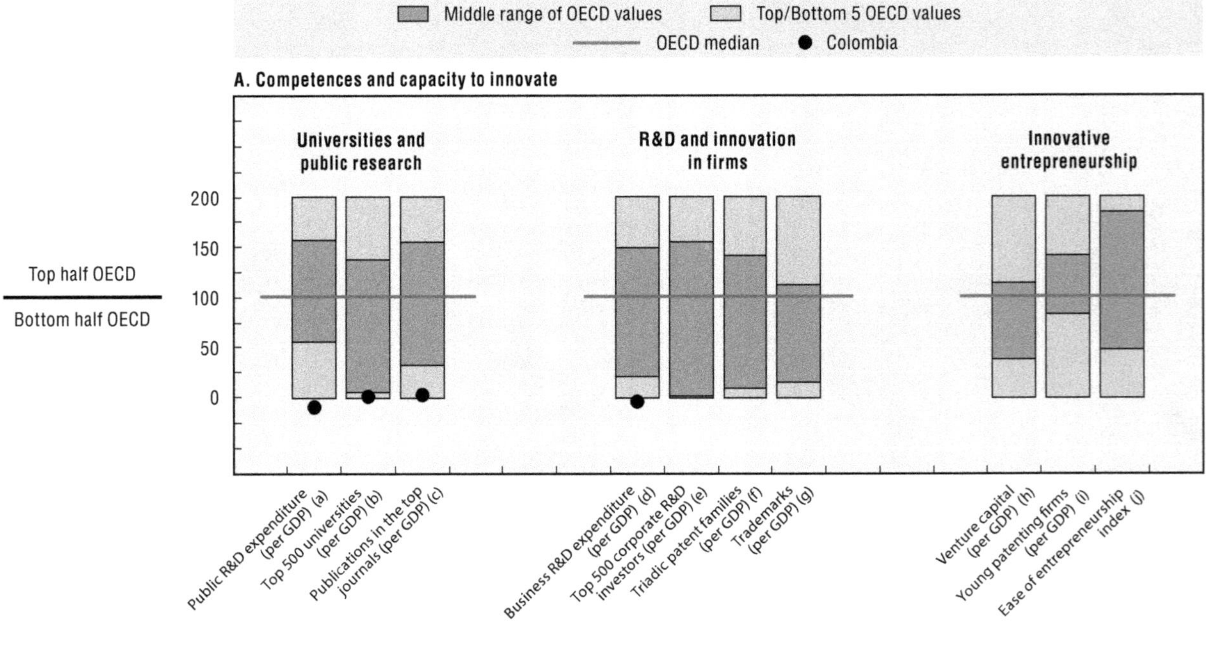

Figure 4.1. Comparison of science and innovation performance in Colombia and the OECD, 2014 *(cont.)*

(normalised performance index relative to median OECD values)

(OECD median = 100)

B. Interactions and skills for innovation

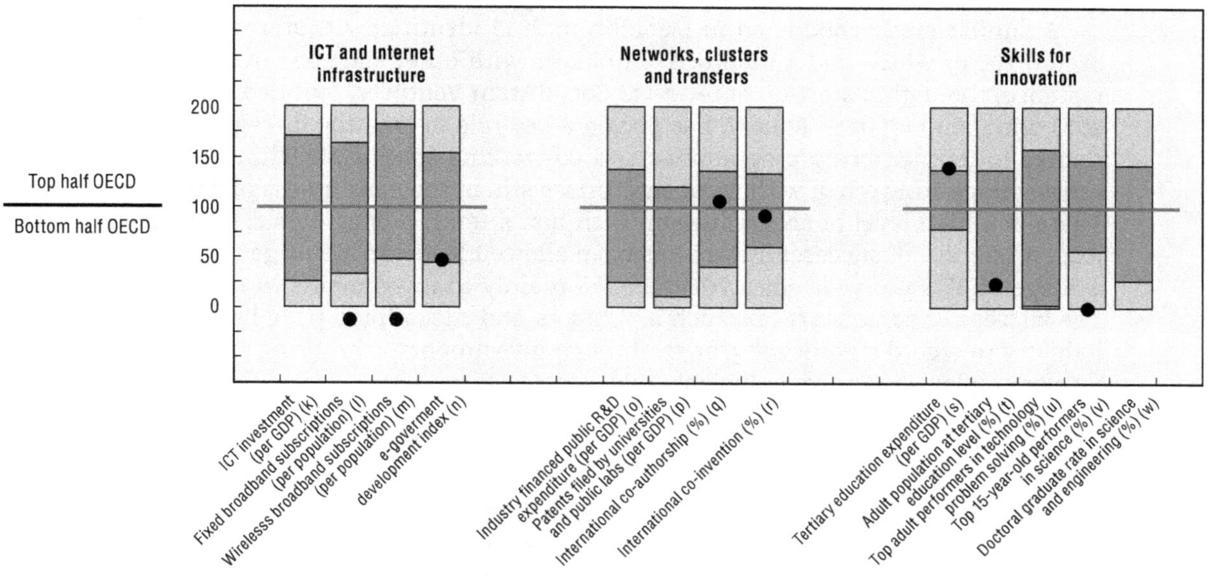

Note: The indicators are adjusted to the size of the country (GDP or population size). The values for Colombia are compared with the median value for OECD countries, i.e. the middle-ranked country of all the OECD countries for which data is available. For more details on the methodology used, see the STI country profiles in OECD (2014).

Source: OECD (2014), *OECD Science, Technology and Industry Outlook 2014*, http://dx.doi.org/10.1787/sti_outlook-2014-en, based on the OECD's *Main Science and Technology Indicators (MSTI)* database, June 2014, www.oecd.org/sti/msti.htm.

Box 4.1. Start-ups in Colombia: Two examples

Launched in 2009 to develop technologies for accessible education, Aulas AMIGAS sells optical boards, interactive tables and educational platforms at prices that are affordable to educational institutions, including those in remote areas located far away from the country's metropolitan areas. In 2011 and 2012, the start-up won the Innova Award as one of the most innovative companies in Colombia. Today, it sells 15 technology products, has 10 registered trademarks and directly employs 98 members of staff in Colombia, Ecuador and Argentina.

Launched in Medellín in 2011, NEDIAR S.A.S. is a technology start-up in the aeronautical sector. The company develops aeronautical engineering solutions for several Colombian-based airlines, including Copa, LATAM and Avianca. For Avianca, Colombia's leading airline, it developed a flight simulator system for training flight attendants. NEDIAR also develops other products, including electronics and equipment for flight operations. Its team of aeronautical and electronic engineers has more than ten years' experience in the sector.

Source: iNNpulsa (2014), *Dinámicos*.

One of the main developments regarding start-ups in Colombia has been the recent emergence of start-up ecosystems in cities. In the space of just a few years, Medellín has transformed its image and has become a place for founding and growing innovative enterprises. Like other Latin American countries, Colombia does not have precise data on the profile and performance of its start-ups, but surveys are generating new data. Endeavor Insight, for instance, conducted a study in 2013 on more than 230 entrepreneurs in the ICT sector in Bogotá. The results showed that the ecosystem is growing: between 2009 and 2013, more than 300 linkages (including mentoring, inspiration, entrepreneurship, investment and former employment) were formed and 150 technology firms began operating (Endeavor Insight, 2014).

A similar study conducted in Medellín in 2015 identified 700 start-ups in the ICT sector, 200 of which had a total of 170 linkages with other start-ups in the sector. For instance, the digital start-up accelerator SocialAtom Ventures, founded in Medellín in 2013 with support from Ruta N, has played a key role in creating linkages in Medellín thanks to its mentoring programmes and co-working spaces. Medellín's ICT start-up ecosystem is still young, with most enterprises still in the early stages of development. There is a high level of concentration, with just a tenth of start-ups creating half the jobs. A handful of successful start-ups have allowed Medellín's linkages to grow by an average of 35% per year since 2010, thanks mainly to investments in new ICT firms. The success of some start-ups such as Ubidots and Alcuadrado have helped the local industry to record significant growth through investments, mentoring and spin-offs of former employees (Endeavor Insight, 2014).

Colombia is restructuring its policy to support start-ups

The 2010-14 National Development Plan ("Prosperity for All") made start-up promotion one of its priorities. As a result, the Bank of Foreign Trade created the Innovation and Business Development Unit and the Ministry of Commerce, Industry and Tourism (MinCIT) launched the iNNpulsa Colombia programme, in both cases, to promote business growth, innovation and entrepreneurship in Colombia. iNNpulsa Colombia issued calls for applications for non-repayable resources in the form of seed capital disbursed to innovative, export-oriented start-ups with high potential turnover. It also provided non-financial support in the form of business training and activities to promote an entrepreneurial culture.

The policy to support start-ups gained fresh impetus in 2015 under the 2014-18 National Development Plan, entitled "Everybody for a new country". Its goals included doubling investment in science, technology and innovation and raising such investment to 1% of gross domestic product (GDP). In 2015, MinCIT reformed Bancóldex to streamline policy implementation, merging iNNpulsa with the Modernisation and Innovation Fund for Micro, Small and Medium-Sized Enterprises and making it an autonomous entity (*patrimonio autónomo*). It also reformed the model under which iNNpulsa supports innovation and entrepreneurship, introducing a voucher scheme in 2016 to run alongside the existing system of calls for applications. Bancóldex launched the Business Hyper-Growth platform (*Crecimiento Empresarial Extraordinario*) to develop the lending market for start-ups and for corporate firms and gazelle companies. Colombia approved the 2016-25 Production Development Policy in August 2016. Drawn up by the National Planning Department, the policy promotes innovation and entrepreneurship as key pillars of the country's long-term vision for production development.

Today, public support for start-ups involves several institutions (Figure 4.2). MinCIT, the Ministry of Labour, the Ministry of Information Technologies and Communications (MinTIC) and Colciencias (the government body in charge of science) draw up policies and implement programmes aimed at different types of start-ups and other stakeholders in the ecosystem.

MinCIT's Vice Ministry of Business Development implements policies to promote start-ups through iNNpulsa Colombia and seeks to link the ecosystem through the regional entrepreneurship networks (*Redes Regionales de Emprendimiento*), which operate as public-private partnerships responsible for designing strategies and taking action. Bancóldex acts as a second-tier bank and runs various programmes for commercial banks with the aim of ensuring the financial inclusion of start-ups. Furthermore, iNNpulsa Colombia seeks to provide financial support and training to start-ups through a voucher scheme. It also runs programmes to promote an entrepreneurial culture with the aim of changing mindsets in the country.

The Ministry of Labour, meanwhile, promotes start-ups with the potential to create jobs by providing them with seed capital and offering training through the National Learning Service (SENA). MinTIC, in partnership with Colciencias, promotes start-ups with digital content through the APPS.CO programme. Additionally, Colciencias supports academic spin-offs through technology transfer offices.

Figure 4.2. **The institutional framework for policies to support start-ups in Colombia, 2016**

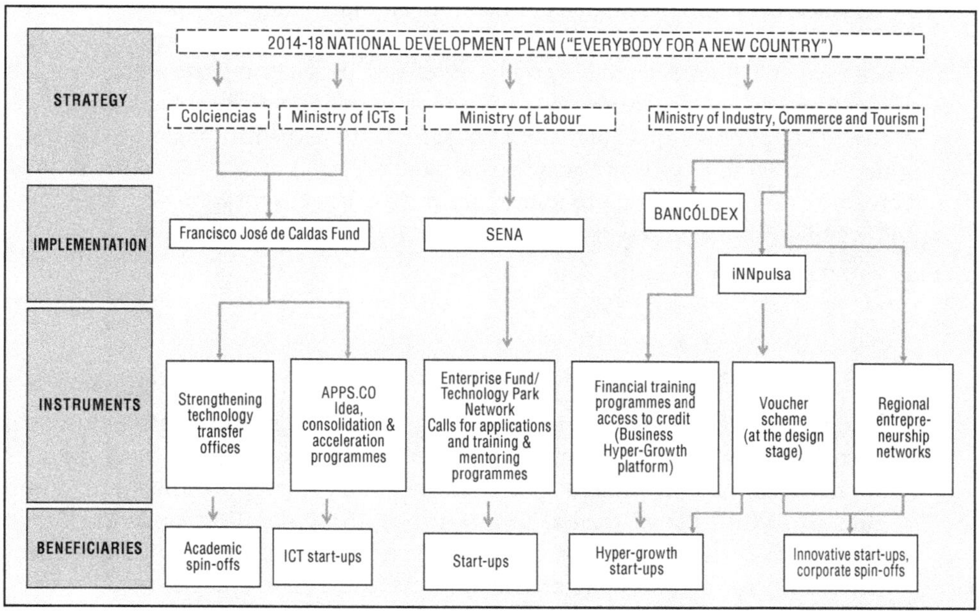

Note: Since 2015, iNNpulsa Colombia has been an autonomous entity (*patrimonio autónomo*) managed by Bancóldex.
Source: Authors' work based on official information from Colombia.

Colombia's policy to promote start-ups has a significant territorial dimension. Medellín is an emblematic case. The city has transformed its image in a short space of time, and since 2000 it has made great strides to position itself as a hub for start-ups in the country and the wider region. Medellín promotes start-ups through public-private partnerships like Ruta N (Box 4.2), which aims to increase the density of the entrepreneurial and innovative ecosystem. The city hosted the Global Entrepreneurship Congress in 2016, and in 2013 it was named Innovative City of the Year by the *Wall Street Journal* and the Citi Group. According to the Office of the Mayor, as of 2015, the public sector had invested COP 5 billion (Colombian pesos) in 142 companies to promote high-impact entrepreneurship. The utility company EPM created the USD 40 million private-equity fund Innovación SP in 2013. The fund is intended to finance science- and technology-intensive projects that offer innovative solutions to public utilities for energy, water, natural gas, ICTs and solid waste treatment. EPM also spends 0.6% of its income on research, development and innovation. The Development and Innovation Management Office (*Gerencia de Desarrollo e Innovación*) identifies innovative projects and helps develop them until there is a prototype or until pilot tests are ready.

Box 4.2. Experimenting to transform cities: Ruta N in Medellín

The Medellín Mayor's Office, UNE Telecommunications and Empresas Públicas de Medellín (EPM) launched Ruta N to promote entrepreneurship and to connect entrepreneurs, businesses, universities and members of public. The corporation provides infrastructure and programmes to support start-ups. Participants can receive training, financing, and support to protect their intellectual property.

Today, 29 companies, 7 high-impact enterprises and 35 social enterprises are benefiting from the corporation's incubation and acceleration services. The Startups Academy programme, supported by Ruta N, provides training to pre-incubation start-ups to help them draw up a validated business model. The programme supported 63 projects and validated 24 minimum viable projects in 2014. Ruta N also has three business development centres that provide specialised support to biotech, digital and high-impact enterprises. The corporation has an integrated support programme, called Development of Innovative Businesses (*Desarrollo de Negocios Innovadores*), for start-ups that can show they have a feasible product and an international plan. Selected start-ups receive financing and mentoring for developing their product, and in gaining access to markets and to private capital. Ruta N financing consists of two parts: one part is non-repayable, and may, depending on the specific conditions of each case, amount to as much as 100% of the project cost; the other part is repayable, and is based on the expenditure to be covered. In 2014, the programme selected 15 projects, which generated turnover of COP 650 million (Colombian pesos) and created 171 jobs according to Ruta N estimates. The corporation also facilitates fundraising to finance high-impact and technology-based start-ups for Medellín.

Source: Ruta N (2016), *Informe de gestión 2015.*

Colombia is reforming its policy mix to support start-ups

Colombia is reforming its policy mix to promote start-ups, shifting towards facilitating access to finance and services (Figure 4.3). To improve access to finance, Bancóldex has introduced financial inclusion programmes and Fundación Bavaria has introduced seed-capital programmes. iNNpulsa Colombia, the SENA and ANDI del Futuro have also introduced business training programmes. Meanwhile, public policy is increasingly focusing on generating a culture of entrepreneurship.

Figure 4.3. Policy mix to support start-ups in Colombia, 2012 and 2016

A. 2012

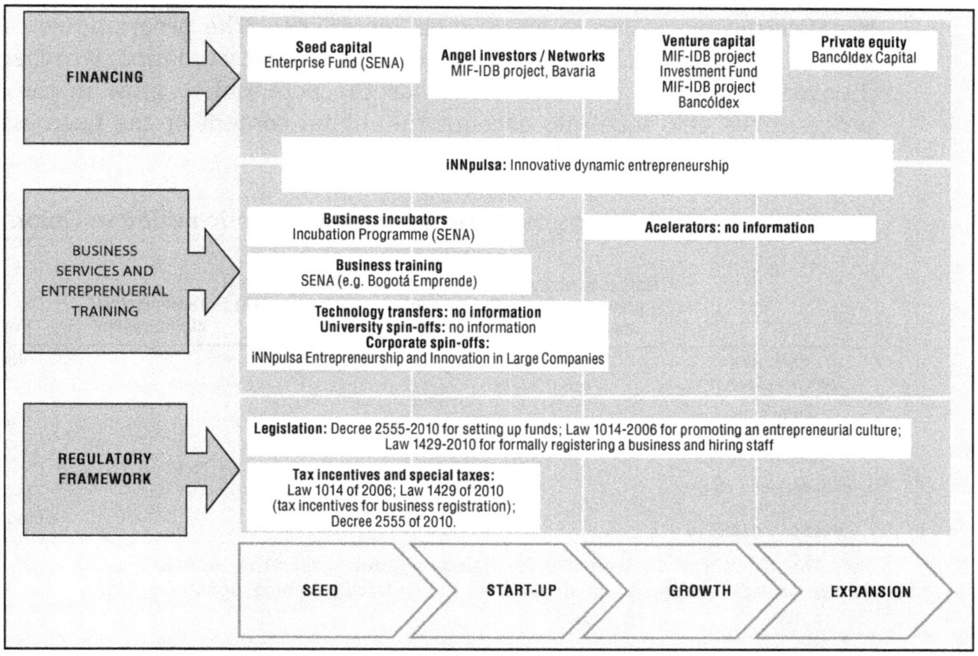

Source: OECD (2013), *Start-up Latin America Latina: Promoting Innovation in the Region*, http://dx.doi.org/10.1787/9789264202306-en.

B. 2016

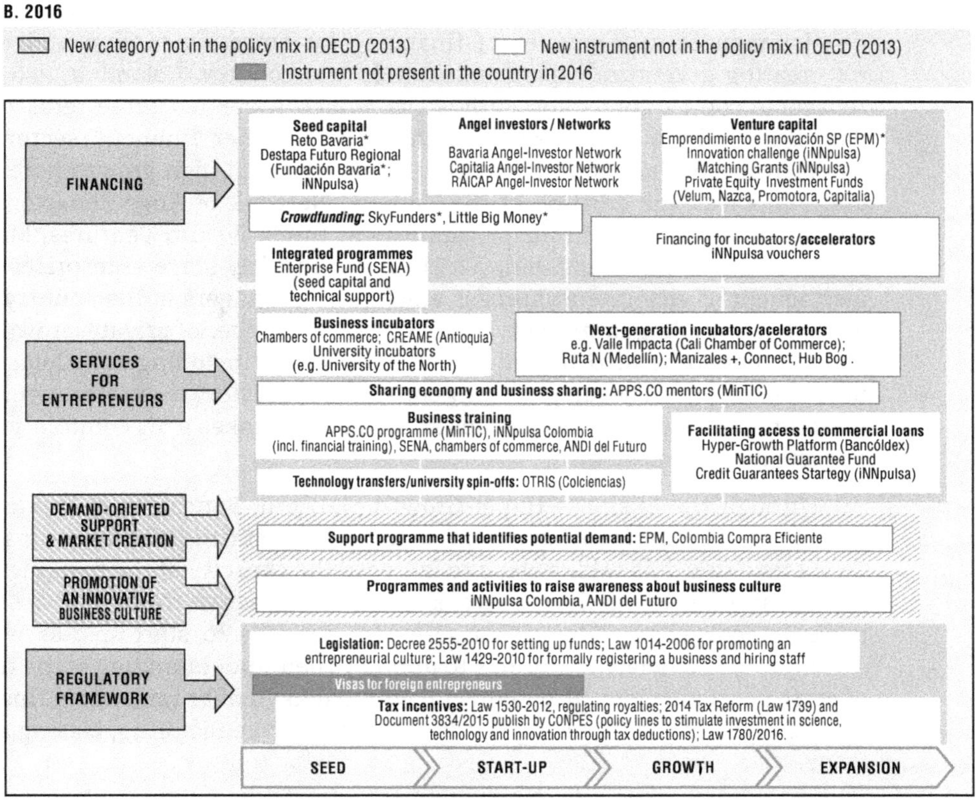

Note: Items marked with an asterisk (*) are private initiatives. The diagram shows information available on some programmes as of May 2016.

Source: Authors' work based on official information from Colombia and MinCIT, as well as information in Corporación Ventures (2015), *Documento de caracterización de herramientas, instrumentos y metodologías existentes para el mercado nacional que atiendan las etapas de identificación y validación del modelo de negocio.*

Colombia is advancing in defining start-ups. Each programme defines its targeted beneficiaries according to specific characteristics. The programmes consider factors such as whether the business has conducted market validation, whether it contributes innovative content, and whether it has the potential to grow in the market. Some programmes also take into account the digital content or the business-development stage of start-ups (Table 4.1).

Table 4.1. **Definitions of start-ups used by public policy in Colombia, 2016**

	Market validation / proven product momentum	Unique market product	Innovative content (unique market product)	Technological/ digital content	Programmes/Tools
Enterprise *(emprendimiento)*	✓	✓	✓	---	iNNpulsa Colombia programmes
Early-stage start-up *(etapa temprana)*	---	---	---	✓	Ideas APPS.co programme
Consolidation-stage start-up *(etapa consolidación)*	✓	---	---	✓	APPS.co Growth and Consolidation Programme

Note: The table shows a selection of the main programmes operating in 2016.
Source: Authors' work based on official information from Colombia, updated in 2016.

Colombia is looking to channel financing towards start-ups

Colombian start-ups receive financing through different channels. Between 2012 and 2015, the main programme, iNNpulsa, focused on creating incentives for the development of new sources of financing for entrepreneurship and innovation and for creating a venture-capital industry in the country. Colombia also provided non-repayable contributions and early-stage equity. It created three rediscount lines with Bancóldex, which were issued through the first-tier financial sector. It also made banks aware of the potential of new enterprises with high growth potential. Colombia also supported the creation of the National Network of Angel Investors (RNAI, led by Fundación Bavaria) and four private-capital funds (Velum Ventures, Mountain Nazca, Atom Ventures and Capitalia), which invest in early-stage enterprises. iNNpulsa has also sought to generate awareness among risk managers at the country's main banks, and it has a credit guarantee system in place. A number of private, crowdfunding-based support networks also began operating recently, including the Colombian platform SkyFunders, which began providing consultancy services to entrepreneurs in 2015. If the entrepreneur raises the target capital, SkyFunders takes a 5% commission, otherwise it charges no commission.

Through the Business Hyper-Growth platform, Bancóldex is looking to develop a lending market that is inclusive and sustainable for start-ups and early-stage enterprises. To achieve this, it is taking steps to increase the capacity of the banking system so that banks can offer loans that are accessible and attractive to start-ups. As a second-tier bank, Bancóldex provides risk-assessment services to start-ups, as well as training activities to financial institutions to improve their understanding of the financing needs of start-ups. Bancóldex also teams up with banks to offer innovative financial products geared towards the financing needs of start-ups, like factoring, leasing and mezzanine loans.

The SENA, for its part, offers integrated support to entrepreneurs through the Entrepreneurship Fund, which provides seed capital and technical assistance. Created in 2002, the fund supports the founding of enterprises by SENA students or apprentices, higher-education students, or Colombians who studied overseas before returning to Colombia. The fund finances up to 100% of project costs, depending on the number of jobs created. The technical support includes consultancy services lasting one year to help start-ups to draw up and implement a business plan. Babson College is currently working with the SENA to modernise the fund.

Open-innovation initiatives such as that of the company Bavaria offer seed capital to start-ups. In 2006, Fundación Bavaria's entrepreneur network introduced the "Destapa Futuro" (Uncover the Future) seed-capital programme. In 2015, the foundation decentralised the programme, with support from iNNpulsa and the Valle del Cauca Regional Entrepreneurship Network (Red Regional de Emprendimiento del Valle del Cauca), creating "Destapa Futuro Regional". The new regional programme selects five start-ups to receive COP 200 million (around USD 68 000) in seed capital. It also provides support and mentoring services and organises a mission to Montreal to connect Colombian and Canadian entrepreneurs. In 2014, Fundación Bavaria also introduced the annual "Reto Bavaria" (Bavaria Challenge) competition, which rewards a start-up that can offer innovative solutions to implement the sustainable development policy of the company Bavaria. The winning entry receives COP 100 million (around USD 34 000) in seed capital and expert support from a mentor from the Fundación Bavaria network. Between 2006 and 2015, the foundation supported 380 start-ups and built a network of 140 mentors. It also delivered training to more than 5 000 entrepreneurs.

Angel investors are emerging in Colombia in response to growing demand for funds to support early-stage enterprises. Colombia opened the Angel Investors Network (Red Ángeles Inversionistas) in 2010 with support from Ruta N and the Multilateral Investment Fund (MIF) of the Inter-American Development Bank (IDB). The network is managed by Capitalia Colombia, a fund and investment bank. The National Angel Investor Network (*Red Nacional de Ángeles Inversionistas*) opened in 2014, with joint support from iNNpulsa Colombia, the IDB and Fundación Bavaria.

Venture capital is expanding in Colombia. The industry has been growing since 2010, when the first fund began operating in Colombia. By 2013 there were four venture-capital funds; by 2015 there were nine, five of which had secured investment commitments for USD 144 million (Bancóldex, 2015). The Colombian Association of Investment Funds, also known as ColCapital, was formed in 2012 from Bancóldex Capital, a programme launched in 2009 to invest in private-equity and venture-capital funds. ColCapital aims to develop the private-equity industry and encourage better practices in Colombia. The association also serves as a meeting point for funds, professional fund managers and professional service providers, all of which are key stakeholders in the industry. As of November 2015, ColCapital had 39 associate members and 47 affiliate members. Venture capital remains small, however, compared to other types of private-investment funds in the country. In 2013, the venture-capital industry's capital commitments accounted for 2% of private investment in Colombia (Figure 4.4).

Figure 4.4. **Capital commitments by fund type in Colombia, 2014**
(percentages of total capital commitments)

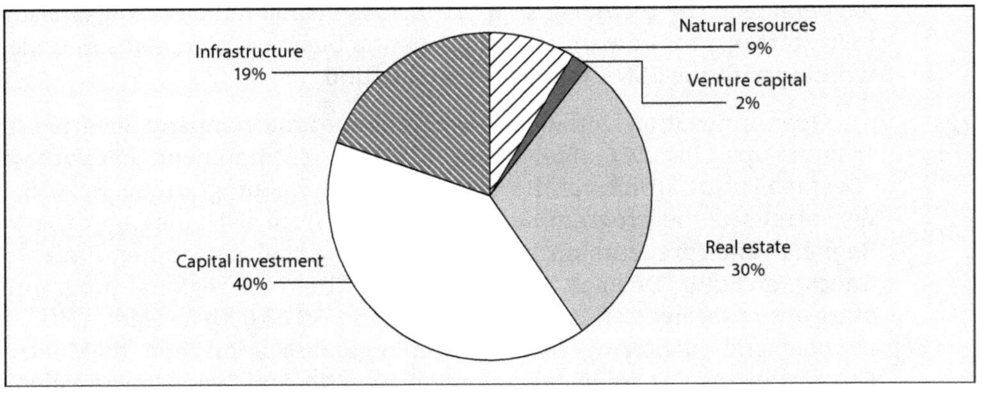

Source: Bancóldex (2015), *Catálogo de fondos de capital privado.*

Colombia's venture-capital industry is still in its infancy compared to its counterparts in other Latin American countries. According to data published by the Latin American Private Equity & Venture Capital Association (LAVCA, 2016), Colombian venture-capital funds accounted for 3.5% of total venture-capital funds raised in Latin America between 2011 and 2015. Chilean venture capital was slightly higher at 5.1%, but both were well below the levels raised in Mexico (15.3%) and Brazil (57.4%). In terms of investments made, Colombia recorded investments by 34 funds, which accounted for 3.3% of total investment in Latin America. One Colombian fund, Velum Ventures, appeared on the list of the 11 most active funds in the region in 2015, having signed seven investment agreements.

Colombia is reforming services and support programmes for start-up growth

iNNpulsa is reforming its system of services to start-ups to create a voucher scheme that will operate alongside the system of calls for applications that began operating in 2012. At the time of publication of this report, the instrument is at the design stage. The vouchers should give start-ups access to services provided by iNNpulsa-certified organisations, including collaborative workspaces. There are also plans to offer online services to entrepreneurs, including tools to self-assess competitiveness potential.

Colombia also has business-service programmes for digital start-ups. For example, in the APPS.CO programme, managed by MinTIC in conjunction with Colciencias, certified institutions provide start-ups with mentoring and training services for a period of eight weeks. The start-ups are selected through the Descubrimientos de Negocios (Enterprise Discovery) call for applications. More than 79 000 entrepreneurs in more than 750 municipalities registered for the programme, which helped develop 2 000 apps between 2012 and 2014.

In the private sector, the National Association of Entrepreneurs (ANDI) runs the ANDI del Futuro network of youth-led start-ups, which has 193 members. It offers pre-incubation, incubation and consultancy services to start-ups at the fundraising stage.

In the regions, the chambers of commerce and universities offer incubation and acceleration services. For instance, Cali Chamber of Commerce and Fundación Bolívar Davivienda have co-operated in running the Valle Impacta acceleration programme since 2012. The programme supports the scale-up of dynamic enterprises, providing technical support, mentoring services, workshops and tailored feedback. Another example is CREAME, one of the country's main incubation programmes. Situated in the Antioquia region, the incubator offers technical support and a workspace for six months and COP 7 million in seed capital. Universities with incubation systems include the University of the North. Its Centre for Entrepreneurship assesses business ideas that connect the university's research activities with the market. The centre then supports the start-ups during the incubation and acceleration stages.

Colombia is investing in promoting a culture of entrepreneurship

The launch of iNNpulsa in 2012 boosted the promotion of an entrepreneurial culture in Colombia. Between 2012 and 2015, iNNpulsa ran a nationwide campaign in which it published stories about inspirational entrepreneurs and provided information about the support programmes available. It created a news agency for the campaign, called Colombia Inn, which sought to raise public awareness via national newspapers. It also arranged for a group of entrepreneurs to tour the country, visiting many municipalities. In 2014 and 2015, iNNpulsa organised the *Heroes Fest* event in partnership with the Medellín Office of the Mayor, the SENA and Colciencias. The purpose of the event was to form networks and an entrepreneurial community (Vesga, 2015). Today, there is a growing entrepreneurial culture in the country. According to the Global Entrepreneurship Monitor (GEM, 2015), more than 70% of Colombia's working-age population (18 to 64 year olds) see entrepreneurship as a good career option and believe that entrepreneurs have a high social status and that entrepreneurship receives media attention (GEM, 2015).

Colombia also promotes an entrepreneurial culture through institutional co-ordination for events that foster networking and circulate information for entrepreneurs. For example, the city of Medellín hosted the 2016 Global Entrepreneurship Congress, which brought together stakeholders from around the world, including regional and national public institutions, international organisations, universities and entrepreneurs. The hosts of the event were the Kauffman Foundation, the Medellín Office of the Mayor, the Global Entrepreneurship Network (GEN) and the ANDI. Another event, the Latin American Venture Forum, took place in April 2016 in the city of Bucaramanga. Jointly organised by the IDB Group's MIF, Bancóldex and the RNAI, the forum connected entrepreneurs with investors.

Colombia is updating its legal framework for entrepreneurship

Colombia began to promote an entrepreneurial culture through the Entrepreneurship Act (Law 1014/2006), which helped to activate regional support for entrepreneurship through chambers of commerce and regional governments. It also introduced the Regional Entrepreneurship Networks, which strengthened the linkages between education and firms. As a result, several regions and universities launched incubation programmes. Colombia has improved its regulations for innovation in firms. Legislative Act 05/2011 and Law 1530/2012, which regulates the organisation and operation of the General Royalties System (*Sistema General de Regalías*), established that 10% of royalties on the extraction of natural resources must go to investment projects involving science and technology. The tax reform introduced by Law 1739/2014, meanwhile, stipulates that investment in technological development and innovation is eligible for a 175% tax break, a measure designed to boost the activities of technology-based start-ups in Colombia. Finally, the National Council for Economic and Social Policy (CONPES) published Document 3834/2015, creating a fast-track scheme for highly innovative firms to access tax incentives for investment in science, technology and innovation. The scheme also allows early-stage firms and small and medium-sized enterprises that generate a net profit to deduct such investment in future innovation from their income tax. Despite these positive steps, risk aversion and the lack of networks among entrepreneurs are still major barriers to the creation of start-ups in Colombia (Vesga, 2015).

Conclusions and challenges for the future

Since the mid-2000s, Colombia has been committed to transforming its economy and laying the groundwork for inclusive growth. Transforming Colombia into a place to do business and to develop innovative products and services is a major challenge. It requires a change of mindset and the introduction of measures to build confidence among stakeholders in Colombia and abroad. Although there has not yet been a sufficient level of structural change and innovation to close the gap with more advanced countries, in some areas, as in the case of start-ups, there have been discernible changes and improvements.

When Colombia created iNNpulsa in 2012, it was joining the growing region-wide wave of interest in start-ups that began with the launch of Start-Up Chile in 2010. Colombia recognises that start-ups could transform the economy, and is aware that they face gaps in the financing chain (CPC, 2015). The current trend is to promote and support start-ups using a model that is tailored to the country's needs. The model focuses on creating conditions and incentives for private-sector entities to team up with start-ups and to channel support and financing towards these potentially high-impact businesses. Colombia has shown that start-ups are not exclusive to capital cities. They can also develop in other ecosystems, such as that of Medellín, and can contribute to urban renewal and youth inclusion. It is still too early to assess the impact of Colombia's strategy and instruments. However, it is clear that this is a dynamic decision-making process in which Colombia makes improvements and sets new priorities. It is also clear that the private sector has been part of the process since the very beginning.

Colombia's main challenges include:

- Continuing to shape the country's image in line with the national vision for inclusive and sustainable development. Reshaping a country's image takes time. It requires continuous efforts and effective communication with society to build trust among stakeholders.
- Establishing mechanisms to monitor and assess new policies, especially given that the country is introducing new instruments such as the voucher scheme, that would need timely evaluations to identify strengths and weaknesses. Since the country's approach is geared towards mobilising private investment, Colombia needs to create mechanisms to identify the needs of innovative enterprises. By doing so, Colombia will be able to detect gaps in terms of access to finance and services, especially for early-stage enterprises with growth potential.
- Strengthening the exchange of experiences with other countries in the region and with more advanced ecosystems so that Colombia can identify and share good practices. For instance, several OECD countries have introduced voucher schemes, and Colombia could learn from their experiences to identify advantages and disadvantages of such schemes. It is also important for Colombia to continue to encourage its cities and regions to share their experiences so that they can learn lessons from each other on policy and identify good practices.
- Improving the legal framework for starting and winding up businesses and simplifying procedures. One major step forward will be the one-stop-shop set to open in 2017, which should allow people to complete business, fiscal and social security procedures for starting a business on a single technological platform. This reform is expected to reduce the number of procedures needed to start a business in Colombia from 8 to 5 and to reduce the time needed from 11 days to 5 days.

References

Bancóldex (2015), "Catalogue: Private equity funds in Colombia", Bancóldex, Colombia.

CPC (2015), Informe Nacional de Competitividad 2015-2016, Consejo Privado de Competitividad, Bogotá.

Endeavor Insight (2015), *Creando el ecosistema de emprendimiento en el sector Tech de Medellín*, Endeavor Global, New York.

Endeavor Insight (2014), *Construyendo el ecosistema de emprendimiento en el sector Tech de Bogotá*, Endeavor Global, New York.

GEM (2015), *Global Entrepreneurship Monitor: 2014 Global Report*, Global Entrepreneurship Research Association, http://www.gemconsortium.org/report/49079.

iNNpulsa (2014), *Dinámicos*, iNNpulsa Colombia, Bogotá, https://www.innpulsacolombia.com/sites/default/files/anexo_7._separatas_dinamicos_sge_2014.pdf.

LAVCA (2016), *Latin America Venture Capital: Five Year Trends*, Latin American Private Equity & Venture Capital Association, http://lavca.org/2016/07/15/new-vc-latin-america-venture-capital-five-year-trends/.

MinCIT and Corporación Ventures (2015), *Documento de caracterización de herramientas, instrumentos y metodologías existentes para el mercado nacional que atiendan las etapas de identificación y validación del modelo de negocio*, Ministerio de Comercio, Industria y Turismo, Colombia.

OECD (2014), *OECD Science, Technology and Industry Outlook 2014*, OECD Publishing, Paris, http://dx.doi.org/10.1787/sti_outlook-2014-en.

OECD (2013), *Start-up Latin America: Promoting Innovation in the Region*, Development Centre Studies, OECD Publishing, Paris, http://dx.doi.org/10.1787/9789264202306-en.

Ruta N (2016), *Informe de gestión 2015*, Corporación Ruta N, Medellín, http://rutanmedellin.org/images/rutan/informes_gestion/informe_gestion_rutan_n_2015.pdf.

Vesga, R. (2015), *El caso de iNNpulsa Colombia. La evolución de una política pública para el crecimiento empresarial extraordinario*, Serie Políticas Públicas y Transformación Productiva, No. 19, Banco de Desarrollo de Latinoamérica, Caracas.

Chapter 5

Promoting start-ups in Mexico

This chapter presents an overview of policies to support start-ups in Mexico. Between 2012 and 2016, Mexico has stepped up its support for start-ups. The country has bolstered institutions to promote start-ups and increased early-stage financing, thus addressing one of the main challenges identified in the first review of policies to promote start-ups (OECD, 2013a). It has also invested in promoting an entrepreneurial culture and creating an image of Mexico as a place for enterprises with a global impact. In supporting start-ups, Mexico is seeing the world as a potential market for exports by its start-ups and as a source for allies and partners for innovative projects.

Introduction

In recent decades, Mexico has taken steps to boost its entrepreneurial ecosystem. Mexico started to reform the legal framework to create an environment that was more friendly towards starting innovative enterprises. For instance, one of the reforms – the 2002 Innovation Act (Ley de Innovación), which came into force in 2009 – gave public research centres greater autonomy in managing intellectual property (OECD, 2013a, 2013b). In 2012, access to seed, venture and angel-investor capital was one of the main barriers to the creation of new technology start-ups in the country (OECD, 2013a, 2013b). In recent years, Mexico has supported start-ups, and the situation has changed significantly since the first studies (OECD, 2013a; OECD, 2013b) were conducted. Not only has the perception changed, with the country having generated and mobilised an entrepreneurial culture, but new instruments have been introduced to strengthen institutions and raise the level of experimentation.

This chapter presents an overview of policies to support start-ups in Mexico, focusing on changes that have taken place between 2012 and 2016 and identifying challenges for the future.

Start-ups in Mexico: The current situation

Despite the progress, Mexico's performance in science and innovation remains below the OECD average (OECD, 2014; Figure 5.1). Nevertheless, although Mexico's innovation system is still not as dynamic as that of the top OECD countries, start-ups are now a reality in the country, even though they are still in their infancy. Although there is a lack of data showing exactly how many start-ups exist, the perceptions of stakeholders in the ecosystem and a number of national information sources suggest that start-ups have begun to emerge in Mexico: data from the Mexican Private Capital Association (AMEXCAP) in 2016 show that Mexico has one centaur (that is, a start-up worth between USD 100 million and USD 1 billion) and 26 little ponies (start-ups worth between USD 10 million and USD 100 billion) (Figure 5.2). According to estimates by the Production Development Corporation (CORFO) in 2015, Chilean start-ups include one unicorn (i.e. a start-up worth at least USD 1 billion), four centaurs (worth between USD 100 million and USD 36 billion) and 36 little ponies (worth between USD 10 and 100 million). These start-ups operate in a range of sectors, including fintech, e-commerce and health (Box 5.1).

Figure 5.1. Comparison of science and innovation performance in Mexico and the OECD, 2014

(normalised performance index relative to median OECD values)
(OECD median = 100).

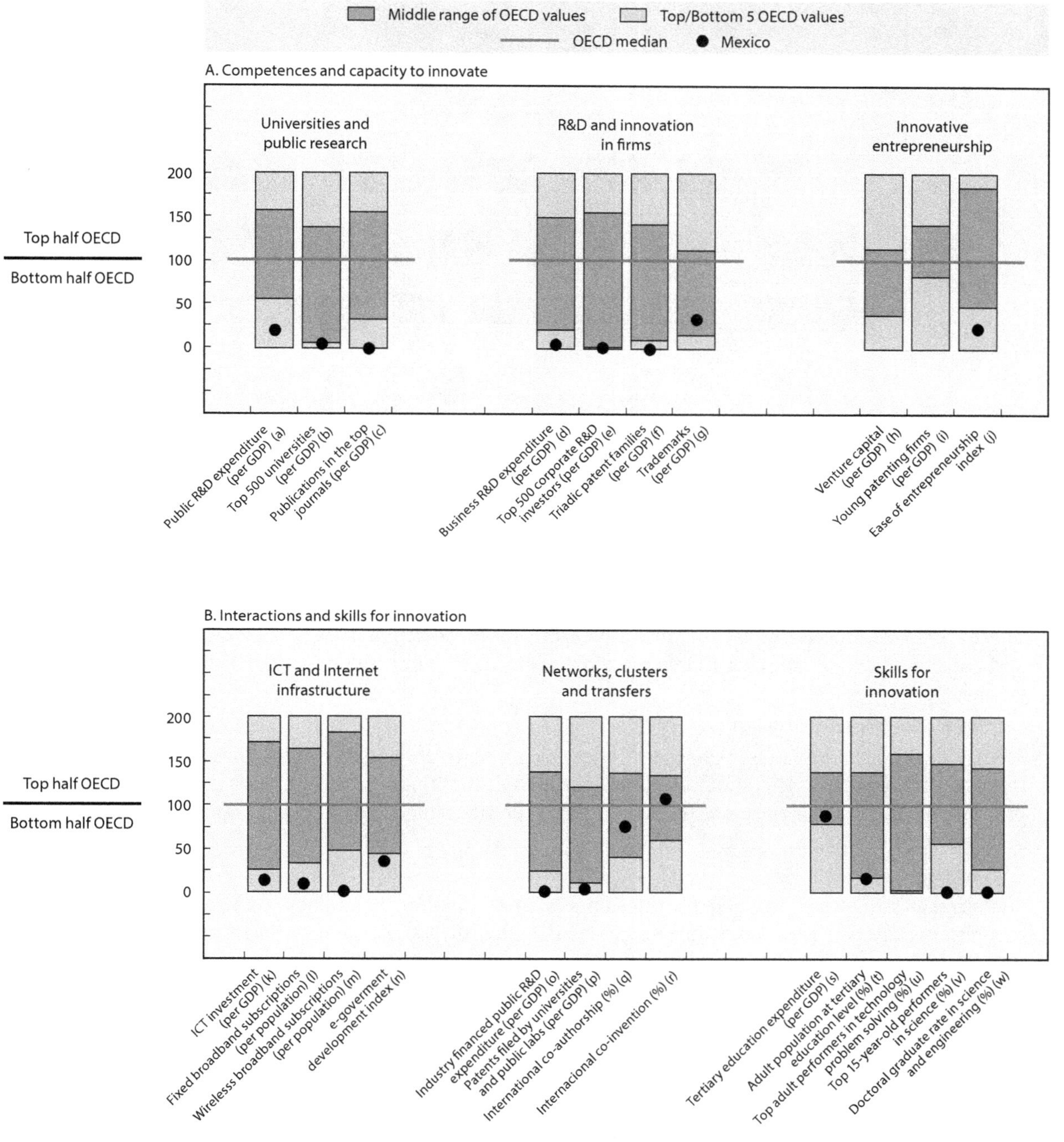

Note: The indicators are adjusted to the size of the country (GDP or population size). The values for Mexico are compared with the median value for OECD countries, i.e. the middle-ranked country of all the OECD countries for which data is available. For more details on the methodology used, see the STI country profiles in OECD (2014).

Source: OECD (2014) *Science, Technology and Industry Outlook 2014*, http://dx.doi.org/10.1787/sti_outlook-2014-en, based on OECD (2014), *Main Science and Technology Indicators (MSTI) Database*, June, www.oecd.org/sti/msti.htm.

Figure 5.2. **Start-ups in Mexico, by value, 2016**

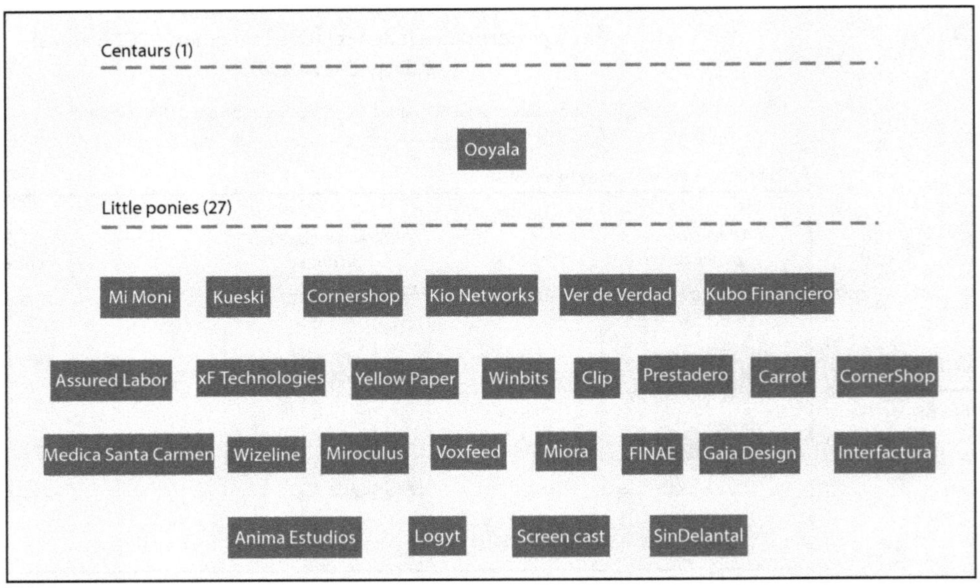

Note: The term "centaurs" refers to start-ups valued at between USD 100 million and USD 1 billion; "little ponies" refers to those valued at between USD 10 million and USD 100 million.
Source: Authors' work based on information provided by INADEM and AMEXCAP, updated in July 2016.

Box 5.1. **Start-ups in Mexico: Some examples**

There are several success stories of innovative start-ups in Mexico that are developing competitive and cutting-edge technologies and helping to transform the country's economy. Below are three examples:

Semka Biomedical Technology:

Semka develops innovative biomedical technology to treat tumour cells, enabling tailored treatment for cancer. The company was supported by the "Support for High Impact Enterprises" programme run by the National Institute of Entrepreneurship (INADEM) and has won several start-up competitions.

Enersureste:

Enersureste specialises in solar thermal energy products and technology applications and is revolutionising the use of renewable energies in Mexico. CONACYT's "Incentives for Innovation" programme supported the company in 2010. In November 2014, Enersureste won the World Summit on Entrepreneurship competition held in Marrakesh. The company has filed more than 10 patent applications.

Ticoy:

Ticoy is an agribusiness firm that processes high-quality food. Launched in 2006, the company has received support from the National Entrepreneur Fund (Fondo Nacional del Emprendedor). Ticoy grew quickly, increasing the size of its workforce from 15 to 150 employees in the space of two years. It is helping to create a high-quality niche in Mexico's traditional food sector.

Source: Authors' work based on company websites and information from INADEM.

Mexico is accelerating the promotion of start-ups

Mexico began to introduce measures to promote the founding of new innovative enterprises in the 2000s. The current Special Science and Technology Programme (PECiTI) was launched in 2000 by the National Council of Science and Technology (CONACYT). The programme introduced measures like the Technological Innovation Fund (FIT) to support innovative entrepreneurship directly and indirectly. Between 2003 and 2009, the AVANCE programme run by CONACYT and by the Enterprise Capital Fund (NAFIN) provided support for exploiting and transferring technology, starting tech firms and accessing seed and venture capital. The seed-capital fund was subsequently abolished, leaving a gap in the financing chain that was recently closed. In the area of private capital, the CONACYT-NAFIN Entrepreneurs' Fund, launched in 2004, was the country's first seed-capital fund. In 2006, the Mexican Capital Investment Corporation (CMIC) was formed, and a year later, it partnered with the Ministry of Economy and CAF – Development Bank of Latin America to launch Mexico Ventures I, a venture-capital fund of funds (AMEXCAP et al., 2015). Mexico was faced with three main challenges to enable start-ups to take off: it needed to ensure the continuity of support mechanisms, improve the co-ordination of programmes and institutions, and close the funding gap, especially in the early stages of business development (OECD, 2013a, 2013b; Ornelas Díaz et al., 2014).

Between 2012 and 2016, Mexico prioritised support for new innovative enterprises through the national competitiveness, innovation and growth strategy. It also strengthened the institutions that promote those start-ups. In 2013, Mexico launched the National Institute of Entrepreneurship (INADEM) as a deconcentrated administrative body of the Ministry of Economy. The purpose of INADEM is to implement and co-ordinate national policies in support of entrepreneurs and micro, small and medium-sized enterprises (MSMEs). Its main priorities are to promote the innovation, competitiveness and national and international visibility of businesses and to connect financing and private investment with production. In 2014, Mexico merged the Entrepreneurs' Fund with the SME Fund to speed up the implementation of entrepreneurship policy. The new body is called the National Entrepreneurs' Fund (Fondo Nacional del Emprendedor). In addition to INADEM, which has become the main channel for promoting entrepreneurs, the development bank Nacional Financiera (NAFINSA) plays a key role in fostering private investment in start-ups. Through venture-capital programmes, NAFINSA invests in four investment funds and supports crowdfunding initiatives.

Mexico's strategy involves promoting start-ups with a global impact. The country sees its potential partners as Latin America, the United States and Europe. Regional and international co-operation is a new priority in Mexican policy for start-ups, and this strategy has good potential. The first step was to create the Mexico-United States Entrepreneurship and Innovation Council (MUSEIC) in May 2013. MUSEIC's goal is to strengthen the binational environment of entrepreneurship and innovation (Box 5.2). Mexico also co-operates with France in promoting start-ups. In 2015, the Mexico-France Council on Entrepreneurship and Innovation (COMFEI) was formed as a result of an institutional agreement between INADEM and Business France. COMFEI has three committees: the Entrepreneurship Committee, which promotes an entrepreneurial culture, the sharing of best practices, and co-operation on high-impact acceleration and incubation; the Innovation Committee, whose aim is to set up the Franco-Mexican Centre for Innovation and Research; and the Strategic Sectors Committee, which focuses on activating productive linkages and linkages between businesses in France and Mexico in sectors such as energy, transport, new technologies, biotechnology, the creative industries, information technologies and innovative tourism.

Figure 5.3. The main institutions and instruments to promote start-ups in Mexico, 2016

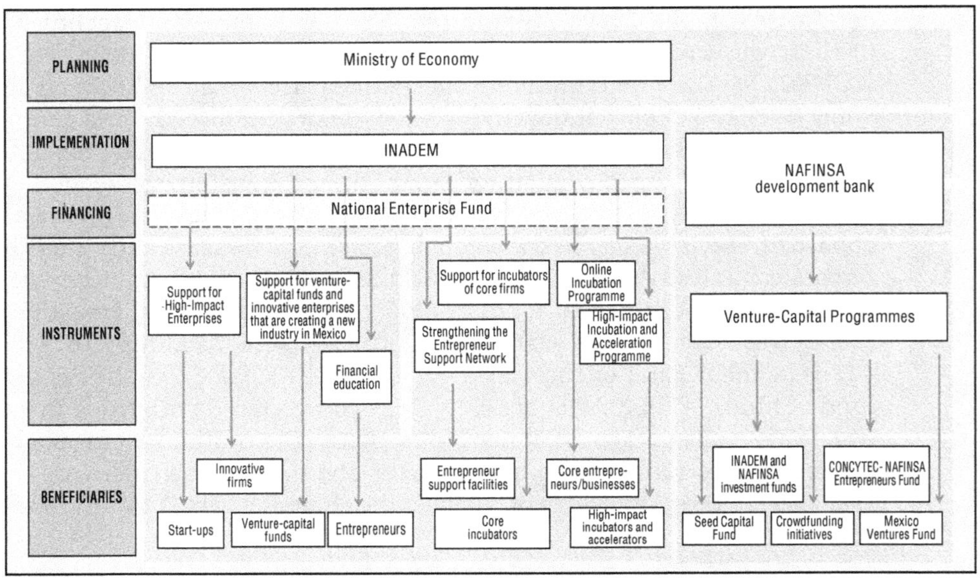

Source: Authors' work based on official data from INADEM and NAFINSA.

Box 5.2. International co-operation in cross-border areas: the iCluster project by MUSEIC

In 2013, the National Institute of Entrepreneurship (INADEM) and the US Department of State created the Mexico-United States Entrepreneurship and Innovation Council (MUSEIC) to increase co-operation between the two countries in supporting innovative entrepreneurship. MUSEIC promotes binational collaboration through joint actions to support innovative entrepreneurship. It has seven sub-committees dealing with topics of interest to both countries, namely innovation clusters, technology commercialisation, women entrepreneurs, infrastructure for MSMEs, the Latino diaspora, access to capital, and energy and sustainability. The committee on the Latino diaspora launched a pitch competition, called La Idea, in 2015 to form linkages between Latin American entrepreneurs and US-based Hispanic entrepreneurs. In the field of technology commercialisation, MUSEIC operates the Intelligent Manufacturing Initiative and the I-Corps Initiative, which promote exchanges between entrepreneurs, scientists, private-sector entities and governments to drive technology commercialisation in key sectors in the United States and Mexico.

MUSEIC also promotes the development of entrepreneurial ecosystems in cross-border regions. Since 2014, for instance, the iCluster project has been supporting start-ups linked to the intelligent specialisation strategies of the territories lying on the border between Mexico and the United States. It encourages the clusters and businesses on either side of the border to share best practices and to draw up joint regional strategies on intelligent specialisation and on linkages between clusters and businesses. The US Economic Development Administration shared its cluster mapping strategy with MUSEIC to align strategies for mapping border-region clusters, thus making it easier to monitor the success and impact of the initiatives. The Mexican cluster map was completed in 2015. Because the methodology was established in co-ordination with the US cluster map, the data shaped economic development strategies in the border regions in both countries. iCluster INADEM is co-financed by the US Department of State and the agencies linked to the project. Seven pilot projects are underway involving 3 600 start-ups in the cross-border regions between Mexico and the United States (the CaliBaja Mega-Region, the Nuevo León-Coahuila-Texas industrial corridor and the Monterrey-Saltillo corridor). Since mid-2016, the Mexican cluster map has been accessible worldwide on a free website.

Box 5.2. International co-operation in cross-border areas: the iCluster project by MUSEIC *(cont.)*

Table 5.1. Member institutions of MUSEIC

UNITED STATES	MEXICO
Department of State	National Institute of Entrepreneurship (INADEM)
Department of Commerce	Ministry of Foreign Affairs
Overseas Private Investment Corporation	National Science and Technology Council (CONACYT), including the Centre for Research and Advanced Studies (CINVESTAV)
Small Business Administration (SBA)	Angel Ventures Mexico
USAID	Crowdfunder México
Kauffman Foundation	Endeavor
National Business Incubators Association	Green Momentum
Omidyar	IGNIA
University of Texas at San Antonio	Impulsa México
UC Berkeley	Latin Idea
United States-Mexico Foundation for Science (FUMEC)	Mexican Technology Platform
WE Connect International	Startup México

Source: Authors' work based on official information from INADEM.

Start-up policies also operate at the state (sub-national) level in Mexico. The most active states are the Federal District, Nuevo León, the State of Mexico, Jalisco and Guanajuato. State programmes, however, tend to have a small budget and rely on additional federal resources, which sometimes support start-ups that address specific local needs. One such programme is the State of Mexico Institute of Science and Technology, which offers a support package for innovative entrepreneurs. Another is the Nuevo León Innovation System, a state public-private programme involving the private Monterrey Institute of Technology and Higher Education (ITESM) and the public Autonomous University of Nuevo León. This programme focuses on promoting innovative activities and supporting technology-based start-ups.

Mexico is broadening and modernising its policy mix for start-ups

Between 2012 and 2016, Mexico has modernised and broadened its range of instruments to support start-ups. INADEM has become the benchmark institution for supporting start-ups in the country. The policy mix mobilises actions aimed at:

- closing the funding gap
- facilitating linkages and providing services
- creating markets
- transforming mindsets
- reforming legal frameworks.

In 2012, Mexico had incentives for venture capital, including through the *Fondo de Capital Emprendedor* (Venture Capital Fund). However, start-ups faced major gaps in early-stage finance as only two funds offered seed capital (the Sectoral Innovation Fund (FINNOVA) and the México Emprende programme) since two major funding lines for seed capital had been abolished (OECD, 2013a). In terms of support services to entrepreneurs, Mexico had the Network of Technological University Incubators (around 200 incubators) and the National Business Incubation System (around 500). The Science and Technology Act (*Ley de Ciencia y Tecnología*), which came into force in 2009, helped to create a more appropriate legal framework for start-ups (OECD, 2013a).

Mexico has improved in three main areas since 2012 (Figures 5.4.a and 5.4.b):

- The early-stage funding gap is now smaller. INADEM has developed instruments to support the financing of start-ups, focusing in particular on supporting venture-capital funds for start-ups in the seed stage. The venture capital industry has taken off, and is now the second most active in all of Latin America according to data released by the Latin American Private Equity & Venture Capital Association (LAVCA) in 2016.
- INADEM is introducing next-generation services to support start-ups. The institute is creating lines to support high-impact accelerators and incubators and providing support for entrepreneurial training, with new features such as financial training workshops. INADEM is also facilitating access to business services through the Network of Business Mentors (*Red de Empresarios Mentores*).
- INADEM is stepping up support to strengthen the start-up culture. It is introducing instruments to change people's mindsets and spread an entrepreneurial culture throughout Mexico. It organises various events like the Entrepreneurs' Week (*Semana del Emprendedor*), and it is strengthening the information points for entrepreneurs in different states and modernising them.

Figure 5.4. **Policy mix to support start-ups in Mexico, 2012 and 2016**

A. 2012

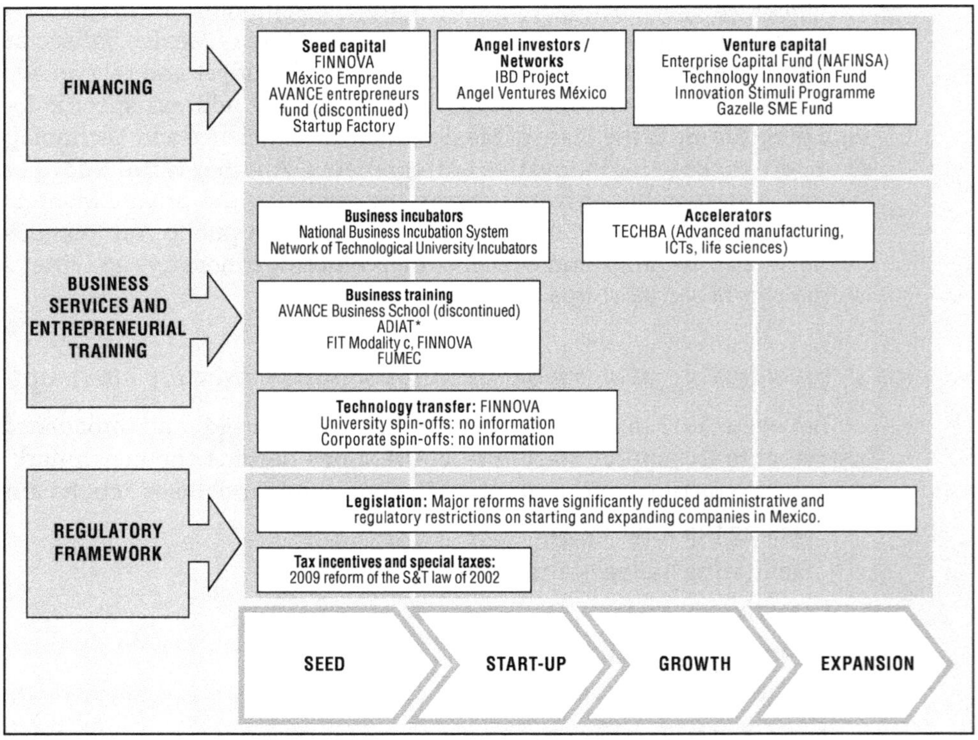

Source: OECD (2013), *Start-up Latin America: Promoting Innovation in the Region*, http://dx.doi.org/10.1787/9789264202306-en.

Figure 5.4. **Policy mix to support start-ups in Mexico, 2012 and 2016** *(cont.)*

B. 2016

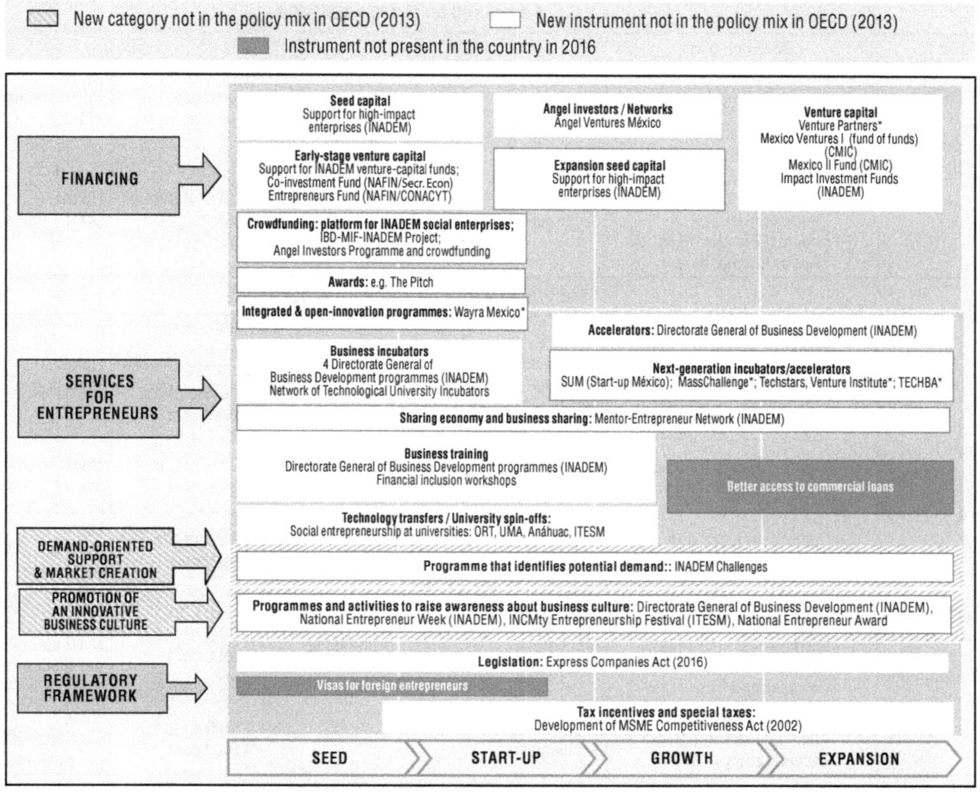

Note: Items marked with an asterisk (*) are private initiatives. The diagram shows information available on some programmes as of May 2016.

Source: OECD (2013), updated and expanded in May 2016 using official sources from Mexico.

Mexico has instruments that address start-ups in a specific stage of development. Some tools provide direct support to start-uppers, some to intermediary support institutions such as incubators, and some to institutions providing financial support or investment (Table 5.1). As Mexico has strengthened the matrix of instruments to support start-ups, it has also refined how it defines them and how it determines which are eligible for each support instrument. Mexico's definition of a start-up is that of an enterprise with a high impact, based on the nature of the business. It then draws a distinction among businesses that have been operating for different lengths of time (less than or more than two years) and among businesses at a different stage of development (Figure 5.5).

Table 5.2. Examples of policy instruments to support start-ups in Mexico, 2016

INSTRUMENTS	GOALS AND FOCUS	BENEFICIARIES	TYPE OF SUPPORT		AMOUNT	INTRODUCED IN
FINANCING for ENTREPRENEURS						
Support for High Impact Enterprises	(1) Developing or acquiring technologies or software for business operations; (2) Issuing product, process, service or human capital certification; (3) Providing financial, administrative and commercial consultancy services; (4) Acquiring machinery	Start-ups	Co-financing	70% of the total cost for each category	Up to MXN 3 million in total	2013
		Scale-ups		60% of the total cost for each category	Up to MXN 4 million in total	2016
SUPPORT for the ECOSYSTEM and SERVICES						
Strengthening the Entrepreneur Support Network (RAE)	Opening and equipping RAE points	State governments, agencies, federal institutions, upper-secondary schools and higher education institutions	Co-financing	50% of the total cost	Up to MXN 100 000	2013
	Approving and standardising existing points			80% of the total cost		2013
	Conducting diagnoses for entrepreneurs			70% of the total cost	Up to MXN 250 000	2013
High Impact Incubation and Acceleration Programme	Identifying, starting and growing high-impact firms	High-impact incubators	Co-financing	50% of the total cost	Up to MXN 350 000 per business	2013
	Providing training or consultancy services to strengthen high-impact incubated firms and/or accelerated firms	High-impact incubators/ accelerators		50% of the total cost	Up to MXN 350 000 per business	2014
	Internationalising businesses through acceleration	High-impact accelerators		60% of the total cost	Up to MXN 800 000 per business	2014
SUPPORT for PRIVATE CAPITAL						
Support for Venture Capital Funds and High Impact Firms at the Industrial and/ or Commercial Scale-Up Stage	Supporting venture-capital funds	Fund managers	Co-investment in investment vehicles	40% of the investment vehicle's total capital	Up to MXN 50 million	2013
	Supporting high-impact firms that are scaling up	Businesses showing that they have the potential to scale up a Mexican innovation that will create a new industry in the country	Co-investment in the investment round	49% of the investment vehicle's total capital	Up to MXN 50 million	2013
Ministry of Economy-NAFIN Seed Capital Co-investment Fund (FCCS)	Scheme A: supporting venture-capital funds	Investment funds	Co-investment	50% of the investment vehicle's total capital	Up to MXN 45 million	2012
	Scheme B: directly supporting businesses	Businesses	Co-investment	50% of the total resources required	From MXN 100 000 to MXN 10 million	

Source: Authors' work based on information provided by INADEM, updated in 2016.

Figure 5.5. **Start-up definitions in Mexico, 2016**

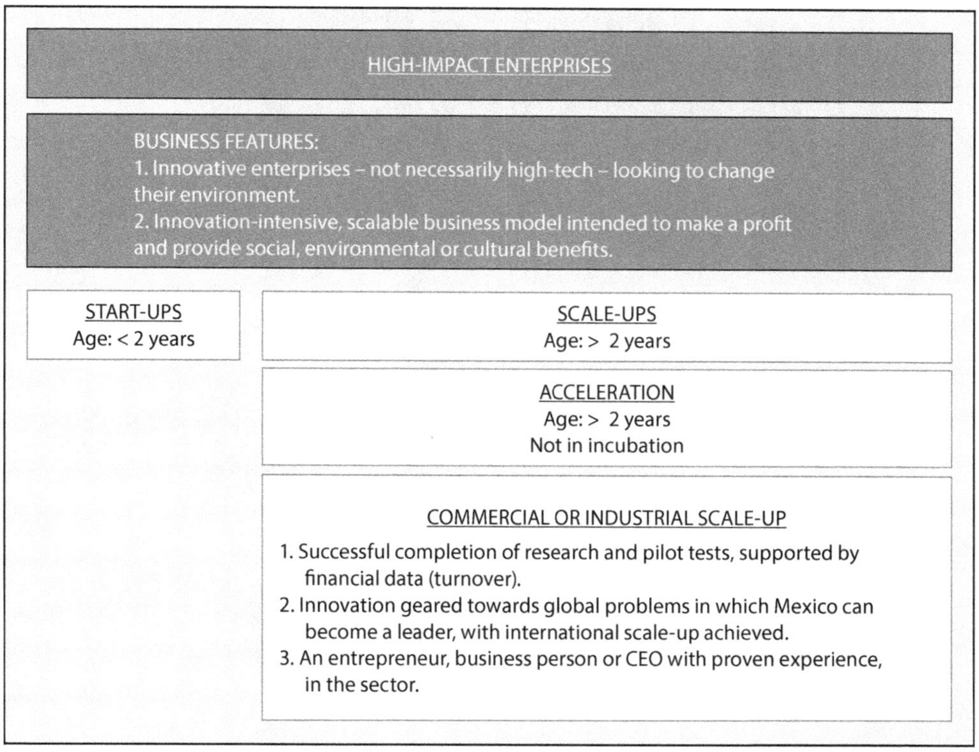

Source: Authors' work based on information provided by INADEM, updated in May 2016.

INADEM's total budget for start-ups in 2016 was MXN 1.96 billion (Mexican pesos, around USD 106 million), which was split between four support lines (Figure 5.6):

- Venture capital
- High-impact enterprises
- Support services and training
- Promotion of an entrepreneurial culture.

Support for venture-capital funds was INADEM's largest budget item for entrepreneurship in 2016, accounting for about 40%. INADEM assigned 15% of its budget to promoting an entrepreneurial culture, and 25% to supporting services to entrepreneurs and training, including the Entrepreneur Support Network (Red de Apoyo al Emprendedor), basic and high-impact incubation and accelerators. Although it is still very early to assess the impact of these programmes, INADEM data for the line to support high-impact enterprises shows that companies have increased their total factor productivity by 16% on average since they began to receive support from the programme.

Figure 5.6. **INADEM budget assigned to lines to support start-ups, 2016**
(percentage of INADEM's total budget for entrepreneurship)

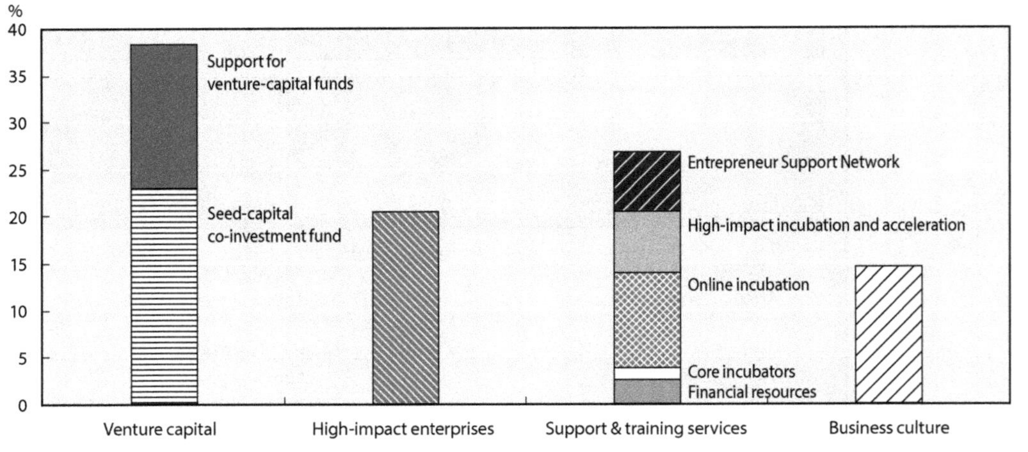

Source: Authors' work based on INADEM data, updated in May 2016.

The following sections look at the main changes in the five action areas of support for start-ups: financing, services, support to boost demand, entrepreneurial culture and regulatory framework.

Mexico is closing the early-stage funding gap

A 2012 assessment of Mexico's set of instruments found that the country needed to improve its financing chain (OECD, 2013a, 2013b). Over the following three years, Mexico rose to this challenge by rolling out new instruments to support early-stage start-ups. INADEM's Support for High Impact Enterprises line has two support schemes: one for high-impact enterprises and one for enterprises with a social or environmental impact. Each scheme supports businesses based on their development stage, distinguishing between early-stage enterprises or start-ups on the one hand, and enterprises that are scaling up on the other. Under each scheme, INADEM offers co-financing for up to 80% of the project cost, up to a maximum of MXN 3 million for projects in the start-up stage and MXN 5 million for projects in the scale-up stage. Firms can spend the money on information and communication technologies (ICTs), consultancy services or certification. There is also a regional scheme for this instrument, in which Mexican states can present projects directly to INADEM. The states provide 10% of the financing and the federal government the remaining 90%. Since 2013, the High Impact Enterprises Programme has supported an increasing number of high-impact projects, i.e. projects with a high growth and innovation potential (Figure 5.7). A survey that Abt Consultores conducted as part of the Economic Policy Programme for Mexico (PROPEM) run by the United States Agency for International Development (USAID) found that 84% of start-ups supported by the programme showed high-impact performance with intensive use of innovation (product and process) and strong growth (sales and employment).

Figure 5.7. **High Impact Enterprises Programme, applications and beneficiaries, Mexico, 2013-15**

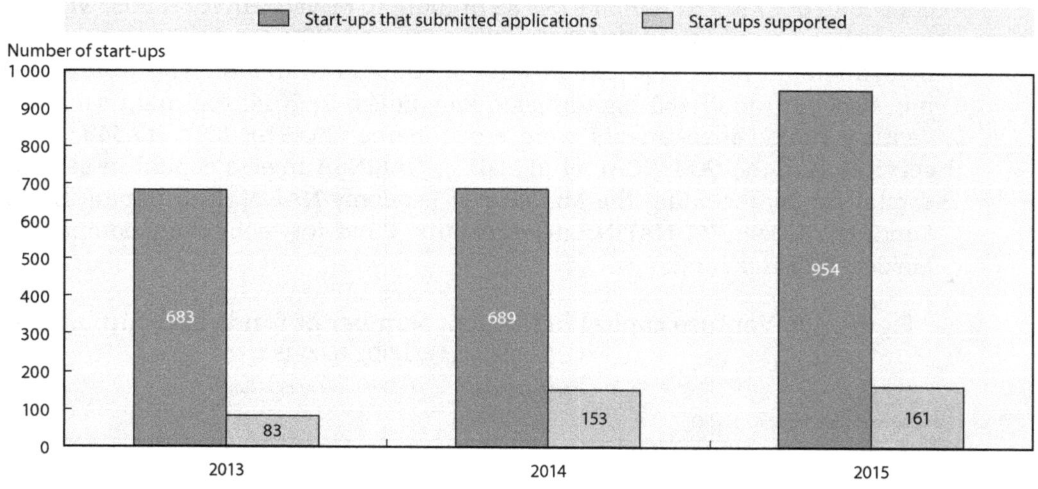

Source: Authors' work based on information provided by INADEM, updated in May 2016.

Mexico is aiming to boost crowdfunding initiatives through support from the Multilateral Investment Fund (MIF), which has launched an angel-investor and crowdfunding pilot programme (MIF, 2014). The programme is a crowdfunding platform specialising in start-ups with a social impact, and it aims to finance up to 20 projects in its initial phase. When the programme launched there were four participating projects, two of which have achieved the amount of capital they sought to raise.

The venture-capital industry is taking off in Mexico. With USD 196 million of capital raised and 17 closure funds in 2015, Mexico is positioned as the second most active market for venture capital in Latin America, behind Brazil, which has traditionally been the region's market leader. Of the 11 most active funds in Latin America in 2015 by number of deals, four were Mexican, namely Angel Ventures (eight deals), ALL Venture Partners (seven deals), Alta Ventures (seven deals) and Dila Capital (seven deals). Venture-capital funds invest not only in technology firms but also in health and energy enterprises (LAVCA, 2016). Between 2012 and 2015, new venture-capital funds were created through the following:

- Seed Capital Co-investment Fund (FCCS), created by NAFIN and the Ministry of Economy in 2012.
- Venture Capital Ecosystem Development programme, created by INADEM in 2013. In July 2016, the programme launched 35 investment funds, which have invested in 76 high-impact firms.
- Fondo México 2 (USD 500 million), launched by the Mexican Capital Investment Corporation (CMIC) in 2013.

INADEM supports access to finance and the creation of venture-capital funds. The programme "Support for Venture Capital Funds and High Impact Firms at the Industrial and/or Commercial Scale-Up Stage" has two financing schemes. The first supports the creation of venture-capital funds by providing joint investment for up to 40% of the investment vehicle's total capital (up to a maximum of MXN 50 million). The second directly supports businesses with the potential to scale up an innovation that will create a new industry in the country by providing joint investment for up to 49% of the total capital required (up to a maximum of MXN 50 million) and up to 70% of the cost of strengthening the corporate structure in preparation for innovation (up to a maximum of MXN 5 million). In 2013, there were just 15 funds in the country, but by 2015 INADEM had provided joint investment for 50 funds (Figure 5.8). As of July 2016, INADEM has contributed MXN 1.52 billion (USD 82 million) to private equity funds, while the private sector has contributed MXN 2.42 billion (around USD 131 million), bringing the total investment to MXN 3.94 billion (around USD 213 million). The funds have directly invested in around 460 high-impact companies. In 2014, the main sectors to receive venture capital investments were e-commerce (20.49%), ICTs (13.54%) and financial services (11.81%) (AMEXCAP et al., 2015). NAFINSA injects capital in several venture-capital funds, including the Ministry of Economy-NAFIN Seed Capital Co-investment Fund, the CONACYT-NAFIN Entrepreneurs' Fund for technology companies, and the Mexico Ventures fund.

Figure 5.8. **Venture capital in Mexico: Number of funds and cumulative capital**

(in millions of USD), 2000-15

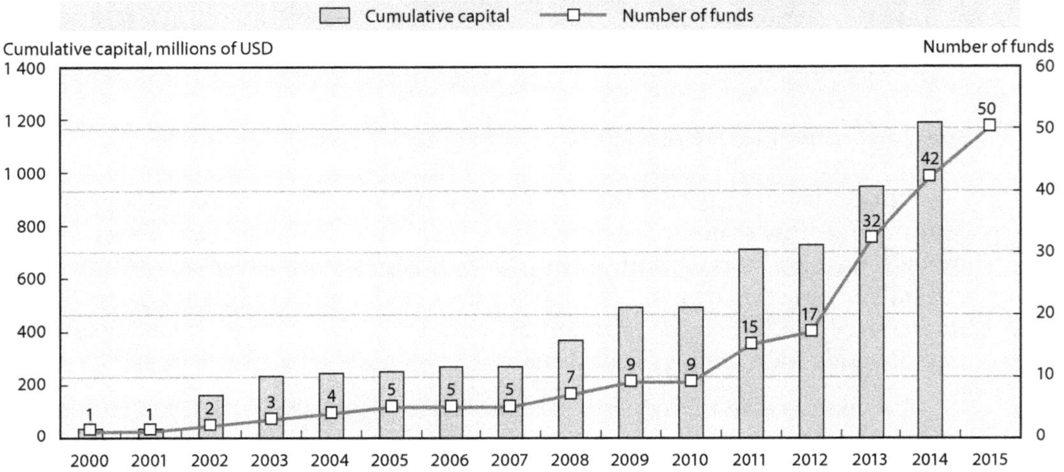

Source: AMEXCAP et al. (2015), *Estudio sobre la industria de capital emprendedor en México.*

Entrepreneur awards are gaining prestige and helping to promote an entrepreneurial culture in the country. INADEM created *The Pitch* in 2015, a contest in which high-impact incubators and venture-capital funds can nominate high-impact entrepreneurs who are in the early stages of business development. The competition provides mentoring services to the entrepreneurs and gives them the opportunity to present their projects to investors. The National Entrepreneur Award, meanwhile, aims to acknowledge and publicise innovative ideas and institutions related to entrepreneurship in the country. For start-ups, the award includes categories for innovative ideas, women entrepreneurs, high-impact enterprises, institutions in the ecosystem and education establishments that boost the entrepreneurial culture.

Mexico is looking to introduce next-generation services for start-ups

Mexico is committed to introducing next-generation instruments to support start-ups. Mentoring networks are becoming widespread as flexible tools to support start-ups, and are considered more effective and cheaper to manage than traditional incubators. In 2014, the Entrepreneur Support Network included a new Network of Mentor and Collaborator Entrepreneurs in its strategy. Business people, academics and officials who are part of the network provide professional support and guidance to entrepreneurs on a voluntary basis. INADEM also provides financial training services to start-ups and MSMEs to better prepare them for receiving financing. Meanwhile, INADEM continues to support incubators and accelerators that provide services to entrepreneurs. The institute assesses the incubators and accelerators based on the number of entrepreneurs they support and on improvements to how they are run. High-impact incubators have doubled in number between 2014 and 2016 (Figure 5.9). Furthermore, some of these incubators and accelerators, including Startup México, are increasingly focusing on innovation-based start-ups with high growth potential (Box 5.3).

Figure 5.9. **Support services to entrepreneurs in Mexico, 2014-16**

(number of incubators and accelerators)

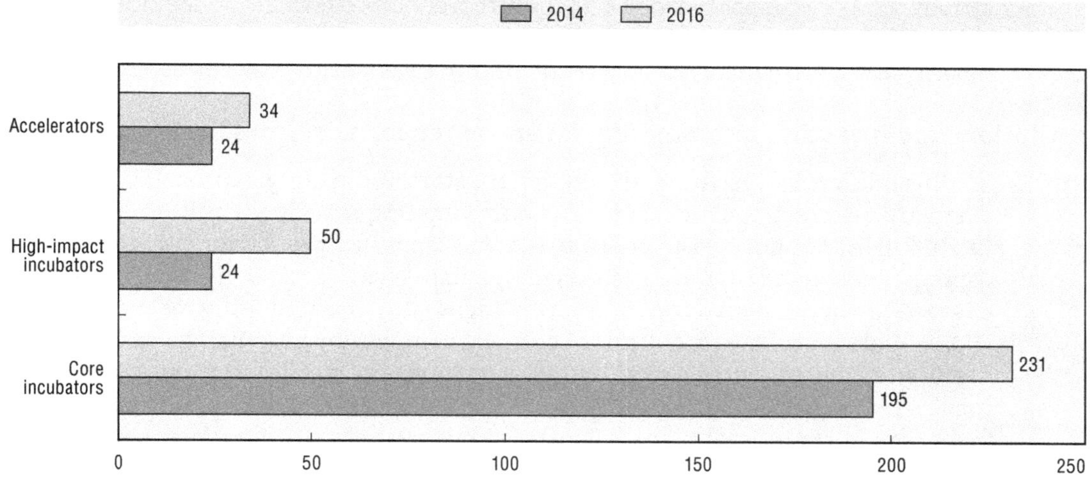

Source: Authors' work based on AMEXCAP et al. (2015), *Estudio sobre la industria de capital emprendedor en México*; and Red de Incubadoras INADEM (2016).

The Entrepreneur Support Network co-ordinates with state governments in Mexico to provide support to start-ups. The Strengthening the Entrepreneur Support Network competition organised by INADEM's Directorate General of Business Development supports the development of the business service centres (puntos de atención empresarial) in the various Mexican states. These service centres provide information geared towards entrepreneurs and give them the opportunity to develop new contacts and forge business ties. INADEM has a MXN 214 million budget for 2016 (around USD 11.6 million) to strengthen the Entrepreneur Support Network and other entrepreneur support facilities in the regions, such as the Advisers Network (Red de Asesores) and the Women Moving Mexico centres (Mujeres Moviendo México). Public support also includes contributions for opening new business service centres and updating and improving the activities and the management of existing centres.

Box 5.3. **High-impact accelerators and incubators in Mexico**

Startup México (SUM) is an incubator that acts as a platform providing integral support to new, high-impact companies. SUM provides early-stage financing and services to entrepreneurs through co-working spaces and direct mentoring services. SUM operates through calls for applications and has facilities in Mexico City, Mérida and Bajío. Between its inception in 2013 and 2016, SUM has received around 5 000 applications and supported 130 start-ups. Of those start-ups, 113 (86%) are still running, 72 have begun to market their products and 27 are in the process of raising capital.

Another example of support for high-impact firms is the international MassChallenge initiative, which in 2016 will launch a platform in Mexico that will serve as its headquarters for operations throughout Latin America. MassChallenge has a network of accelerators for high-impact start-ups based on the principles of mentoring, business training, collaboration and networking.

Source: Official Mexican data updated in 2016.

INADEM is challenging start-ups to propose innovative solutions to emerging demands

None of Mexico's public procurement programmes envisages bids from start-ups. In 2013, however, INADEM launched the Challenges programme (Retos INADEM:), which activates demand for start-ups through public-private partnerships. The first calls for proposals were for solutions to problems encountered by public bodies, but then several private-sector institutions joined the programme. As of 2015, the programme had launched 15 challenges to problems encountered by 13 public and private institutions, attracting 378 proposals from 1 000 entrepreneurs based in 14 Mexican states. The INADEM Challenges have mainly been in six sectors: the social sector, environment, health, ecology, financial inclusion and improvements to public services.

Institutions are investing in promoting an entrepreneurial culture in the country

In addition to instruments to support start-ups through financing and services, there are also instruments that focus on promoting a business culture in the country. In 2014, INADEM decided to adopt the term "capital emprendedor" to refer to venture-capital, and abandon the traditional Spanish term "capital de riesgo", which was deemed to have negative connotations of high risk, since it literally means "risk capital". INADEM also promotes a culture of entrepreneurship by organising events, prizes and discussion forums, creating a network of business service centres and supporting incubation and acceleration schemes. For instance, INADEM's call for applications for "Organising, running and participating in business and entrepreneurship events that support and strengthen the productivity of a strategic sector" targets state governments and higher education institutions that organise conferences, conventions, seminars, business meetings and exhibitions. INADEM also supports educational institutions, state governments, municipal councils and specialist civil associations that promote entrepreneurial learning using INADEM-approved methodologies. These methodologies include entrepreneurial-talent spotting, learning exchanges, business simulators for entrepreneurs and the Mx Lean Startups entrepreneurial methodology. In addition to the government, some Mexican universities, including the ITESM, play an important role in promoting an entrepreneurial culture in the country (Box 5.4).

Box 5.4. Promoting new mindsets: The ITESM's experience

The Monterrey Institute of Technology and Higher Education (ITESM) is one of Mexico's leading private universities in terms of linkages between science and technology and the production sector. It has a portfolio of over 200 patents, more than any other higher education institution in Mexico. The ITESM is known for facilitating the movement of academic and research staff between the university and industry.

In 2013, the ITESM opened the Eugenio Garza Lagüera Institute of Entrepreneurship to activate its community of students, faculty, researchers, alumni and business families and provide them with training in entrepreneurship. The institute co-ordinates existing activities and programmes to support entrepreneurship on ITESM campuses nationwide. As of 2016, the institute's network has 33 business incubators (25 high-tech, 8 low-tech), 17 accelerators in 12 states, and state technology parks. The institute provides business training through the Entrepreneur Programme, consultancy services and mentoring for entrepreneurial families. Through its Capital Funds scheme, the institute also provides financial support in the form of seed capital to ITESM network members participating in incubation and acceleration.

Box 5.4. Promoting new mindsets: The ITESM's experience *(cont.)*

One of the Eugenio Garza Lagüera Institute's primary goals is to change the business mindset and the perception of failure in business. The institute firmly believes that knowing how to reposition oneself in response to failure is part of the learning process, so its programmes include this skill, which is vital to the success of start-ups. In 2014, it worked with the Institute of Failure (Instituto del Fracaso) on an investigation into the causes of business failure in Mexico. The Institute of Failure encourages entrepreneurs to share knowledge and to learn lessons from failed business projects. It wants them to understand that business failure is part and parcel of the creative process. In a joint research project, the Eugenio Garza Lagüera Institute and the Institute of Failure conducted qualitative analysis on a focus group of 24 people whose businesses had failed, and quantitative analysis through a survey of 409 unsuccessful entrepreneurs. According to the research, the top five causes of failed businesses in Mexico are low turnover, insufficient goal indicators, insufficient performance indicators, the failure to conduct analysis, and poor planning.

Source: Official Mexican data in 2016 and Instituto del Fracaso (2014), *El Libro del Fracaso*.

Mexico is continuing to simplify its regulatory framework, but tax incentives remain a weak point

Mexico is continuing to reform the regulatory framework for starting and winding up businesses. In February 2016, it introduced reforms to the Ley General de Sociedades Mercantiles, or General Corporations Act, to create a new type of business, the sociedad por acciones simplificadas (SAS), or simplified joint-stock company. It also passed the Express Companies Act (Ley de Empresas en un Día), which simplified procedures for starting a business. Thanks to the latter, Mexicans can form a company and register it on the government's digital platform free of charge in a single day. New digital technologies, especially e-signatures, made this reform possible.

Mexico is yet to reintroduce the tax incentives for innovation that would place the country on an equal footing with many OECD countries, where in addition to direct incentives for innovation and for starting a business, there are also tax incentives for innovation (OECD, 2015). It also needs to reform the regulatory framework for MSMEs, which are currently regulated by the 2002 MSME Competitiveness Development Act (*Ley del Desarrollo de la Competitividad de la Micro, Pequeña y Mediana Empresa*). This 2002 legislation should benefit from synergies with the 2015 Sustainable Productivity and Competitiveness Gains Act (*Ley para Impulsar el Incremento Sostenido de la Productividad y la Competitividad de la Economía Nacional*).

Conclusions and challenges for the future

Despite the persistent innovation gap with more advanced countries, in recent years Mexico has stepped up support for start-ups and has boosted the entrepreneurial ecosystem. It has increased early-stage financing, thus achieving one of the main challenges identified in OECD (2013a). Mexico is also investing in forging international partnerships so that it can learn and share new practices and increase the visibility of its start-ups. The country is also seeking to promote an entrepreneurial culture and to portray Mexico as a place to run innovative, high-impact, technology-based businesses.

Mexico's main challenges in supporting start-ups include:

- Improving the evaluation and monitoring capabilities of the various programmes and identifying good practices for assessing public procurement proposals. Mexico needs to develop an effective mechanism for creating a network of independent evaluators to determine which projects deserve public support and to find mechanisms that will mobilise joint private investment in early-stage businesses.
- Streamlining and boosting public support. Start-ups are highly dynamic, so support programmes need to keep up with the market situation by paying out quickly and making swift decisions.
- Consolidating and scaling up the support provided to investment funds for start-ups. So far, Mexico has been making relatively small contributions to rather small investment funds.
- Identifying mechanisms to boost angel investment, which still hardly registers on the radar in Mexico.
- Updating intellectual property protection and regulatory frameworks and standards so that start-ups in different sectors and industries can operate beyond Mexico's borders, both regionally and internationally.

Mexico must look to strengthen and simplify support programmes and instruments for start-ups and to improve co-ordination among national, state and private stakeholders and programmes. Mexico is promoting start-ups through new policies, so it needs to accompany this experimentation with mechanisms to monitor and assess the impact of policies so that it can identify good practices, reform programmes and incentives, and, where appropriate, show that an instrument needs to be scrapped. Progress in supporting start-ups, however, will not depend exclusively on better start-up policies. Changes will also be necessary in areas like industry, innovation, digitisation and ICTs, and private-sector attitudes to investment and risk aversion will need to change.

The start-up ecosystem needs to become denser, private investors must become willing to back start-ups, and the country must be willing to strengthen its overall science and technology capabilities. Only then will Mexican start-ups flourish, grow and achieve their potential. Only then will they raise the country's productivity, competitiveness and innovative capacity. Start-ups do not work in a vacuum and successful enterprises operate in the global market using global standards, or at least aspire to do so. Efforts are therefore needed to ensure that the production system and the science and technology system match the potential of innovative Mexican entrepreneurs. It is also important to find ways to enhance synergies between start-ups and production development in Mexico. Certain sectors, such as the automotive industry, are crucial for the country and are undergoing major changes in terms of their overall business model and demand as a result of new manufacturing techniques, the growing electronic content of vehicles, and the spread of alternatively powered cars. These changes could open up opportunities for Mexican start-ups if the country draws up a suitable strategy. To seize these opportunities, Mexico will need to find synergies with the open-innovation strategies of large companies and connect science and technology developments with start-ups. Greater co-ordination and dialogue across Latin America will also be essential.

References

AMEXCAP/INADEM/EY (2015), "Estudio sobre la industria de capital emprendedor en México", Instituto Nacional del Emprendedor, Mexico.

Instituto del Fracaso (2014), *El Libro del Fracaso*, Instituto del Fracaso, Mexico City.

LAVCA (2016), *Latin America Venture Capital: Five Year Trends*, Latin American Private Equity & Venture Capital Association, http://lavca.org/2016/07/15/new-vc-latin-america-venture-capital-five-year-trends/.

MIF (2014), *Crowdfunding in Mexico: The Power of Digital Technologies to Transform Innovation, Entrepreneurship & Economic Inclusion*, Multilateral Investment Fund, Inter-American Development Bank, Washington, DC, http://www.fomin.org/en-us/Home/Knowledge/Publications/idPublication/104681.aspx.

OECD (2015), *OECD Science, Technology and Industry Scoreboard 2015: Innovation for growth and society*, OECD Publishing, Paris, http://dx.doi.org/10.1787/sti_scoreboard-2015-en.

OECD (2014), *OECD Science, Technology and Industry Outlook 2014*, OECD Publishing, Paris, http://dx.doi.org/10.1787/sti_outlook-2014-en.

OECD (2013a), *Start-up Latin America: Promoting Innovation in the Region*, Development Centre Studies, OECD Publishing, Paris, http://dx.doi.org/10.1787/9789264202306-en.

OECD (2013b), *Knowledge-based Start-ups in Mexico*, OECD Publishing, Paris, http://dx.doi.org/10.1787/9789264193796-en.

Ornelas Díaz, I., F. Poli and A. Primi (2014), "Emprendedores y startups: agentes de la innovación en Iberoamérica", Conclusion from the policy dialogue organised by INADEM in August 2014, Mexico City.

Chapter 6

Promoting start-ups in Peru

This chapter presents an overview of policies to support start-ups in Peru. Start-ups are still an emerging phenomenon in the country. In line with the wave of interest in start-ups in Latin America, Peru began to prioritise support for start-ups in 2012, when it introduced Start Up Perú. Between 2012 and 2016, Peru has advanced in structuring its policies to promote start-ups, making Start Up Perú its main support programme. The country has introduced seed capital for entrepreneurs and incentives for incubators and angel-investor networks. Peru has also promoted the launch of science start-ups to solve key problems in the country in the areas of health, agriculture and the environment. For start-ups to flourish and contribute to Peru's productivity, the start-up ecosystem needs to become denser, private investors must become willing to back start-ups, and the country needs to strengthen its overall skills in science and technology.

Introduction

When the "Start-Up Latin America: Promoting Innovation in the Region" report was published in 2013, Peru was enjoying high economic growth and was looking at how to channel some of its resources from the extraction of natural resources towards innovation and regional production development. Start-ups were an emerging topic in this context. The country was working to create a new start-up programme, called Start Up Perú, which would offer financing and advice to new businesses. Peru was also considering introducing new lines of seed capital in the national fund for innovation. The challenges that laid ahead for Peru were to strengthen these initiatives, co-ordinate them better with existing public and private initiatives, and support the regions to make start-ups a viable option in the regions beyond Lima. Three years later, in 2016, Peru has improved its measures to promote start-ups. It has structured Start Up Perú to provide various lines of support and introduced seed capital for start-ups. It has also sought to co-ordinate private-sector initiatives, which have been pioneers in the support they offer to start-ups, with public initiatives that provide financing and services to entrepreneurs.

This chapter presents an overview of policies to support start-ups in Peru, focusing on changes that have taken place between 2012 and 2016 and identifying the main challenges that lie ahead.

Peru is structuring its policy to promote start-ups

In line with the wave of interest in start-ups in Latin America, Peru began to prioritise support for start-ups in 2012, with the introduction of Start Up Perú. At the time, there was no seed capital for starting a business in Peru, and the country's innovation and production development policies placed no special emphasis on start-ups. Since Start Up Perú was launched, under the responsibility of the Ministry of Production (PRODUCE), it has embodied the country's commitment to innovation and private-sector development. The programme initially sought to offer integrated support to new entrepreneurs, issuing calls for technology start-ups to apply for seed capital and business training. The initiative was implemented in 2013, with a USD 50 million budget. The programme would co-finance up to 80% of the cost of launching start-ups and support new firms in their international expansion. As of 2016, Start Up Perú has cemented its position as the main programme for promoting start-ups. In addition to providing seed capital to innovative entrepreneurs and high-impact enterprises, the programme also supports the strengthening of incubators and promotes angel-investor networks. Until Start Up Perú was launched, the only support for entrepreneurs creating start-ups was in the form of a few private initiatives. For instance, the pioneering Wayra initiative introduced by Telefónica in 2011 provided integral support to entrepreneurs through a combination of seed capital, services and infrastructure.

Between 2012 and 2016, Peru improved the structure of its policy to support start-ups and introduced reforms to strengthen the Start Up Perú programme as part of its production development and innovation policies (Figure 6.1). One of the main reforms was the launch of the Fund for Innovation, Science and Technology (FOMITEC) in 2013. The fund consolidated the various existing lines of financing for innovation (OECD, 2015), including four lines for start-ups: Start Up Perú, Ideas Audaces (Bold Ideas), run by the National Science and Technology Council (CONCYTEC), the lines targeted at venture capital and the ones for financial and technical support for patenting innovations (Figure 6.2). The other FOMITEC instruments are the centres of excellence, the research networks, and training for advanced human capital (including doctoral programmes and programmes to attract talent). Lines to promote start-ups were allocated PEN 285.3 million (new Peruvian soles) for the period from 2013 to 2020, equal to 35.5% of the FOMITEC budget for that period (Figure 6.2). According to recent official estimates, resources to support start-ups represent 6% of the total consolidated budget for innovation in Peru (about PEN 1.5 billion).

Since 2014, Start Up Perú has been part of the Innóvate Perú programme, created by PRODUCE for the implementation of the National Production Diversification Plan (*Plan Nacional de Diversificación Productiva*). Up to and including 2015, Start Up Perú was financed by the Fund for Innovation, Science and Technology II (FINCyT II) through a loan agreement between the Government of Peru and the Inter-American Development Bank. In 2016, Start Up Perú began to receive its funding from FOMITEC instead of FINCyT II, and was allocated PEN 50 million (around USD 15.7 million) to be spent between 2013 and 2020. Start Up Perú consists of various lines of action aimed at entrepreneurs, incubators, accelerators and angel-investors. The programme aims to promote innovative, technology-intensive enterprises that are targeting an international market and have the potential to create jobs. In 2016, Start Up Perú incorporated a line to support an angel-investor network and a line to support business accelerators. As of 2016, in four calls for proposals, Start Up Perú has assessed 2 054 proposals, of which 172 were selected as beneficiaries. The line for strengthening the ecosystem has benefited 14 incubators. CONCYTEC, meanwhile, has promoted the founding of science start-ups since 2014 through the CienciActiva initiative and the Ideas Audaces contest. Both Start Up Perú and Ideas Audaces have been earmarked 10% of FOMITEC resources for the period from 2013 to 2020. Since its inception, Ideas Audaces has conducted two calls for proposals, as a result of which it has supported 60 start-ups. Peru's development bank, COFIDE, is monitoring the country's interest in supporting start-ups. In addition to entrepreneurial training, the development bank is also co-financing investments in investment funds and is looking for ways to channel private investment towards start-ups. COFIDE has included support for innovative entrepreneurship among the strategic goals in its 2016-21 Strategic Plan, demonstrating its desire to increase its support for the promotion of start-ups.

Figure 6.1. **Institutions and instruments to promote start-ups in Peru, 2016**

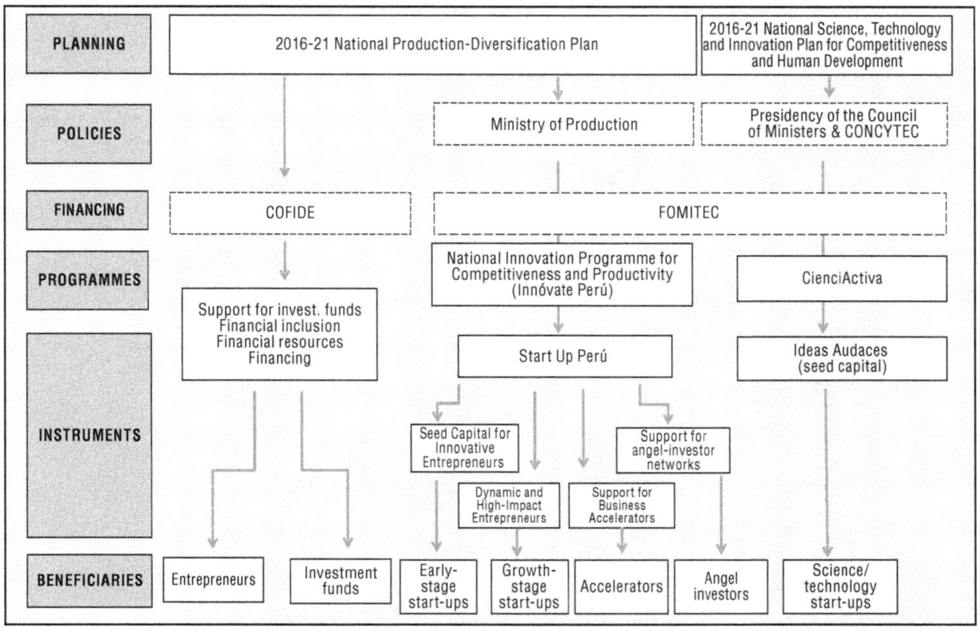

Source: Authors' work based on official data from Peru as of May 2016.

Figure 6.2. **Fund for Innovation, Science and Technology (FOMITEC), 2013-20**
(percentage of the total budget allocated to each instrument for the period from 2013 to 2020)

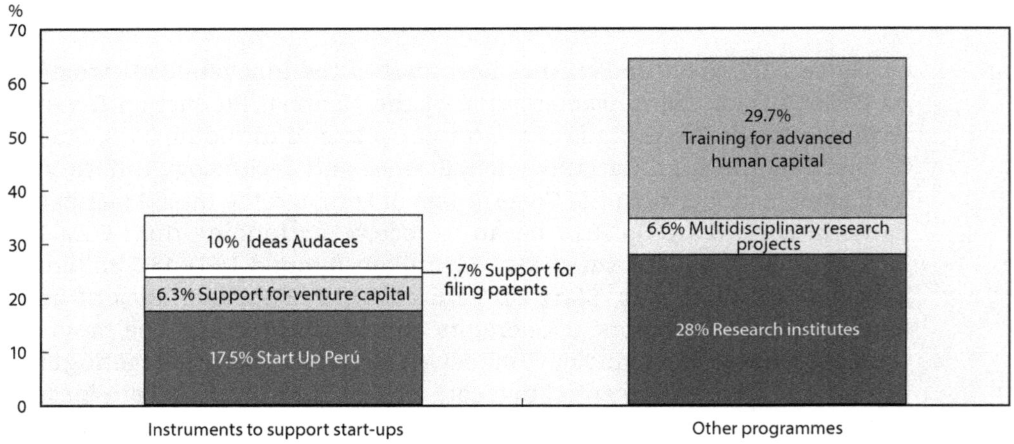

Source: Authors' work based on data from PRODUCE and CONCYTEC, as of May 2016.

Peru is expanding its policy mix and strengthening Start Up Perú

Between 2012 and 2016, Peru has stepped up its support for start-ups, expanded its policy mix and strengthened Start Up Perú's role as the main programme for promoting start-ups (Figures 6.3.a and 6.3.b). In the area of financing, Start Up Perú provides seed capital for founding and growing start-ups and supports the formation of angel-investor networks. Ideas Audaces, meanwhile, provides seed capital for growing science and technology enterprises in the agriculture, environment and health sectors. In the area of services to entrepreneurs, Start Up Perú provides support for strengthening business accelerators and incubators. COFIDE and PRODUCE run training programmes in business and finance. COFIDE also acts as a second-tier bank and provides support to the country's venture capital funds (Figure 6.1).

Three main developments took place between 2012 and 2016 (Figures 6.3.a and 6.3.b):

- Peru introduced seed-capital instruments to help close the early-stage funding gap and financing mechanisms to support dynamic, high-impact enterprises.
- Peru designed and implemented new pro-startup instruments, including co-working spaces.
- Peru invested in promoting an entrepreneurial culture.

Figure 6.3. **Policy mix to support start-ups in Peru, 2012 and 2016**

A. 2012

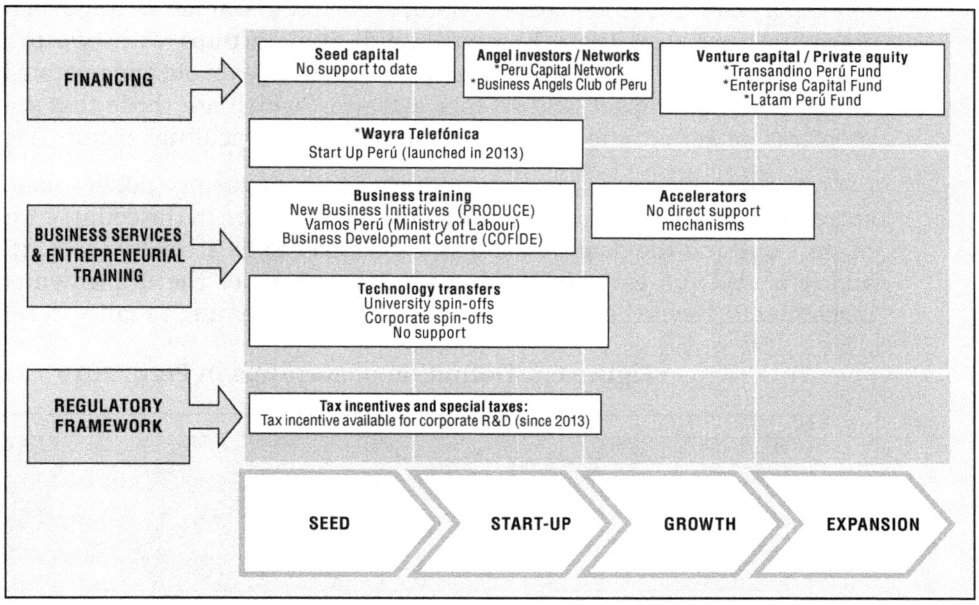

Source: OECD (2013), *Start-up Latin America: Promoting Innovation in the Region*, http://dx.doi.org/10.1787/9789264202306-en.

B. 2016

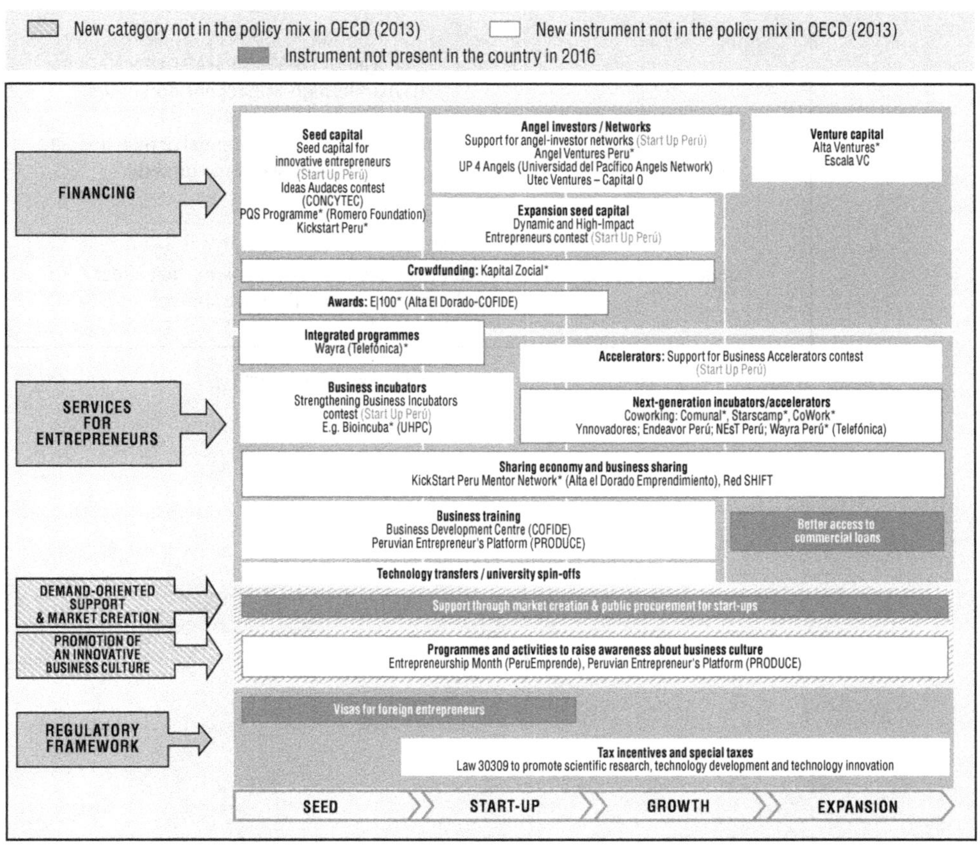

Note: Items marked with an asterisk (*) are private initiatives. The diagram shows information available on some programmes as of May 2016.

Source: OECD (2013), updated and expanded in May 2016 using official sources from Peru.

As Peru structures its policy for start-ups, it is also refining its definition of start-ups for the purposes of public policy. Each programme determines which businesses to support based on their age and nature. The programmes distinguish between: early-stage start-ups (less than three years old) and start-ups with two to five members; growing start-ups, which are between one and five years old and operate in sectors with a high potential impact; and science start-ups, which are those that seek to solve key problems for Peru in the health, environment and agriculture sectors (Figure 6.4).

Although Peru has made progress in structuring public policy to support entrepreneurship, start-ups remain a new phenomenon in the country. The critical mass of start-ups and the deal flow are still too small to be attractive to venture capitalists, and it is still too early for an impact assessment of the implemented policies and instruments. Nevertheless, start-ups seem to be becoming a reality in Peru (Box 6.1).

Figure 6.4. **Definition of start-ups in Peru, 2016**

START-UPS

BUSINESS FEATURES:
Firms with innovative products, processes, services or sales methods.

EARLY-STAGE START-UPS
(Innovative enterprises)
Age: < 3 years
No. of staff: 2-5

GROWTH-STAGE START-UPS
(Dynamic, high-impact entrepreneurs)
Age: 1-5 years
Business with growth potential or high impact
(35% annual income growth)

SCIENCE and TECHNOLOGY
Science and technology firms geared towards solving problems that affect Peru in three sectors: health, agriculture and the environment.

Source: Authors' work based on official data from Peru as of May 2016.

Table 6.1. **Selected instruments to support start-ups in Peru, 2016**

<table>
<tr><th colspan="2">INSTRUMENT</th><th>INSTITUTION/ PROGRAMME</th><th>TYPE OF SUPPORT</th><th>BENEFICIARIES</th><th>PERCENTAGE OF SUPPORT</th><th>MAXIMUM AMOUNT</th><th>YEAR INTRODUCED</th></tr>
<tr><td colspan="8">FINANCING FOR ENTREPRENEURS</td></tr>
<tr><td colspan="2">Seed capital for innovative entrepreneurs</td><td rowspan="2">PRODUCE/ Start Up Perú</td><td rowspan="4">Co-financing Seed capital</td><td>Early-stage start-ups</td><td>70% of the total cost</td><td>Up to PEN 50 000</td><td>2013</td></tr>
<tr><td colspan="2">Dynamic and high-impact entrepreneurs</td><td>Growth-stage start-ups</td><td>70% of the total cost</td><td>Up to PEN 20 million</td><td>2013</td></tr>
<tr><td rowspan="2">Ideas Audaces (Bold Ideas)</td><td>Phase 1: business plan development & prototype</td><td rowspan="2">CONCYTEC/ Cienciactiva</td><td rowspan="2">Technology/ Science-based start-ups</td><td>---</td><td>Up to PEN 146 900</td><td>2014</td></tr>
<tr><td>Phase 2: transition to industrial scale</td><td>---</td><td>Up to PEN 2.6 million</td><td>2014</td></tr>
<tr><td colspan="8">SUPPORT FOR THE ECOSYSTEM and SERVICES</td></tr>
<tr><td colspan="2">Support for business accelerators</td><td>PRODUCE/ Start Up Perú</td><td>Co-financing</td><td>Business accelerators</td><td>70% of the total cost</td><td>Up to PEN 700 000</td><td>2016</td></tr>
<tr><td colspan="8">SUPPORT FOR PRIVATE CAPITAL</td></tr>
<tr><td colspan="2">Support for angel-investor networks</td><td>PRODUCE/ Start Up Perú</td><td>Co-financing</td><td>Private entities that run angel-investor networks.</td><td>70% of the total cost</td><td>Up to PEN 700 000</td><td>2016</td></tr>
</table>

Source: Authors' work based on official data from Peru as of May 2016.

Box 6.1. **Examples of start-ups in Peru**

iFurniture:

iFurniture is a pioneering digital carpentry firm in Peru. This technology firm is transforming the traditional carpentry sector in Peru, combining computer numerical control (CNC) routers and digital manufacturing (Fab Lab). iFurniture uses digital technologies to design and manufacture custom-built furniture. The firm was part of Start Up Perú's second generation of initiatives in 2015 and has a registered trademark with the National Institute for the Defence of Competition and Protection of Intellectual Property (INDECOPI).

Maraná:

Maraná specialises in manufacturing high-quality chocolate using traditional methods. The company began operations in 2015 as part of the business incubation programme Emprende UP run by Universidad del Pacífico. As of 2016, it has 35 points of sale in four regions in Peru, and it is currently preparing its internationalisation strategy. Maraná is positioned in the niche market for high-quality, organic chocolate and its mission includes a social focus with a strong commitment to the development of local farmers.

Qaira NANO+7:

Qaira develops drone technologies to monitor air quality and ionising radiation, and it uses nanotechnology to reduce pollution. It took part in the business incubation process run by the Business Innovation and Development Centre at the Pontifical Catholic University of Peru (CIDE-PUCP) and received support from CONCYTEC's Ideas Audaces seed-capital programme. Quaira has two utility model patents pending and was selected by the Seedstars initiative in 2015 to represent Peru in the 2017 Seedstars World competition.

Source: Authors' work based on information from the businesses' websites.

The following sections look at the main changes in the five action areas of support for start-ups: financing, services, support to boost demand, entrepreneurial culture and regulatory framework.

Peru is introducing seed capital and support for angel-investor networks

New innovative firms face many barriers in accessing capital in Peru. Peru has introduced seed capital for start-ups, completing the financing chain with incentives for creating angel-investor networks, and crowdfunding is emerging as a means for early-stage businesses to raise capital. The Peruvian crowdfunding platform KapitalZocial was launched in 2013 with a focus on social enterprises. The Seed Capital for Innovative Entrepreneurs competition co-finances 70% of the project costs of technology start-ups with market potential, up to a maximum of PEN 50 000 (around USD 15 000). The Dynamic and High Impact Entrepreneurs competition provides 70% co-financing, up to a maximum of PEN 137 000 (around USD 43 000), for the commercial scaling up of innovative enterprises that have been operating for between one and five years and are showing potential for rapid growth. Since Start Up Perú was launched in 2013, there have been three calls for proposals, from which 172 start-ups have received support. FOMITEC has allocated Start Up Perú a PEN 50 million budget (about USD 15.7 million) until 2020. Up to and including the fourth call for applications, in 2016, Start Up Perú had spent PEN 20 million from this budget. In addition to Start Up Perú, there are private initiatives. The Romero Foundation, run by the Romero Business Group, has a seed-capital contest called Para Quitarse el Sombrero, which awards seed capital for up to PEN 500 000 (around USD 157 000) to young entrepreneurs with innovative ideas.

Ideas Audaces provides financing to science and technology enterprises in three priority sectors: health, environment and agriculture. Run by CONCYTEC, this programme was introduced in 2014 to provide seed capital to help the market launch of science start-ups that either operate in the three sectors mentioned above or provide solutions to social problems affecting vulnerable sectors of society. The programme is split into two phases. The first provides seed capital for up to PEN 146 900 (around USD 46 000) to co-finance a proof of concept or feasibility study. Projects with a high technical and economic feasibility enter the second stage, in which they transition to industrial-scale production. During the second phase, Ideas Audaces provides seed capital for up to PEN 2.6 million (around USD 818 000). In its first edition, in 2014, the programme focused on enterprises in the health sector and was co-financed by the Grand Challenges Canada foundation. It selected 22 projects for the first phase, of which four have been sufficiently developed to move into the industrial-scale production phase. In the 2015 edition, 40 projects were selected, and those projects have been going through the first phase in 2016. The two main seed-capital instruments – Start Up Perú and Ideas Audaces – have supported a total of 230 start-ups since 2013 (Figure 6.5). Start Up Perú has also supported 14 business incubators between 2013 and 2016.

Figure 6.5. **Number of start-ups receiving seed capital, Peru, 2013-16**

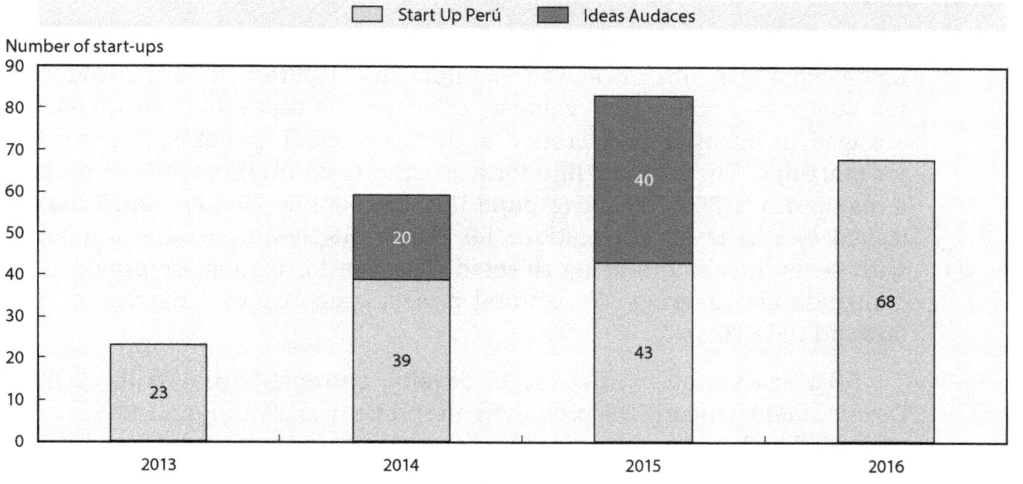

Source: Authors' work based on official data from PRODUCE and CONCYTEC, as of May 2016.

In 2016, Start Up Perú introduced the Support for Angel Investor Networks contest. This instrument provides 70% co-financing in the form of non-repayable public contributions for up to PEN 700 000 to private entities that run angel-investor networks. The aim of the programme is to encourage the development of networks, facilitate private-equity investment in innovative start-ups with growth potential, and develop a culture of investment in start-ups. The private-sector is also supporting angel investment in Peru. The Angel Ventures Peru network, for instance, was launched in 2014 as a franchise of Angel Ventures Mexico and has a co-investment fund. Through a business accelerator, it provides entrepreneurs with mentoring, consultancy and various other services, as well as infrastructure. In May 2016, Universidad del Pacífico's entrepreneurship centre, Emprende UP, launched the UP 4 Angels angel investment network. By June of the same year, the network had 12 registered angels supporting nine enterprises in Peru and four elsewhere in Latin America. The network hopes to increase the number of angels to 50 by the end of 2016. The network operates in Lima and in four regions: Arequipa, Cajamarca, Cuzco and Trujillo.

Peru's venture capital industry is still in its infancy. Investments by venture capital funds in Peru totalled USD 33 million between 2011 and 2015, accounting for 1.6% of total investment in Latin America (LAVCA, 2016). By contrast, this figure was USD 68 million in Colombia and USD 85 million in Chile. Private-sector initiatives include Alta El Dorado Emprendimiento, the result of a strategic alliance between private-equity institutions Alta Ventures and El Dorado Investments. Alta El Dorado's programmes include the COFIDE-sponsored Kickstart Perú venture capital fund, which provides capital and the services of a mentoring network during the early stages of high-impact projects, thus facilitating access to seed capital for start-ups. Faced with the challenge of developing a venture capital industry, public policy to support the industry was introduced in 2016. Furthermore, PRODUCE is forecasting the approval of PEN 18 million of financing by FOMITEC to support instruments that will promote venture capital for innovative, high-impact enterprises. The COFIDE development bank's 2016-21 Strategic Plan includes support for investment funds among its priorities. As of 2016, these instruments are in the design phase.

Peru is introducing public services for entrepreneurs to complement private initiatives in this area

In addition to offering direct support to start-ups, Start Up Perú also provides funds for developing incubators and accelerators. In 2016, Start Up Perú introduced the Support for Business Accelerators contest, offering non-repayable resources to institutions engaged in business-acceleration activities, including looking for private investment for start-ups. The support line for accelerators co-finances 70% of project costs up to a maximum of PEN 700 000 (around USD 220 000). In 2014 and 2015, Start Up Perú also issued two calls for applications for the Strengthening Business Incubators contest, with seven incubators being selected. The line for incubators provides non-repayable contributions covering 70% of total project costs, up to a maximum of PEN 725 000 (around USD 227 000).

Peru has various initiatives to develop entrepreneurial skills. COFIDE's Business Development Centre (CDE) provides entrepreneurial training and advice to entrepreneurs and small and medium-sized enterprises. The CDE is committed to regional development and is expanding entrepreneurial training services to its offices outside Lima. Meanwhile, in 2015, the Ministry of Production created the Peruvian Entrepreneur's Platform (*Plataforma Emprendedor Peruano*), which offers free training courses to entrepreneurs to improve their business knowledge and attitudes. The Peruvian Entrepreneur's Platform currently has 11 face-to-face and distance courses in areas like neuromarketing, soft skills for entrepreneurship, finance management and information and communication technologies (ICTs).

Mentoring networks are emerging in Peru thanks to private-sector initiatives. There is no specific public support for mentoring networks in Peru, but some private initiatives are driving support for entrepreneurs, a new trend that already exists in other countries in the region, such as Chile and Mexico. Alta El Dorado Emprendimiento, for instance, has the Kickstart Peru Mentor Network, as well as the StartUp Academy, which emerged from the Peruvian Association of Internet Entrepreneurs and Innovators (Lima Valley) and offers mentoring programmes for technology start-ups. Wayra Perú and Endeavor Perú have also established mentoring networks to support entrepreneurs in their programmes.

Universities play an important role in supporting start-ups in Peru. Under Law 30220/2014 (*Ley Universitaria*, or Universities Act), universities must provide consultancy services and make campus facilities and infrastructure available to encourage students to start businesses. Several Peruvian universities run activities to support start-ups, and some universities have opened entrepreneurship centres. The Bioincuba centre at Cayetano Heredia University, for example, benefited from Start Up Perú's financing line for incubators in 2014. The centre focuses on life sciences and environmental conservation and promotes the commercialisation of technologies developed at universities. Universidad del Pacífico has the Emprende UP entrepreneurship and innovation centre, which provides business training, disseminates a university business culture, and organises the THASKI contest for start-ups offering solutions to social problems. Emprende UP launched its own network of angel-investors, UP 4 Angels, in 2016. At the University of Applied Sciences (UPC), the StartUPC business incubator runs the "Made in UPC" incubation programme. Furthermore, since 2011, the UPC, in collaboration with the International Youth Foundation and the Sylvan/Laureate Foundation, organises the UPC Champions of Change award for young entrepreneurs with social start-ups. So far, 50 young social entrepreneurs have received the award. The University of Engineering and Technology (UTEC) has the UTEC Ventures accelerator, which specialises in technology and engineering projects in Peru. The EmprendeAhora programme, organised by the

Instituto Invertir in conjunction with the Center for International Private Enterprise and the University of Lima, aims to promote entrepreneurship among young people in all regions of the country, awarding scholarships to the most outstanding students at universities. The winners benefit from a four-month training programme covering various aspects of business management. They also receive mentoring in drawing up their business plans. In the 2014 edition, 130 winners were selected from 40 universities in 24 regions.

Public-private networks support the development of a business culture in Peru

Institutions join networks to promote collaboration and an entrepreneurial culture in Peru. PeruEmprende comprises public and private institutions and organises activities and events to strengthen the entrepreneurial ecosystem and disseminate a culture of innovation and entrepreneurship in Peru. Since 2014, PeruEmprende organises an Entrepreneurship Month every November. In the first edition in 2014, 53 institutions participated in more than a hundred events in 12 cities throughout the country, including workshops, conferences and fairs. The Shift network brings together institutions that promote business innovation through initiatives for businesses to share best practices. These networks involve public-sector bodies like PRODUCE, private-sector companies like PwC and Telefónica, and several universities.

The private institution Alta El Dorado and COFIDE collaborate with Start Up Perú and the Multilateral Investment Fund in organising the E|100 competition for forming networks. The competition aims to encourage linkages among start-ups to create a solid entrepreneurial ecosystem. The entire entrepreneurial community plays a leading role during the process, since nominations for the competition are made through open collaboration or crowdsourcing among academic, public-sector and private-sector entities. A vote then takes place to determine which of the nominated start-ups will be recognised by the E|100 programme. Currently, there are E|100 networks in Lima and Arequipa. In the first edition in 2015, 76 entrepreneurs were selected to form the Lima E|100 network and 49 to form the Arequipa E|100 network.

The regulatory framework could be more business friendly

There are still barriers to starting businesses in Peru, but tax incentives for business innovation are improving. Law 30309, which was passed in 2015 and came into force in January 2016, is designed to promote scientific research, technological development and technological innovation, granting a 175% tax deduction to private investors for the expenses they incur. Under the previous legislation (Law 30056/2014), the tax deduction was limited to 100% of expenditure on research, development and innovation. Despite this additional incentive, procedures to start a business in Peru remain complex, and bureaucracy is still a barrier to the founding of start-ups in the country (GEM, 2014).

Conclusions and challenges for the future

Peru is making progress in boosting the entrepreneurial ecosystem and encouraging the founding of innovative enterprises with a high economic or social impact. The reform of financing for innovation and the strengthening of Start Up Perú has been a significant step forward. Several key challenges lie ahead for Peru:

- To assess existing programmes and use the resulting data to measure the dynamics of start-ups in the country and to assess the impact of policies.
- To continue promoting a business culture and to find mechanisms to increase the flow of innovative proposals in order to mobilise private investment.

- To reform and simplify the legal framework for starting, winding up and expanding businesses, to increase access to ICTs and to introduce reforms to facilitate the operation of web-based businesses, such as by introducing e-signatures which, in Chile and Mexico, have significantly reduced the number of days needed to start a business.

At the same time, progress needs to be made in diversifying the economy and developing production to create a better environment for starting and expanding new businesses. One of the challenges already identified in OECD (2013) has still not been achieved: finding mechanisms to mobilise entrepreneurial talent throughout the country and creating an entrepreneurial ecosystem that stretches beyond the boundaries of the city of Lima. It remains vital to co-ordinate with regional governments and mobilise them in supporting start-ups, given the growing role of the regions in the country's innovation and competitiveness agenda.

Like in other countries in the region, for start-ups to flourish and contribute to the productivity, competitiveness and innovative capacity of Peru, start-up ecosystems must become denser, private investors must be willing to back start-ups, and the country must strengthen its science and technology skills.

References

GEM (2014), *Global Entrepreneurship Monitor: Perú (2014)*, http://www.gemconsortium.org/country-profile/97 , accessed in March 2016.

LAVCA (2016), *Latin America Venture Capital: Five Year Trends*, Latin American Private Equity & Venture Capital Association, http://lavca.org/2016/07/15/new-vc-latin-america-venture-capital-five-year-trends/.

OECD (2015), *Multi-dimensional Review of Peru, Volume 1. Initial Assessment*, OECD Development Pathways, OECD Publishing, Paris, http://dx.doi.org/10.1787/9789264243279-en.

OECD (2013), *Start-up Latin America: Promoting Innovation in the Region*, Development Centre Studies, OECD Publishing, Paris, http://dx.doi.org/10.1787/9789264202306-en.

ORGANISATION FOR ECONOMIC CO-OPERATION AND DEVELOPMENT

The OECD is a unique forum where governments work together to address the economic, social and environmental challenges of globalisation. The OECD is also at the forefront of efforts to understand and to help governments respond to new developments and concerns, such as corporate governance, the information economy and the challenges of an ageing population. The Organisation provides a setting where governments can compare policy experiences, seek answers to common problems, identify good practice and work to co-ordinate domestic and international policies.

The OECD member countries are: Australia, Austria, Belgium, Canada, Chile, the Czech Republic, Denmark, Estonia, Finland, France, Germany, Greece, Hungary, Iceland, Ireland, Israel, Italy, Japan, Korea, Latvia, Luxembourg, Mexico, the Netherlands, New Zealand, Norway, Poland, Portugal, the Slovak Republic, Slovenia, Spain, Sweden, Switzerland, Turkey, the United Kingdom and the United States. The European Union takes part in the work of the OECD.

OECD Publishing disseminates widely the results of the Organisation's statistics gathering and research on economic, social and environmental issues, as well as the conventions, guidelines and standards agreed by its members.

OECD DEVELOPMENT CENTRE

The OECD Development Centre was established in 1962 as an independent platform for knowledge sharing and policy dialogue between OECD member countries and developing economies, allowing these countries to interact on an equal footing. Today, 27 OECD countries and 24 non-OECD countries are members of the Centre. The Centre draws attention to emerging systemic issues likely to have an impact on global development and more specific development challenges faced by today's developing and emerging economies. It uses evidence-based analysis and strategic partnerships to help countries formulate innovative policy solutions to the global challenges of development.

For more information on the Centre and its members, please see *www.oecd.org/dev.*

OECD PUBLISHING, 2, rue André-Pascal, 75775 PARIS CEDEX 16
(41 2016 17 1 P) ISBN 978-92-64-26565-3 – 2016

www.ingramcontent.com/pod-product-compliance
Lightning Source LLC
Chambersburg PA
CBHW061218240926
51846CB00006B/1268
9789264265653